SLEEP PLAY LOVE

SOPHIE ACOTT

Photography credit: Damien Noble Andrews

www.nobleandrews.com

Formatting credit: Kristen Forbes

www.deviancepress.com

CONTENTS

ACKNOWLEDGMENTS

In this present moment, I wish to acknowledge you, the reader. Thank you for choosing me to help guide you on your journey toward a deeper parent-child connection, and healthy, sustainable sleep habits for you and your family. Thank you for taking the time out of your busy schedule to commit to making change on a conscious level. Education is the most powerful weapon which we can use to change the world, and I sincerely appreciate you for supporting me in my mission to help normalize sleep (and behavioral) challenges, ease the burden of parental guilt, and restore some rest and harmony to families everywhere.

To my husband, Ben; without your tireless encouragement, support, and love, this book would not have been possible. You are my best friend, my soul mate, and the most inspirational father and role model to our children. From the bottom of my heart, thank you.

To my four beautiful children; Leila, Bodhi, Jett, and Luca: thank you for choosing me as your mom and for the daily lessons of patience, gratitude, forgiveness, and humility. You are the inspiration for this book, and I will never stop striving to be the best version of myself, and mother for you.

To my parents, Robyn and Jack: thank you for your unconditional love, support, and being the best parents you could be for me and my brothers. I have a deep respect and appreciation for you both—and for the blessed childhood you worked relentlessly to gift us.

To my tribe of strong, inspiring women near and far; you know who you are. I acknowledge you for the profound influence you have had in my life and my parenting journey. Thank you for your trust, support, advice, for listening to me, and for sharing your own struggles and hardships—I am eternally grateful for your courage, honesty and friendship.

To the pioneers whom have inspired and influenced my personal journey, and my professional method and practices; Patty Wipfler (Hand in Hand Parenting), Magda Gerber and Janet Lansbury (RIE), and Althea Solter (Aware Parenting). Thank you for your years of research, dedication, and generosity in sharing your invaluable knowledge—and for our shared vision of helping parents to connect more deeply and meaningfully with their children.

To the families that I have worked with over the years; thank you for entrusting me to help your children (and you) sleep better. I acknowledge you for your courage, vulnerability, and determination—and for affording me the opportunity to learn and grow from our time together so that this book could be made possible.

And finally, I wish to acknowledge parents all over the world for the incredible job you do every day. This parenting gig is the most important, yet underresourced job on the planet, and I offer you my eternal respect, support and love as you go about this journey. I hope that the following pages provide you with comfort in knowledge, or simply in the understanding that you are not alone. You are a good parent, you are doing your best, and you are enough.

FOREWORD

It is a great pleasure and honor to write the foreword to Sophie's book, *Sleep Play Love*, which offers families sustainable solutions to the modern-day child-sleep and parenting challenges.

Sophie and I met through my organization, the International Maternity and Parenting Institute, where she embarked on her journey to become a holistic maternity and child-sleep consultant. Not only did Sophie successfully obtain her certification but she also established herself as a reputable parent coach, helping hundreds of families all over the world with their children's sleep challenges, difficulties, and transition into parenthood.

As a mother herself, Sophie understands the various challenges and demands of parenthood—especially when it comes to child sleep. Her practical, holistic, and down-to-earth approach is heavily influenced by the philosophies of Parenting by Connection (Hand in Hand Parenting), RIE, Aware Parenting, and also the International Maternity and Parenting Institute's Holistic Sciences Sleep Method.

Sophie's style, perceptions, and experience offers a wealth of knowledge and comfort to parents of young children who are "doing it tough" in the sleep department. Unlike most other one-size-fits-all approaches that only serve to provide solutions from one extreme to another, Sophie knows very well that what works for one family does not work for another. She has conceptualized the Sleep Play Love Method to provide a refreshing perspective to parenting and child sleep—a welcome, sustainable alternative to the traditional (or boxed-in) methods of "sleep training."

With the parent-child connection at the heart of her approach, Sophie addresses in detail how to prepare for change holistically, providing a very supportive approach—not only for the child but also for the parents and caregivers. Sophie focuses heavily on the parents' awareness unfolding and awakening, helping them to understand their role in sleep and behavioral difficulties and how they can be more conscious of their behavior and time with their children.

In addition to age-appropriate routines, optimizing the sleep environment, and tips for managing inevitable life transitions, this book provides for all families the perfect balance between practicality and heart with proven methods to successfully and respectfully overcome sleep patterns that are no longer serving the child, parent, or family—such as rocking, feeding, holding or patting to sleep, cosleeping, and weaning from the breast, bottle, or pacifier.

This book provides inspiration, practical tools and guides, relief, and support—in a way that helps to normalize what is happening, in all the challenges that parents are facing today. It helps to give families another perspective on how to work with children, encouraging independent, happy, sleeping, and confident kids in the long term.

My hope is to see Sophie's approach and book reach families far and wide, who are in need and seeking an alternative holistic approach.

- Mar De Carlo Oscategui, *CBP (IABPP) CGP (IMI)*

Founder of the International Maternity and Parenting Institute and the Association of Professional Sleep Consultants.

Author of *The Baby Planner Profession: What You Need to Know!, Green Body Green Birth,* and *Awakening through Sleep.*

INTRODUCTION

Parenting is the most important, yet the most challenging job on the planet. It takes us on a psychological, emotional, and spiritual journey, which can bring out the very best—and the worst—in us. While unequivocally joyful, wondrous, and rewarding, it can be equally contrasted with fear, guilt, and exhaustion. And the latter ensue irrespective of the detrimental impact that sleep deprivation can have on all areas of our lives: physical health, energy, emotional well-being, relationships, and psyche.

Sleep, or lack thereof, continues to be one of the most talked-about (and contentious) topics of parenthood—among expectant, new, and seasoned parents alike. In fact, over the last ten years, Google trends depict that "baby sleep" search-engine queries have more than doubled.

Research demonstrates that over 60 percent of parents with babies aged less than twenty-four months get no more than three and a quarter hours of sleep each night! While for some this may only last for a season (or two), for others, sleep deprivation can lead to a breakdown of the family unit, postnatal depression, stress, anxiety, and a host of other mental and physical health issues. Society's unrealistic expectations of baby sleep (and parenting in general) are undoubtedly to blame, setting parents up for failure in their quest for the unattainable holy grail of a seven-to-seven routine and sleeping through the night—not to mention any futile attempts to keep up with the Joneses with respect to developmental progress and capabilities.

The sheer abundance of generic sleep advice at our discretion these days, coupled with lack of support (or a "village") is undeniably overwhelming; cry it out, or no cry? Breast milk or formula? Pacifier or no pacifier? Cosleep or crib? Despite the current trends, which only seek to appease our insatiable appetite for a quick fix, there is no such thing, nor any one-size-fits-all approach for our children—sleep, behavior, or otherwise.

A favorite mantra of mine is this: nothing is a problem unless it is a problem for *you*, or alternatively, if it ain't broke, don't fix it! Just because your neighbor's baby is sleeping through the night from six weeks of age, don't assume that your baby should, would, or could. Guilt, albeit part of the (parental) job description, has many of us pursuing parenting choices that don't necessarily serve the greater good, but rather only our (or society's) pressure-fueled beliefs of what is the most successful sleep method or parenting strategy.

Despite the myth, what is best for our children isn't always what is best for the parents or family unit, and vice versa. We must be aware of our own limitations, expectations, and agenda, with consideration to our child's genes, temperament, age, and physical and emotional well-being. As parents, we are all doing the very best that we can with the resources we have available to us, and we do not deserve the judgment of others, least of all ourselves.

While I don't believe in "training" children to change sleep patterns, I don't pass any judgment on parents who have, or will resort to behavioral methods to improve sleep for their family. I understand both personally and professionally that sometimes we all do things we never thought we would do—due to time constraints, compliancy, lack of knowledge and/or help, or sheer exhaustion. I have the utmost empathy for how arduous parenthood can be—let alone conscious parenting—in the midst of sleep deprivation. We all have different emotional and physical thresholds, levels of support available to us, degrees of sleep and behavioral challenges, circumstances, expectations, commitments, family dynamics, and number of children. There is no wrong or right—only what feels intuitively right, or what works best for you and your family at the time.

The truth is we can't train a child to sleep any more than we can train him or her to breathe. Most children are capable of sleeping well *and without* parental intervention, provided that they feel safe enough to do so. Like any other milestone such as learning to crawl or walk, sleep ability is a combination of nature and nurture. There are biological, emotional, genetic, environmental, and psychological influences that are outside of our control, and each child will learn these skills according to his or her innate timetable. Some children simply take longer to learn than others and may need more parental intervention to achieve each milestone. In any case, trust, which begins as a secure attachment in the early weeks, must continue to be encouraged, while connection, safety, and responsiveness are paramount.

While the concepts within this book are nothing new, I believe that we are currently at the forefront of a paradigm shift—away from the rigid, traditional parenting (and sleep training) methodologies, toward a more conscious (and effective) framework.

In my years of practice as a sleep consultant, I have successfully supported hundreds of parents all over the world on their journey to better sleep with the methods, routines, and recommendations within this book. Of the families whom I have consulted using the Sleep Play Love Method, the long-term improvement to their child's sleep ability —and overall well-being of the family unit—far surpasses any other existing behavioral (or "sleep-training") method I have used. Ultimately when we know better, we do better, and as such, I am excited to share with you some of the tools that have quite literally transformed my own parenting journey, my relationship with my children, and the lives of many families around the globe.

My intention is to provide a gentle, yet realistic, achievable, and sustainable solution to better sleep for parents and child, while offering flexible solutions to meet the unique needs (and circumstances) of each individual family. I hope that this book empowers and inspires you, and helps to restore some confidence, joy, and calm to the all-too-common confusing, stressful, and exhausting reality of modern-day parenting.

Love,
Sophie

Disclaimer: The information in the following chapter; "Why Won't My Baby Sleep" may be triggering for some parents. In no way is this intended to harm, blame, or shame; but rather to provide an holistic overview of some (not so widely understood) causes for sleep and behavioral difficulties. Some ideas may be considered unconventional, or controversial at best (as is the topic of sleep and parenting in general), and should be considered as insight once all other sleep foundations have been appropriately addressed—refer to "The Seven Sleep Foundations." If you suspect that the catalyst for your child's ongoing sleep (or behavioral) difficulty does stem from (for example); "unfilled needs," "prenatal experience," or "birth experience and early trauma," know that you are not alone. Your child is not damaged, and you are not broken (albeit, I know it may feel so at times). Nothing is ever "irreversible." Simply your awareness of these factors can shift any associated negative implications they may have on your (or your child's) emotional well-being and/or sleep ability. I have included tools, resources, and solutions throughout this book to enable you and your child to heal as necessary from such experiences, so that you can cultivate positive, sustainable change for your family's health and well-being; now and for the future.

SECTION I
WHY WON'T MY BABY SLEEP?

There are countless variables that impact our children's sleep quality, duration, habits, patterns, behavior, and capabilities. Some factors we can control (to an extent), but there are many we can't, and these are simply an inevitable part of life—developmental milestones, leaps, illness, teething, and life transitions. While we can be as consistent as possible with (our child's) sleep associations, routine, environment, and our parenting approach, this doesn't always reflect consistency in their sleep patterns. It may seem at times as though you are engaged in an infinite, frustrating tango of one step forward and two steps back —especially in the first twelve to twenty-four months, when so rapid is their learning, growth, and development. Some sleep solutions may be simple and fast and others far more complex and time consuming. Sometimes, a child's inability to sleep transcends all logic and compels us to look outside the square concerning possible catalysts and solutions.

THE FOUR PILLARS TO OPTIMAL SLEEP ABILITY

A child's sleep ability is directly influenced by four main areas:

1. The family unit: including family dynamics, routine, persistency, parenting style, genetic expression, and temperament—of parent and child alike.
2. Emotional and physical well-being: including physical health, nutrition, parent-child connection, and birth and prenatal experience.
3. Age and developmental stage: including age-appropriate physiological and cognitive readiness, opportunities, and capabilities.
4. Environment: including physical, emotional, and genetic—or epigenetic—considerations (i.e., their subconscious memory, past trauma, and a child's programmed perceptions about the world).

Figure 1 demonstrates these key factors (among others) and highlights the considerations and action tools that we, as parents, can implement to ensure minimal impact on our children's sleep and behavior. These tools are discussed in further detail throughout this book, and in a practical, step-by-step format as outlined in "The Sleep Play Love Method."

THE FAMILY UNIT

Parent's support network
Family dynamics and demographics
Parenting style
Control patterns and habits
Parent's expectations, agenda, and
readiness for change
Routine, time, and commitment
Parent's relationship and synergy with
parenting philosophy
Genes and temperament of parents
and child

PHYSICAL AND EMOTIONAL WELL-BEING

Predictable, regular bedtime routine   Parent-child connection tools
Minimize environmental stress   Optimal, age-appropriate nutrition
and overstimulation   Regular self-care for parents

ENVIRONMENT

Light exposure
(red/blue/white/natural)
Light/darkness of sleep space
Noise
Temperature
Stimulation
Distractions
Toxins
Stress
Genetics/Epigenetics

Nutrition of parent and child
Teething
Illness
Parent's current emotional state
Parent's physical and emotional bandwidth
Trauma, stress, and unmet needs of parent
and child (conception, pregnancy, birth,
infancy, and childhood)
Parent-child connection
Medical conditions
Sleep disorders
Allergies
Food intolerances

OPTIMAL
SLEEP ABILITY

Optimal, age-
appropriate; sleep
environment, routine,
clothing, and bedding
Positive sleep associations
Adequate sunlight exposure

Secure attachment
Age-appropriate routine
and physical activity
Optimal, age-appropriate
nutrition
Time and space to practice
new-found skills without
intervention

Age of the child
Ability to self-settle
Developmental stage, readiness, and ability
Gestation (full-term versus premature birth)
Developmental leaps and milestones
Day and night routine
Nutritional intake and expenditure
Co-regulation
Need for physical closeness and touch
Sleep training methodology

AGE AND STAGE

Figure 1: The Four Pillars to Optimal Sleep Ability

Parenting Style

Parenting style is a combination of nature versus nurture. We naturally navigate to a certain style on the basis of how we were parented, whether we are predominantly an A- or B-type personality, the temperament of our children, and our environment. From my experience, there tends to be a correlation between an attachment or a more gentle-parenting style and the prevalence of sleep difficulties that rely on parental or "hands-on" intervention such as feeding, rocking or holding to sleep (and back to sleep), cosleeping, and habitual night waking.

To the contrary, parents who have been more structured and consistent with routine from birth—most commonly A-type personalities—typically demonstrate more persistence and experience greater consistency with sleep overall, hence less regression at times of change. However, these children—and parents—are often less adaptable and may experience increased stress or anxiety when exposed to unanticipated changes to routine or structure.

Unfilled Needs

As parents, it is our job to be attuned to our children's needs and what they are trying to communicate to us. It is our role to eliminate any source of hurt and to ensure that our children's immediate primary needs have been met (i.e., warmth, safety, emotional connection, hunger, stimulation, thirst, discomfort, pain, physical touch, and closeness).

Meeting our children's basic needs in a timely manner ensures trust and confidence in us as their caregiver and in how they perceive and relate to the world around them—laying the foundations for secure attachment.

Sleep is often a reflection of what is, or what isn't, happening during our children's waking hours. If children are not receiving sufficient stimulation, age-appropriate physical or developmental activity, nutrition, or emotional connection by day, they can wake overnight to fulfill these needs. It is also important to note that *too much* stimulation, nutrition, physical—or developmental—activity can lead to an overstimulated nervous system, which can equally prevent a child from sleeping well.

It's impossible for any parent to meet all their child's (physiological and emotional) needs, all of the time. However, by tuning into your intuition and your baby's communication cues, you can be assured that you're doing the very best possible in that very moment.

Incorporating just five to ten minutes of quality one-on-one time per day and listening to tears and tantrums—instead of distracting—can make a significant difference to children's ability to sleep. These tools encourage a safe environment for children to release their past or present fears and tension, and heal from early trauma. Baby wearing, cosleeping, and swaddling are additional ways to help a child feel safe and secure emotionally and physically, and can help establish secure attachment in the early weeks. Refer to "The Seven Sleep Foundations: Emotional and Physical Well-Being" for the practical application of these connection tools.

Control Patterns and Sleep Needs

Any action or object that children *habitually* turn to as a source of comfort (or distraction) at times when they may feel bored, insecure, anxious, overtired, or in pain—provided that their immediate needs have been satisfied—is likely to be a *control pattern* or habit, and not a *real need*. Common examples include; television, smart phones and tablets, the pacifier, feeding for comfort (not hunger), movement, or a special toy/lovey. Control patterns can interfere with a child's ability to sleep in two main ways: 1) because they are often used as a diversion for tantrums and to stop crying, emotions are repressed (or stored) rather than felt and released. Unresolved feelings often surface overnight, manifesting in sleep issues such as frequent night waking, screaming, nightmares, and night terrors; and (2) it is also common for control patterns to develop into sleep needs—i.e., children will rely on certain actions or objects to distract them from feeling afraid or anxious when falling asleep at bedtimes, and/or when they wake overnight—often requiring repetitive parental intervention to provide comfort in the form of their associated control pattern or sleep need. *Refer to "The Sleep Play Love Method" for step-by-step instructions to help you transition your child toward independent sleep by alleviating the reliance on control patterns and sleep needs.*

The Parent's Preconceived Ideas and Agenda

Parents with less rigid ideas about how and where their babies should sleep are generally much happier and far less likely to be disappointed when their children cannot perform the way they are "supposed to" i.e., sleep through the night.
   —James McKenna, cosleeping expert

It is important to recognize that the past does not equal the future. What worked yesterday isn't guaranteed to work tomorrow, and what was instrumental in helping your first child sleep won't necessarily be successful for your second, third, or fourth. Each child is unique, and therefore we cannot compensate for our past perceived parenting failures by adopting parenting choices that only serve to fulfill our own ego, or alleviate our fears or regrets.

Babies and children are continually growing, learning, and developing—and as such, their sleep needs and reliance on us as their parents also continue to change. Just as we respect the ebb and flow of nature without judgment or question, we must surrender to the as-is-ness or the fluid nature of our children *without* controlling, manipulating, or tainting the experience with our own needs, desires, or conveniences. We must evolve with, and adapt to, our children instead of attempting to mold them to fit *our* agenda or the movie we are playing in our head of the "perfect" child, parent, or family.

As parents, we are often unwilling to surrender to the spiritual, emotional, and psychological commitment that parenthood demands of us, and therefore, many of us passionately resist our current reality —or are compelled to spend every waking moment trying to change it. It's in our nature to want answers and to deconstruct our children's behavior and their sleep patterns. We feel helpless and out of control when we are unable to predict our child from one day to the next, or when things don't go according to plan. But when we are operating from a place of fear, our desire to control, compare, and analyze ensues the unobtainable pursuit of perfection, an unhealthy attachment to our past, and a resistance to what is. The thing is, no matter how hard we try, other people are one thing we can't control. We can, however, control our perspective, perception, attitude, expectations, and our level of acceptance.

Fear

Fear of the dark, "monsters," separation (or a break in connection) from a parent, being alone, and change (or the unknown) are among the predominant catalysts for most sleep and behavioral difficulties. Children's ability to sleep (well) is directly proportionate to their perceived level of safety and the opportunity they are afforded to regularly heal their fears and insecurities in the supportive and loving presence of a caregiver. Nightmares, night terrors, crying/screaming at bedtimes and/or overnight, and disturbed sleep in general are common ways for children to process their fears when they are unable to integrate and recover momentarily from the big—or little—things that bother them during their waking hours. As parents, we have been conditioned to believe that when we encounter sleep issues, the cause is behavioral, and therefore the most effective solution is to "train" a child to sleep. However, sleep is not a behavioral process. In fact, *the majority* of sleep difficulties arise because of (a) biological unreadiness (i.e., age, developmental stage, and ability) and/or (b) unmet emotional needs—or fear (e.g., lack of connection, insecurity, trauma, or general upset). Children's emotional needs will always be heightened at times of transition, milestones, and change to routine—so additional mindfulness, empathy, and patience may be required at these times. Implementing the connection tools as detailed in the following chapter; "The Seven Sleep Foundations: Emotional and Physical Well-Being" will help parents to consciously support their children to heal and recover from their fears without distraction, punishing, shaming, ignoring, or the use of "control patterns"—enabling them to sleep better and independently for the long term.

Prenatal Experience

Our prenatal and birth experiences set the foundation for our life—ultimately impacting our physical, emotional, and psychological health. Through our early interactions with our infants—from conception to pregnancy, birth, and infancy—we imprint the way in which they will perceive and respond to the world and those around them; will they evolve to be trusting or fearful? Calm or anxious? Disempowered or confident?

A fetus in the womb obtains feedback about his or her external environment solely through the mother's perception and her behavior in response to her environment. This includes hormone fluctuations, stress levels, thought patterns, emotional state, and physical health. The baby's nervous system absorbs and downloads all this information in his or her subconscious, and these early impressions and sensations can remain with the child throughout his or her entire lifespan—otherwise referred to as "limbic imprinting."

Whist it is natural for every woman to experience momentary or incidental stress while pregnant, there is a correlation between chronic or ongoing maternal stress—including trauma, toxins, certain medications, depression, grief, and anxiety during pregnancy—and an increased incidence of colic-like symptoms (e.g., persistent crying and fussiness), and sleep and behavioral difficulties in babies following birth and throughout early childhood.

Birth Experience and Early Trauma

According to a 1995 study by Dr. William Emerson—a pioneer in the field of birth trauma—95 percent of all births in the United States are considered traumatic, 50 percent rated as "moderate," and 45 percent as "severe" trauma. Emerson states, "Most parents and professionals consider it ordinary for infants to awaken during the night, cry for long periods, have gastrointestinal distress, or be irritable. Few parents or professionals have seen trauma-free babies, so few have experienced babies who are symptom-free. In addition, few have glimpsed the human potential that is possible when babies are freed from the bonds of early trauma."

Complications to the mother (and/or baby) during birth, medical interventions, medication (or drugs), induction, breach birth, illness, parental separation, environmental toxins, complications with vaccinations, hospitalization, premature birth, injury, illness, circumcision, surgery, lip- or tongue-tie corrections, dietary imbalances or sensitivities, and the actual birth process itself (i.e., a prolonged or fast second stage of labor, C-section, or vaginal) may contribute to excessive crying, an inability to settle (such as colic), sleeping difficulties, developmental delays, sensory processing disorders, retained reflexes, and a host of emotional and behavioral issues in babies and children.

The specific nature of our birth can affect us physically, emotionally, and psychologically—the effects being experienced from infancy and potentially into adulthood (if left unhealed). For example, a child who endured a prolonged second stage of labor, or was "stuck" in the birth canal, may express a fear of confined spaces (e.g., crying, screaming, or thrashing when placed in a car seat, high chair, or stroller). Or a child who was born with the umbilical cord wrapped around his or her neck may become distressed, anxious, or panicky when anything touches their neck area. Similarly, children who have experienced a long and stressful separation from their mother either at birth, or during infancy, may express prolonged separation anxiety at sleep times or amid life transitions—many relying on parental presence to fall asleep and remain asleep.

We are all born with the ability to heal from trauma. If something happens to us that is too big to integrate at the time, we dissociate from it, and then it comes up later in little bits to be healed. Birth is often traumatic to babies, which is why they cry so much in the first three months. Starting from birth, mothers can learn the difference between crying that says, "I am hungry" (or expresses some other need in the present) and the kind of cry that means, "Please hold me in your loving arms and let me cry about something that hurt me in the past so I can heal from it." Babies who can do this whenever they signal the need, also get the

chance to cry about all the little frustrations that build up every day, and they
tend to sleep better at night, waking only when they are hungry.
    —Aware Parenting

While some interventions are unavoidable, providing psychological and physical comfort, and acknowledging our baby's innate need to cry to relieve stress and to heal from trauma is integral to their well-being and development. Listening is a powerful tool to support our children to offload their heavy feelings, which can be triggered in different ways: perhaps when overtired or overstimulated, or when experiencing a change to routine or certain life transition which may leave them feeling disempowered, insecure, and vulnerable—the very feelings associated with their birth or early trauma experience that they perhaps were unable to fully release or integrate (and therefore heal from) at the time.

About Birth (www.aboutbirth.com.au) is a great online resource that supports parents with the physical, emotional, and psychological aspect of pregnancy, birth, and the postpartum journey. With practical tools and tips, this comprehensive program educates parents about the birth process and how to create a positive and empowering birth experience.

If you have experienced birth trauma or you suspect a certain life event is impacting on you and/or your child's ability to sleep, the following modalities or resources may support you: craniosacral therapy, neuro emotional technique, kinesiology, somatic experiencing, and "Children and Trauma—What to Expect, and What to Do" by Aletha Solter (Aware Parenting).

Coregulation

The human infant is the most vulnerable, contact dependent, slowest developing and most dependent primate-mammal of all, largely because humans are born neurologically premature, relative to other primate mammals. For the human infant to safely pass through its mother's small pelvic outlet, the infant has to be born with only 25 percent of its adult brain volume. This means that its physiological systems are unable to function optimally without contact with the mother's body, which continues to regulate the baby much like it did during gestation. The mother's body is the only environment to which the human infant is adapted.

—James McKenna, cosleeping expert

From birth, babies are extremely sensitive and attuned to their environment—energetically, emotionally, physically, and via visual and verbal cues. Albeit that children learn to gradually regulate their own thoughts, feelings, behavior, and emotions over time, in the early years, they look to a caregiver to determine how they "should" react in any given situation.

A child can pick up on a parent's emotional cues within milliseconds and will often mirror the emotional state of those closest to him or her. If you are relaxed, your child is likely to be calm. If your child is surrounded by tension and stress, he or she will feel threatened (fight or flight) and may express such feelings through off-track behaviors (e.g., crying and tantrums) and sleep difficulties.

Infants also rely on parents to help regulate their physical state. Being physically close to a parent stimulates a baby's nervous system and aids antibody production at times of teething and illness. This can explain infants' strong desire to be held when they are upset, unwell, in pain, or frightened—and consequently, the increased "clinginess" that parents experience at these times.

Regular self-care, a reliable support network, and a listening partnership are vital to parents' well-being and their ability to parent consciously—especially in the early months where the demands of parenthood can be emotionally and physically demanding.

Age

Age is a significant consideration for determining how often to feed our babies, how we respond to their needs, and how long they can sleep during the day and overnight.

- Newborns have an inherent physiological and biological requisite to wake more often day and night for growth, development, the mother's milk supply, and for basic survival.

- Biologically, a child's circadian rhythm (internal body clock) is underdeveloped in infants younger than three months of age, and therefore, inconsistencies in sleep patterns such as catnapping, day-and-night confusion, and frequent night waking are extremely common in the early months.

- Until six months of age, a child will spend 50 percent of his or her sleep time in REM (light/active sleep). This explains why infants awaken more easily and are far more susceptible to changes in their sleep environment than older children.

- At six months, the overall time spent in REM sleep reduces to 30 percent. Because an infant's daytime sleep patterns are the last to be established—sometime between six to seven months—it is very common to experience inconsistencies with day sleep until this age, particularly catnapping.

- Babies have a shorter sleep cycle when compared to older children and adults (i.e., forty-five to fifty minutes), and therefore, they may wake more often day and night as they cycle regularly through light- and deep-sleep stages.

- In my experience, babies under six months are not physiologically capable of sleeping through the night without feeds—this seems to be a more consistent pattern between eight and ten months (parents will often experience an improvement in night sleep when they abstain from feeding overnight from this age). Other variables include whether the child is breastfed or formula fed, their weight, overall health, a premature versus full-term birth, developmental stage, nutrition, temperament, environment, routine, and so on.

Retained Neonatal Reflexes

The Moro, rooting, and sucking reflex are among the reflexes our babies are born with and that commonly integrate between the first two to six months of life. If a reflex is unintegrated (i.e., it remains active), it can create a host of health, behavioral, developmental, and sleep-related problems including sensory processing issues, poor coordination and/or motor skills, ADHD, allergies, weak immune system, pacifier reliance, aggressive behavior, fatigue, bed-wetting, and vision impairment—to name a few.

For example, a child with a retained Moro (startle) reflex may experience increased difficulty transitioning out of the swaddle—and sleep may regress significantly as a result. Similarly, children with a retained sucking reflex may struggle weaning from the pacifier, causing sleep regression, heightened clinginess or withdrawal, crying, tantrums, and behavioral issues.

The birth process is a key factor in the integration of these reflexes, particularly a prolonged or fast second stage and births requiring medical intervention. Other common causes for retained reflexes include prenatal stress, early trauma, illness, injury, lack of proper movement in infancy (e.g., overuse or rotation of high chairs, jumpers, activity centers, and swings), and dietary imbalances or sensitivities. If you suspect your child may suffer from a retained reflex, you can test for these at home (www.retainedneonatalreflexes.com.au) or engage the help of a professional such as a pediatric chiropractor, osteopath, physiotherapist, or kinesiologist to diagnose or prescribe integration exercises.

Premature Versus Full-Term Birth

Preterm birth typically refers to babies born between twenty and thirty-seven weeks. Premature babies often have some degree of early trauma due to the increased likelihood of hospitalization, parental separation, medical intervention, complications, and health issues—which can compromise development and sleep quality and duration. It is not uncommon for babies born early to exhibit increased sensitivity, persistent crying, fussiness, or inability to settle at sleep times or sleep well overnight. They also require more regular milk feeds and have a heightened need for closeness, warmth, and touch for regulation.

Most health-care professionals advise to refer to the corrected age (actual age in weeks minus the number of weeks premature) for scheduling and anticipating developmental ability, sleep, and feeding requirements up to the age of twelve to twenty-four months. *Cosleeping, feeding on demand, and baby wearing may be effective solutions in the early months.*

Sleep Disorders

Common ones include sleep apnea, bed-wetting, sleep walking, and night terrors. Some children will engage in head banging or body rocking for comfort or pain relief (commonly if they have been previously rocked to sleep as an infant). Albeit disturbing for parents to witness, many of these do not have long-term effects on health or well-being and may be improved significantly with a consistent, age-appropriate day-and-night routine, adequate sleep, regular connection tools (play, listening, and quality time), and by avoiding overstimulation where possible. *Always consult with a health-care professional prior to starting a sleep program if you suspect your child may have a sleep disorder.*

Medical Conditions

This can include numerous ailments—from the common cold to eczema, allergies, colic, reflux, and disease. Pain and discomfort can impact sleep a little or a lot—depending on the severity of symptoms, the child's temperament, a parent's responsiveness, and how the symptoms are treated. If you or your partner suffers from allergies such as eczema, asthma, or hay fever, or if there is a family history of allergies, there is an increased likelihood that your child may also experience symptoms. Lip- and tongue-ties (often diagnosed by a lactation consultant) are also common in infants and can lead to poor latch, difficulties feeding, excess wind, colic-like symptoms, hunger, and fussiness—consequently affecting sleep quality and duration both day and night. *If at any time you are concerned about your child's health or suspect that there may be a medical condition affecting your child's ability to sleep, seek advice from your health-care provider.*

Teething

The average age that most babies cut their first tooth is between six and seven months. Most children will have all their milk (baby) teeth by two and a half years. Despite many professionals claiming that teething doesn't affect sleep patterns or behavior, I couldn't disagree more. A tooth erupting through the surface of the gum creates a localized inflammatory response, subsequently triggering an immune response. Symptoms of illness may present if bacteria enter the inflamed, open gums—extremely common due to the fact that babies at these times chew on anything and everything they can find. Depending on the child, their age, temperament, which teeth (and how many) are coming through at the time, the pain and effect on sleep and behavior can vary in intensity and duration. From my experience as a mother, and from the accounts of hundreds of other parents

I have worked closely with, the physical and emotional symptoms, albeit varied, are real: fever, drooling, biting, diarrhea, vomiting, diaper rash, sleeplessness, hyperactivity, teeth grinding, irritable behavior, fatigue, fears, anxiety, croup, ear and throat problems, sinus congestion, a runny nose, and even a cough. Refer "Common Sleep Difficulties and Solutions: Teething and Illness" for symptoms, common effects on sleep, and solutions.

Breast Milk Versus Formula

Breast milk is more easily digested than formula, and therefore, breastfed babies may wake more frequently from hunger and for the added primal comfort (i.e., skin-to-skin contact and the hormones in breast milk such as oxytocin). For this reason, breastfed babies *generally* take longer to night wean and to sleep longer stretches overnight without feeds. The added ease of breastfeeding to settle a baby back to sleep (day or night) may also become habitual—that is, babies may begin to wake more frequently for comfort rather than nutrition.

The Parent's Level of Readiness and Commitment to Change

When it comes to making changes in any area of our lives, it's always the pleasure-pain principle: we will do more to avoid pain than we will to gain pleasure.

Therefore, until the pain—or perceived challenge—of *not changing* sleep habits outweighs the perceived pain of *making the change*, a parent may not be ready to commit to moving forward. Many of us continue to tread water for the longest time—often attributed to our lack of knowledge, confidence, or support.

Most sleep issues don't resolve without us making change on some level. We must be cautious not to sacrifice our own well-being (and sanity!) for the fear of "rocking the boat." Children are intrinsically resilient and adaptable—and most of the time, any undesirable sleep habits are just as much the parent's as the child's. We must assume personal responsibility—accepting *our role* in the problem before we can offer a solution. If things aren't working, or are unlikely to be sustainable in the long term, we must have the honesty to acknowledge it and the willingness, commitment, and support to change it.

Intake Versus Expenditure

If the consumption of food and/or milk is consistently greater than the physical output (e.g., activity, growth, and development), sleep quality and duration may be compromised.* Some parents unknowingly rotate their child between one apparatus to the next by day (e.g., from activity center to high chair, to baby carrier, to stroller, to crib, and so on), which can impede on physical development and cause children to wake more frequently overnight to "burn" stagnant, stored energy—or practice developmental skills. The effect on sleep can be minimized by providing an opportunity for children to explore their environment during the day and allowing them the time and space to acquire new physical skills such as rolling, crawling, cruising, and walking. Avoid the impulse to snack or demand feed your child after six months of age to encourage more adequate, full feeds less often—day and night.

This seems to be more prevalent in babies who continue to be fed on demand or comfort fed day and night, or when feeding is used as a settling method for frequent night waking (in babies over six months of age).

Food Intolerances and Allergies

Food allergies, sensitivities, and intolerances can impact sleep either marginally or dramatically, and may be challenging to diagnose.

Symptoms Can Include the Following:

- Hyperactivity or restlessness
- Colic-like symptoms such as wind and bloating
- Flushed skin or rash
- Face, tongue, or lip swelling
- Vomiting and/or diarrhea
- Coughing or wheezing
- Difficulty breathing
- Loss of consciousness

The most common culprit for children is cow's milk protein (found in milk, cheese, and yoghurt). Other common allergens include wheat, soy, corn, eggs, chocolate, seafood, and nuts. *Approximately 50 percent of infants who are allergic to cow's milk protein are also allergic to soy-bean protein. Goat's-milk (formula) is a hypoallergenic alternative.*

There are also numerous additives, preservatives, and chemicals that are hidden in our children's packaged snacks and everyday pantry items such as bread, milk, cheese, and sauces, which can have adverse effects on behavior, sleep, and little immune systems. Breastfeeding mothers are also advised to avoid high-allergen foods as they are often transferred to the baby via breast milk.

The Food Intolerance Network (fedup.com.au) and Little Stomaks (littlestomaks.com) are great resources for ingredients to avoid when buying prepackaged foods.

SECTION II
THE SEVEN SLEEP FOUNDATIONS

1. Emotional and Physical Well-Being
2. Routine
3. Environment
4. Nutrition
5. Positive Sleep Associations
6. Developmental Stages, Milestones, and Transitions
7. Temperament and Genetics

EMOTIONAL AND PHYSICAL
WELL-BEING

Sleep and emotional well-being are synonymous. If a child is feeling insecure, frustrated, overwhelmed, or distressed, it's almost a guarantee that you will see these feelings manifest in sleep and behavioral difficulties such as tantrums, crying, raging, bedtime resistance, dependence on a parent to fall asleep—and back to sleep—heightened clinginess, nightmares, night terrors, and frequent night waking. Undesirable parenting choices or sleep habits often ensue (especially where parental self-care may be lacking), and this can place undue stress on the family unit.

With the exception of medical conditions or sleep disorders, at the core of *most* sleep difficulties is fear—often disguised as insecurity, anxiety, grief, withdrawal, or aggression. Fear often peaks at times of transition, during developmental leaps and milestones, and when a child is faced with a change to his or her sleep routine, habits, or patterns. Consequently, we experience separation anxiety (fear of separation or abandonment), irrational behavior (insecurity/unsafety), and resistance to (or grieving) the loss of someone or something to which the child has become attached.

The following tools, when implemented regularly, will help you connect with your child—ultimately minimizing sleep regression and off-track behavior, and ensuring a smoother transition (and increased resilience) at times of change.

Follow Your Intuition

Often confused with instinct, intuition can be described as a gut feeling—or a "hunch"—awareness, love, connectedness, or an innate knowing of what is right for the highest good of all involved. On the other hand, instinct refers to something that we do automatically without consciously thinking about it. Of biological and primal origin, it serves as a caveman-like survival mechanism, which can sometimes be a detriment to our overall physical and emotional well-being (e.g., our fight or flight response, and instinct to distract or stop children from crying).

Use your *intuition* to determine what your child may be trying to communicate to you, what he or she needs in the moment, and how you respond to them. Avoid becoming overwhelmed with milestone timelines, the plethora of baby advice, or comparing your child to others of his or her own age. Rest in the fact that you aren't supposed to have all the answers, all the time. Indeed, there will be *many* times where you will be unable to discern an obvious reason as to why your child is upset, crying, or experiencing sleep regression—and this is okay. Holding the loving intention to offer your warm and supportive presence and employing your best efforts to attune to your child's needs will be enough. You always know your baby best, and your intuition is better than any sleep program ever written.

Connect

Our children's sense of connection is the foundation of their confidence. Connecting with children when they express their emotional experience supports the essential elements of the parent-child relationship.
—Hand in Hand Parenting

Connection is the cornerstone of success, and establishing trust and security is the most powerful antidote for fear—which is at the core of *almost every* sleep (and behavioral) difficulty.

Children thrive on a close relationship with their parents; this enables them to successfully handle stress, upset, and conflict in their everyday lives. Children actively seek out connection from their parents throughout the day—and often overnight—so they can feel safe and secure. When a child feels connected, all parts of his or her brain are able to work together—that is, the prefrontal cortex (responsible for thinking, impulse control, memory, logic, and reasoning), the brain stem (which manages reflexes, heart rate, breathing, and other basic bodily functions), and the limbic system (which governs all aspects of social and emotional functioning, coordinates the communication between all parts of the brain, and signals to the body that "all is well"—i.e., there is no threat to one's safety). When children are connected, they can learn, think, and remember. They can be flexible about their needs and demands, demonstrate empathy toward others, and can be their inherently easygoing, cooperative, and joyous selves. Connection literally builds a child's intelligence and enables them to access the innate intelligence they already have. The result? An increased sense of well-being, a harmonious parent-child relationship, and the ability for a child to reach age-appropriate milestones and sleep well.

To the contrary, disconnection commonly occurs when a parent's attention and energy shifts from the child. When a child's sense of safety and connection is compromised, the child experiences some degree of hurt (e.g., worry, sadness, shame, loneliness, or anger). When these feelings consume a child, he or she is unable to think and cannot cooperate, listen, or learn. There can be many things, big or small, that can break a child's connection: a parent being ill, a family member moving away, a parent talking on the phone, separation from a parent (e.g., the child is left in the care of someone else, or the parent leaves the child temporarily), or when a parent's emotional state may be compromised (e.g., he or she is distracted, frustrated, or stressed).

When a child feels disconnected, the prefrontal cortex (the thinking part of the brain) shuts down, and the limbic system is unable to effectively coordinate all parts of the brain to maintain emotional equilibrium.

Children may respond to feelings of disconnect in one of two ways: they may have a spontaneous emotional release—tears, tantrums, laughter, trembling, or perspiring—or they engage in off-track (attention-seeking, or "bad") behavior to let a parent know they need help to restore their thinking, security, and confidence.

Some disconnections may be small and can be easily repaired with a parent's loving attention and touch. Others may be major—often if the child has previously experienced a real loss or danger, which is evident when he or she may express big feelings over small or trivial things. In such cases, the child may cry and tantrum intensely and for longer periods.

Children are innately resourceful and clever. When gripped by big feelings, they may attempt to remedy this by setting up a situation that will elicit an emotional release so they can recover and heal. Some children may relentlessly test boundaries with undesirable behavior—with the intention that the parent will set a limit for them to rage against. Alternatively, children may simply seek out their parents' warm embrace to make them feel connected once more—as the limbic system responds positively to nonverbal cues.

As a parent, the three most effective ways to provide connection are; move close, stop any off-track—or inflexible—behavior, and listen. This creates safety and gives our children permission to offload the emotional tension that is causing the break in connection.

Support Tears and Tantrums

Let feelings be. Accept tantrums, meltdowns, whines, neediness, disappointments, sadness, major and minor complaints without judgment. Our children's feelings and desires are involuntary and do not belong to us. Managing, calming, or otherwise "fixing" them is not our responsibility, nor is it helpful to them.

    —Janet Lansbury

Children cry for two reasons:

1. To communicate an immediate need such as hunger, holding, thirst, cleanliness, sleep, or stimulation.

2. To recover (or heal) from emotional stress and/or physical pain, for example:

- prenatal stress
- birth trauma
- unfilled needs
- overstimulation
- developmental frustrations
- physical pain
- frightening events such as loud noises
- separation from parents and parental stress

When we have met our children's primary needs, crying serves as an innate healing mechanism that enables children to maintain emotional equilibrium.

Biochemist and "tear expert" Dr. William Frey discovered that emotional tears allow the body to excrete stress hormones and other toxins, and stimulate the production of endorphins—our body's natural pain killer and "feel-good" hormones.

When held in the attentive, loving arms of their parents, and *not left to do so alone*, crying promotes healing of past or present hurts, fears, and trauma and is an effective release for everyday stresses and tensions—especially beneficial in the early years when our children are evolving very rapidly and hence transition, change, and developmental frustrations are inescapable.

Most of us have an aversion to hearing babies and children cry, mainly because of the uncomfortable feelings it evokes within us from our own upbringing—particularly anxiety, fear, sadness, and a sense of failure. Parents will do almost anything to stop their child from crying: distraction, pacifier use, feeding, holding, rocking, patting, or driving in the car for hours on end.

Albeit that we are often motivated by instinct (different from intuition), and our intentions may be genuine, such actions become our children's sleep crutches, needs, habits, and control patterns, which negatively impact their ability to self-settle or sleep well in the long term.

For adults and children alike, we all must regulate ourselves physiologically to maintain overall health and well-being. For example, anything we consume must be digested, assimilated, and the waste eliminated. The same applies to our emotions. Any uncomfortable feelings, stresses, or tensions triggered by an earlier life event or experienced in the current moment must be efficiently processed and released—or eliminated—for emotional regulation and our ability to effectively manage stress, change, and transition.

Children are highly sensitive and aware. They are biologically programmed to release uncomfortable or painful feelings freely and vigorously in the present moment; this often explains how infants and toddlers can transform from a contented and happy disposition to raging, crying, laughing, or screaming quite literally at the drop of a hat. If children are supported to release these feelings freely—without distraction, shame, or punishments—their limbic system can work to restore the brain's broken connection, and they can effectively (and efficiently) return to their innate joyful, cooperative, and enthusiastic self.

To the contrary, unreleased feelings are stored away in a child's "emotional backpack" and often culminate in irrational behavior, tantrums, excessive crying, or screaming at times when a child may be feeling distressed, overwhelmed, overtired, or something in the current moment triggers similar painful emotions from a past event.

Ever wondered why your child behaves like an "angel" when in the care of others (e.g., grandparents or at childcare), but as soon as they are reunited with you, they will cry and tantrum incessantly? Rest assured—this is a universal parenting phenomenon! Albeit frustrating, it is a compliment that your child feels most safe and secure with you to show you his or her true feelings. Children often reserve their most passionate emotional expressions for those closest to them, and this often succeeds times when separation has occurred and the child has felt somewhat insecure to release his or her heavy feelings momentarily while in the care of others.

If children are not supported to release these feelings by day, they often surface overnight when a child is in an altered state of consciousness—and unable to exert the physical energy required to keep these feelings suppressed. Repressed feelings become the catalyst for bedtime resistance, nightmares, night terrors, habitual catnapping, frequent night waking, and long-term inconsistencies with sleep in general.

Listen

Listening to Children

> "By deleting from our parenting job description the responsibilities to 'soothe', 'correct' and 'control' our kids' feelings and replacing them with 'accept', 'acknowledge' and 'support', both parent and child are rewarded and liberated."
> —Janet Lansbury

Listening is vital for connection and a powerful tool for changing sleep patterns. When we offer our loving presence and *really* listen to a child as they express their emotional experience—without judgment or prejudices triggered from our own upbringing—we communicate to them that they are safe, they are loved, and they are accepted.

Whether infants, children, or adults, having someone listen to us allows us to effectively offload tensions and stresses and heal trauma from our past, which otherwise depreciates our intelligence and inhibits our thinking, learning, and development.

You can help a child heal from physical or emotional hurt by listening as he or she cries, for as long as the child needs to cry for—ideally without distraction, becoming agitated (or triggered), and/or "taking on" our children's mood or feelings. Offering gentle validation of the child's emotional experience intermittently, while holding a safe space for them to offload their feelings (i.e., stating what you see *without* judgment, shame, or trying to "fix" the situation) helps a child to feel acknowledged and understood—expediting the healing process. When you listen to your child's upset, his or her feelings may temporarily become more intense. Crying may evolve to thrashing or screaming but will eventually dissipate if a parent counters this with his or her warmth, love, closeness, and undivided attention. As prefaced earlier, there can be no reasoning or logic at times where a child is experiencing an emotional upset because the thinking part of the brain (i.e., the prefrontal cortex) has shut down. Connection—by listening—is the most effective way to help a child release the tensions that consume him or her, helping the child to restore broken connection and function optimally. After a period of intense listening, it is common for children to demonstrate cognitive and physical skills that they were previously unable to master—because tensions consume a child's attention and energy, which can otherwise be more efficiently directed toward learning, growth, and development.

My husband was leaving for work one morning when my three-year-old became unexpectedly upset—begging him not to go. My husband gave him a kiss-and-cuddle good-bye and reassured him that he would return before dinner time. As he shut the door behind him, my son's protest quickly escalated to a full-blown cry as he fell to the floor in a flood of tears. I assumed a position beside him on the floor and warmly acknowledged that he was having a hard time. "I know you don't want Daddy to go," I said in a calm, loving tone. "Daddy has gone to work, and you want him to stay here with you." He proceeded to cry harder.

Each time I validated him, he would lash out with undeniable aggression. I attempted to move closer to place my hand on him, but each time he would become more upset and move away from me. Honoring his request for space, I assumed my position close to him but far enough so that he did not feel threatened or disrespected. Knowing that he was undoubtedly feeling an accumulation of big emotions (we had recently relocated from Australia to San Diego and were also "potty training" at the time), I continued to offer further reassurance: "I am not going to leave you while you are so upset. I am going to stay with you until you feel better. I am here for you, and I love you very much." All the while, he cried and cried.

Every five minutes or so, I would attempt again to offer some physical comfort, but this only made him cry harder as he shied away. We sat together on the floor for close to an hour before his tears started to gradually dissipate. It was at this moment that I offered him a cuddle, which he graciously accepted. I thought some laughter might lighten the mood, so I proceeded to sniff in his ear and lick his cheek (pretending to be a puppy). He began to smile and giggle, and his demeanor completely transformed —from fear, isolation, and grief to a relaxed, happy, and carefree child. He then stood up and used the potty completely unassisted—when only an hour earlier, he was afraid to do so.

Listening Partnerships for Parents

Just as children need to be supported to release their feelings regularly to remain on track, happy, and cooperative, we too need to have this opportunity so we can connect with our children and parent effectively. Put simply, how can we listen to our children if no one listens to us?

Imagine how *you* would feel if you were experiencing emotional upset and all you wanted was your partner to acknowledge you, but instead, he or she patted you on the back and said, "Shush! You'll be okay—don't worry." This would almost certainly evoke further upset. Consequently, because of feeling unsafe to cry—release and heal—in the present moment, you brush these feelings under the carpet, the by-product of which is commonly the accumulation of feelings such as anger, resentment, and sadness. It is common for adults in such moments to rely on *their* control patterns to temporarily distract themselves from the pain of feeling—for example, unloved, unsupported, or unheard. Common methods of repression include drugs, alcohol, aggression, withdrawal, and self-destructive behavior. Unfortunately, because of the law of regulation—which sustains what goes in must come out—these stored feelings will remain in check, often resurfacing the next time you and your partner have an argument, or you feel triggered by similar hurtful feelings. You may also experience disturbed sleep or nightmares as you subconsciously attempt to process and release these uncomfortable emotions to self-regulate.

Now, imagine this scenario differently: your partner sits down with an arm around you, looks at you lovingly in the eyes, and in a warm tone, says, "Darling, it sounds like you have had a really hard day. I can see how upset you are. I am here for you, and I love you. We will get through this together." Your partner's kind reassurance promotes the safe environment you need in order to cry and offload the heavy feelings that have been burdening you. A while later you stop crying, and a feeling of relief sweeps over you—as if a weight has been lifted off your shoulders. You feel a contented tiredness and later fall into a deep, sound slumber. *Emotional release often encourages a deep and restorative sleep—for children and adults—allowing the brain to integrate, recover, and heal.*

Many of us are harboring negative emotional patterns—unresolved hurts, fears, grief, and trauma from our own childhood and upbringing —and when left unhealed, these feelings infiltrate the way we connect with our children and others. Our past hurts are commonly triggered in moments where our resolve may be compromised (e.g., when we are feeling exhausted, unsupported, emotional, or hormonal), and by our children's behavior (anything from crying, tantrums, or language —to simply a look), which leads to us feeling out of control, angry, and frustrated. Our fear and disempowerment in such situations often result in undesirable parenting choices: spanking, yelling, threats, and punishments—because *our* prefrontal cortex shuts down. *History usually repeats itself. If you were spanked as a child, unconsciously you may default to spanking in challenging moments.*

A listening partnership is an agreement between two persons who take turns in listening to each other. It is a relationship that is built on mutual trust and respect and is free from judgment. It is not a conversation, nor is it an opportunity for the listener to provide advice, react, share his or her similar personal experiences, or attempt to offer solutions. The role of a listener is just that—to listen. The listener assumes the role of a "counselor" and provides a safe and nurturing space for the other person—or "client"—to offload his or her frustrations, tensions, fears, and hurts, whether past or present. A listener believes in the intrinsic intelligence of their partner, and that they are completely capable of unearthing the answers and solutions to his or her own affairs—given the space, attention, and empathy to do so. It is not just listening with ears and mind, but with the heart.

Being listened to empowers us by directing our awareness from the current situation (the event) to the source of our past hurts or trauma (emotional patterns and feelings) so that we can consciously integrate and heal from painful memories. In doing so, this liberates us from the intensity and frequency of our emotional triggers, allowing us to truly connect with, and listen to our children more effectively when they experience upsets—without restimulation from our past, or *reacting* to our children's feelings.

A listening partnership helped me to identify the reason why I felt so triggered when my children would "dawdle." I would become very frustrated and angry. "Hurry up!" "quickly!" and "we are going to be late!" frequented my vocabulary at least one hundred times per day—or so it seemed. With the help of my listening partner, I uncovered the root of my impatience: my inability to be still and enjoy the present moment. I real-

ized that I very rarely stopped to celebrate the little wins in life—rather constantly distracting myself by focusing on the next thing to do or place to be. My listening partner guided me toward a more empowering mantra: "it is okay to be exactly where I am." This has been a transformational realization and shift in awareness. It has enabled me to be more present and more mindful of the external circumstances that lead to me becoming so frustrated with my children's actions. Instead of constantly rushing my children (and life in general), I have made a conscious effort to be more organized and to plan in advance so that I am not pressured by time constraints, which is a trigger in itself for me and many parents alike. I also found that regular self-care was instrumental in resolving these feelings, in particularly yoga practice and regular listening time. Listening time has allowed me to free myself from my own relentless race against time, so that I can simply just "be" with my children without distraction or incessantly having to always have an end goal.

For help with finding a listening partnership, refer to: handinhandparenting.org/how-to-find-a-listening-partner.

Regular Self-Care for Parents

Parenthood is the most important job on the planet, yet the most severely underresourced.

> "To give to our infant on demand is an enormous psychological and emotional responsibility that has the potential to drain us of energy and sanity—especially if we have no additional help. If we are also juggling a career, it can exhaust us beyond all conceivable limits, pushing us to our psychological edge."
> —Dr. Shefali Tsabary

Infants and children rely heavily on their parents for emotional regulation, and they often mirror the energy states, emotions, and behavior of those closest to them. A child's limbic system subconsciously gauges the level of attention that an adult's limbic system has available; therefore, our children's emotional state is a direct reflection of *our* current inner state. Awareness of this fact shifts our focus from the external (our children and their behavior) to the internal, that is, what we are feeling, our triggers, what we are lacking—commonly sleep, rest, support, and self-care—and what we need to counteract this and achieve a more balanced state.

To truly connect with, and support our children—emotionally and on their journey to better sleep—we (the parent) must come first. It is impossible to tend to our children's constant emotional and physical needs or demands if our "cup" is empty. Off-track behavior often results from a disconnect between the parent and child. For parents to maintain a calm disposition and be present at such times, *we must be connected.* Taking time out to rest and recover, pursue passions, and to be truly listened to within a listening partnership can have a profound effect on our ability to cope with the everyday parenting struggles.

Start by taking time out each day. As a minimum, I recommend three breaks of at least ten minutes during the day to enjoy some *"you" time*: a cup of tea (hot, not cold!), a nature walk, grounding exercises, breathing, a quick meditation, or stretching. You may even have a couple of listening partners on hand whom you can text or phone for a quick five-minute check-in when needed throughout the day. Domestic tasks should wait until after your break is over. This will also be an invaluable lesson to model for your children: as you take time to nurture and respect yourself, they will learn to do this for themselves (and you) too. *Give your child 80 percent of your presence during their waking hours, and the remaining 20 percent is all yours.* This will also help you fill up your cup—as it is impossible to support others if you are running on empty.

All good parents have bad days. However, parents who commit to regular self-care are less likely to burn out or become triggered by their children's behavior—ultimately making for a happier, more harmonious family unit.

Establish Limits Without Punishments

"Fifty years of studies show that physical punishment and verbal threats make children's behavior more challenging, and interfere with their ability to learn."
  —Hand in Hand Parenting

Children need us to set kind, but firm, limits for them to feel secure and to keep them safe—both physically and emotionally. It is important that we validate our child's emotional experience and acknowledge the various catalysts for off-track behavior such as disconnection from a parent, hunger, low blood sugar, overtiredness, changes to routine, life transitions, and dehydration—or otherwise, feelings of fear and insecurity.

Setting limits usually elicits an emotional release, and crying and tantrums often ensue. It's the quintessential blue-bowl versus pink-bowl analogy: your child wants his or her breakfast in a pink bowl. You calmly let them know that the pink bowl is in the dishwasher but today he or she may have the blue bowl instead. If the child is feeling otherwise happy and connected, albeit a little disappointed, he or she will graciously accept the blue bowl as a substitute. If your child has stored feelings that need to be released—most common if overtired, lacking one-on-one time with a parent, or during times of transition and developmental change—this scenario will most likely result in a major meltdown. In such circumstances, a parent's initial reaction is to either (a) locate the pink bowl to "keep the peace" or (b) punish, shame, scold, or dismiss the child's feelings by telling him or her that "it's only a bowl," "don't be silly," or "if you're going to behave like this, you can leave the table."

As a parent, if you observe that your child becomes irrationally upset over a small incident during the day, this is the *perfect* opportunity to remain firm with the limit (i.e., do not give in). For example, even if you can easily locate the pink bowl, you may say instead, "I'm sorry, sweetheart, there is no pink bowl today; you can have the blue bowl." The color of the bowl merely serves as a pretext for the child to release any stored feelings, which are always better out than in.

A child who is feeling tension carried over from earlier difficult times may have an intense emotional release over what appears to be a trivial issue. If a child has major unhealed feelings from a previous life event (e.g., he or she has endured life-threatening circumstances, birth trauma, or hospitalization), such episodes of intense release will reoccur more frequently—usually when the child is placed in situation that triggers similar feelings from the earlier memory. An example of this may be a child who experienced a traumatic separation from his or her mother at birth. This child may continue to feel threatened or sad every time he or she is separated from a parent. In such circumstances, open communication and connection is key. Proceed with connection tools such as regular quality time and play as detailed later in this chapter. When big feelings surface, listen lovingly—pouring in warmth and intimacy so your child can continue to feel safe to heal their hurts.

"Letting your child have his emotion and letting him know that you understand it's hard not to get what he wants is the kindest and most helpful thing you can do for your child at that moment."
—Dr. Dan Siegel and Mary Hartzell, *Parenting from the Inside Out*

There is no such thing as a naughty or bad child. It is not our child's intention to be hurtful, manipulative, or disrespectful; in fact, most undesirable behavior is unconscious—attributed to some degree of disconnect between parent and child. Therefore, connection is the foundation for creating positive, sustainable change—for behavior, and sleep alike.

When a child's sense of safety is threatened, their limbic system—or reptilian brain—is activated, triggering a stress response. During fight or flight, there can be no reason, logic, thinking, or memory. Incredibly, up to 50 percent of a child's intelligence can be suppressed when experiencing environmental stress.

Attempting to reason with a child at this time, therefore, becomes impossible, and any lessons we try to instill will be futile. For example, your two-year-old knows not to pull the cat's tail, but you are preoccupied with house chores—disconnection sets in—and lo and behold, he pulls the cat's tail right in front of you! It is parents' instinct to become frustrated or angry and question why their usually "well-behaved" child may display such "naughty" behavior when they know better—given you have told them a thousand times not to do that very thing!

The tradition in most cultures is to blame, scold, lecture, and enforce punishments. However, this does little to change behavior in the long term. Instead, it shames and isolates children and ignores the root of the undesired behavior. These are also lost opportunities to connect with your child, intensifying—not improving—undesirable behavior over time.

If we want to create a long-term change in behavior and reconnect, we must move in close and offer our unconditional love and acceptance. Physical touch can expedite the healing process by reducing stress and increasing oxytocin and endorphins, which promote a feeling of well-being. If your child responds positively to a cuddle or being held at times of upset, then do so. Some children may become physically aggressive if you attempt to move close (fear). In such cases, honor their need for space and hold an attentive presence at a short distance while listening lovingly. Reassure your child that you will not leave them alone while they are feeling so upset. Tell them that you love them dearly and will stay with them until they are feeling better. Put aside the lessons and "I told you so" for when they have calmed down and the prefrontal cortex—thinking part of the brain—is back in the driver's seat.

> My two-year-old son was starting to make a habit of constantly opening the fridge and taking food out—some of which he ate, and some he didn't. Knowing that this was beginning to serve as a diversion for boredom or emotional release (as opposed to satisfying genuine hunger), one morning after breakfast, I decided to set the limit.
>
> I made sure that he couldn't be hungry—I had witnessed the sheer quantity of food he had consumed prior to this so-called "intervention." With

a gentle hand on his, I knelt-down, looked deeply into his eyes, and said gently; "no more food for now sweetie."

"No!" he screamed, as he desperately tried to get around me and open the fridge. I could see that he was becoming agitated and some heavy emotions were beginning to surface. I remained firm, and with a hand against the fridge (holding it closed) I said; "I am sorry honey, I know you're not hungry. Let's move away from the fridge now and you can have something more to eat a little later." With that, he proceeded to scream and cry—lashing out to hit me, which luckily, I anticipated, raising my hand to meet his in front of my face.

I knew that he had an accumulation of frustrations; being the third—and youngest—child meant that he was continually either left out, or bossed around by his older siblings—not to mention that developmentally, he had been trying so hard to communicate verbally, but much of the time he couldn't quite find the words to express himself effectively.

I remained close beside him as he continued to cry facedown on the kitchen floor. It was some time before he stopped—all the while I was unable to offer any physical comfort or move closer without him becoming more upset and aggressive. Intermittently, I provided warm and loving reassurance; "I love you. I won't leave you while you are so upset. We will get through this difficult time together."

When he finally did stop crying, he peeled himself off the floor and gave me a big cuddle and kiss. It was his nap time, so I tucked him into his bed and he fell asleep instantly—exhausted from all the crying. He slept for two and a half hours straight—his longest nap in weeks.

In the days that followed, I noticed remarkable advances in his vocabulary–new words, and even some sentences! He was more content, and he stopped opening the fridge completely. This experience—and transformation in my son's behavior—made me more aware of the little diversions (or control patterns) that our children develop to help them deal with change to their routine and amid life transitions. This also cemented the importance of setting limits (and listening) as a valuable connection tool to support our children to release and heal from the big—or little —things that bother them.

Quality One-on-One Time

Remember this: quality, not quantity. Just five to ten minutes per day of one-on-one time can work wonders to build connection, trust, and confidence for children of all ages—effective in reducing off-track behavior during the day and disturbed sleep overnight. Quality time means time spent without distractions and it does not include doing things like morning/bedtime routines or house chores. It is recommended to time the play by using a stopwatch so that your child has definitive boundaries for when quality time begins and ends.

Empower your older child by allowing him or her to choose the activity (within reason!) and avoid your impulse to teach lessons, correct, or manipulate the play—unless you perceive it to be a threat to your child's (or your) safety. Encourage silliness, laughter, and the opportunity for your child to lead, win, or be the master of the activity.

If you have a young baby, engage with him or her by using plenty of eye contact, age-appropriate physical play, touch, singing, reading, and affection. Babies between seven and twelve months of age may be able to pass you a book or toy, or begin directing the play by signaling "come catch me!" as they crawl or walk away from you.

Children are innately intelligent and resourceful. They know when they have something that needs to be healed and will seek out the opportunity to recover from such feelings—either through play (laughter) or an alternative emotional release, such as crying or tantrums. When children are given the opportunity to direct the play, you will notice that they quite literally "act out" their own fears in their attempt to heal from the things that bother them. Therefore, it is common for some big feelings to arise either during or following quality time. Be prepared to listen if laughter turns to tears—it's better for these feelings to be released during the day than overnight!

Don't beat yourself up if some days you are simply unable to schedule this time. Instead, try using the ordinary interactions with your child—or daily tasks—as an opportunity to engage, be playful, and affectionate. Use plenty of eye contact, physical touch, and enthusiasm—embracing every opportunity to create laughter. For example, you may strategically place underpants on your head when folding the laundry, playfully tackle your child when getting him or her dressed, or make up a silly song or dance as you go about your routine activities (e.g., changing diapers, cleaning up toys, or eating meals).

My three-year-old son was having nightmares regularly over a week or two. When he cried out in the early hours of the morning, I would go to him and offer comfort. When I questioned him about what he was afraid of, he informed me that there were animals in his closet. He wouldn't elaborate as to which animals or whether there was anything that had triggered such fears—and to my knowledge, I couldn't think of any movie, book, event, or anything else that might have been the catalyst for the disturbed sleep.

We had been doing quality one-on-one time regularly. One day, I informed him that it was "quality time" and asked him what he wanted to do. He replied with "I want to play the baby rhino (rhinoceros) game." Okay, I thought to myself! I asked him to lead the way. What he did quite literally astounded me. He asked me to kneel on the floor, and he proceeded to hide behind me. My role was to pretend I was looking for the baby rhino: "Where is that baby rhino? I know he is here somewhere— baby rhino, where are you?" After twenty seconds of calling out, my son appeared from behind my back, where I acted surprised to see him, but also greeted him with love and cuddles. This game continued for the entire twenty minutes of our time together, and we played the "rhino game" every day for one week. From the first day that we began playing this game, my son began sleeping much better, and the nightmares stopped. This was the first time I had witnessed just how innately clever our children could be at literally "playing out" their fears—given the safety, trust, and opportunity to do so.

When first introducing quality one-on-one time, don't be alarmed if your usually contented child begins tantrum or cry—or does so more regularly in the days that follow. This is a healthy sign that he or she is shifting some previously stored emotions, enabled by the closeness and safety that quality time brings. Regular emotional release helps engage children's full intelligence. It can accelerate their physical and cognitive ability and enable them to reach developmental milestones more efficiently. At times of transition, or when changing sleep patterns, increasing the amount of quality time per day can help children adjust with greater ease and cooperation.

Play

The Importance of Laughter

> "Laughter is the shortest distance between two people."
> —Victor Borge

Promoting laughter through play builds trust, connection, and confidence—consequently releasing (past or present) stress and tension. Laughter is especially beneficial for children who have developed fears of the dark—or bedtime in general—or who may have insecurities around certain life transitions such as introducing a new sibling, beginning childcare, potty training, or facing a change to their sleep routine.

Laughter is generally the icing on the cake; when melted away through play and close attention, it helps to reveal more intense feelings of fear, grief, and hurt to be healed under the surface. If you notice that something particularly creates laughter for your child, do more of that! Some children will indulge in a deep belly laugh when a parent pretends to fall over or walks into the wall. Similarly, funny faces, silly dance moves, or basic horse play can be a healing experience for children to laugh away their fears, which may otherwise be the catalyst for nightmares, night terrors, or disturbed sleep in general.

Roughhousing Play

Roughhousing is spontaneous, boisterous, and interactive play that is both physically and mentally stimulating because it recruits the body and the brain. It has been said to improve emotional intelligence, memory, learning, and logic, and it is especially effective when making a change to routine or during any transition that may evoke feelings of insecurity. Because roughhousing helps to reduce stress and encourages emotional release, it is particularly effective for separation anxiety, breaking habits, and changing sleep patterns.

Various play ideas can include pillow fights, rough-and-tumble, jumping on the bed, hide-and-seek, chasey, and horseback rides. My kids particularly love playing "duck, duck, goose" before bedtime, which is a great opportunity for the whole family to be involved, have a laugh, and let off some steam—both physically and emotionally. Play is also effective at lightening the mood and relieving parents and children from the monotony of the everyday bedtime routine.

> **Tip:** Refrain from tickling to elicit laughter as this is forced as opposed to child led and may cause some children to feel trapped, vulnerable, and disempowered. Instead, try wiggling your fingers just above their belly or underarms—this usually instigates laughter simply in the anticipation of being tickled.

It is common for laughter to transform to tears following connected and playful moments, so make allowances for some listening time if your child becomes emotional.

Roughhousing preceding bedtime can be especially effective at minimizing bedtime resistance and improving overall sleep duration as it enables children to offload any stored tensions, frustrations, disappointments, or upsets from their day (attributed to a combination of past and/or present events, separation, or lack of connection). Supporting our children to release these feelings before sleep times significantly reduces the need for children to wake overnight in order to process—and release—such emotions.

Aim for at least five to ten minutes per day. Although many children respond positively, you may want to avoid this at least twenty to thirty minutes preceding bedtimes if you notice that your child becomes hyperactive or has increased difficulty falling asleep.

Role-Playing

For children eighteen months and older, role-playing can be an effective tool to create laughter, release fears, and strengthen the parent-child bond. Using dolls, teddies, figurines, or simply your own imagination (i.e., creative play) to normalize your child's struggles can work wonders to encourage security at these times—acquiescing somewhat heavy moods or emotions and helping you to facilitate change more easily and organically.

My son was two and a half years old and had been attending childcare (quite happily) three days per week, when one day, he decided that he didn't want to go anymore. This sudden change of heart did not come as a huge surprise; we had recently welcomed our third child into the family, and there was certainly some adjusting to a new family dynamic and a shift in the attention I once shared equally between him and his sister.

Acknowledging that undoubtedly he was feeling a mix of heavy emotions, I knew that I had to dig deep in my "parenting toolbox" to support him (and myself) through this challenging time.

One morning, we pulled up at childcare, and I could see that he was starting to cry. I decided to try a "role reversal." In a small, shaky voice, I said, "I don't want to go into childcare today—I am scared." My son's expression changed from fear and sadness to concern, as he said, "Mommy, it's okay; don't be scared." I proceeded to ask him if he could come in and hold my hand and look after me so that I would feel safe—of which he happily obliged. That morning we walked hand in hand into childcare together; no flood of tears, no resistance—for the first time in two weeks! After staying with him for some time, I told him that it was time for me to leave, to which his response was to cry and tell me not to go. I reassured him that I would be back soon, and he would be safe with Natalie, his carer.

The fear of not wanting to go eventually dissipated over another week or so with a combination of various connection tools, including quality time (before and after care), listening, and more role-playing. But this day was certainly a defining moment for me. I was not confident that a role reversal would work in the moment (seeing as it was the first time I had tried it), but it was extremely successful at empowering my son and instilling the confidence necessary to help him overcome his fear of separation.

Avoid Behavioral Approaches Such As "Cry It Out"

Sleep is a biological and emotional process, not a behavioral one. Behavioral sleep issues develop when a child's emotional needs remain unmet. Therefore, if parents desire sustainable changes to sleep patterns, they must focus on connection as the priority.

Otherwise referred to as controlled crying, controlled comforting, or responsive settling; the most popular variations of cry it out (CIO) were pioneered by Daniel Weissbluth and Richard Ferber.

Weissbluth's *extinction* method instructs parents to leave their baby to cry alone for up to an hour at nap times (indefinitely at bedtime), while Ferber's method of *graduated extinction* is a modified version of this—leaving the child to cry for intervals of three, five, and ten minutes (for up to twenty minutes) whilst checking on them intermittently to resettle and offer comfort.

Such "sleep training" methods are generally not recommended for children younger than six months, and although some parents may experience quick results, these are rarely long-term, or without drawbacks.

Children are fast learners. If you leave them to cry alone with minimal intervention over a period of three days or more, they will stop crying eventually; it's cause and effect, and in fact, a survival instinct. However, it is largely debatable whether such methods are successful in changing sleep habits, or whether this is just attributed to learned helplessness.

Some experts claim that cry it out can compromise secure attachment. Others have linked such methods (that involve a child crying for extended periods in isolation) to raised cortisol levels, causing undue stress and rise in blood pressure—and in extreme cases, developmental delays, poor social skills, and a higher risk of behavioral and psychiatric disorders later in life.

I have worked with many families who have endured varying degrees of sleep regression after implementing cry it out. It is also very common for babies to experience some level of trauma after being left to cry alone, and consequently, a child may begin to resist—or become fearful of—their usual bedtime routine, wake more frequently overnight, and/or exert more off-track behavior.

To the contrary, there is also no such thing as a "no cry" approach —nor should this be encouraged. Crying is an effective medium for babies to communicate and is essential for emotional regulation. Because feelings of fear, stress, and overwhelm are often inextricable with (developmental and routine) change, it is important to acknowledge a child's need to cry to enable the release of such heavy feelings during these times.

However, unless our children can release—and heal—their fears and insecurities through crying in the supportive presence of their parents (rather than being left alone to do so behind a closed door), these emotions will continue to be repressed. It is only a matter of time before accumulated feelings resurface, manifesting in sleep regression, behavioral difficulties, and sometimes even physical ailments. Such challenges commonly arise during life transitions, a change to routine, or in the midst of developmental milestones, which often trigger feelings of separation/abandonment, fear/insecurity, and disempowerment—similar feelings associated with being left to cry alone. The degree to which this impacts a child's emotional well-being throughout childhood and well into adolescence is unknown.

Communicate Your Intentions

It is important for us as parents to be transparent and to communicate any changes to sleep patterns and routine *in advance* if we want our children to continue to feel secure. And when we implement these changes, ensure that we do so in a kind, respectful, and gentle manner that encourages their cooperation. Forewarning children of our intentions also ensures that we don't distract or interrupt our children from any task they are highly engaged in, as this may rob them of vital learning opportunities. At times of change and transition, feelings of fear, anxiety, confusion, apprehension, uncertainty, and insecurity are common. Consequently unsettledness, crying, and tantrums can be heightened at these times. Planning ahead—by allowing an extra fifteen to thirty minutes prior to leaving the house or before bedtimes —enables parents to listen more effectively to their child without time restraints and the inextricable feelings of frustration and anger that ensue when we are feeling rushed.

Form a Secure Attachment

A parent's responsiveness to a child's needs—in particular, their basic needs such as hunger, closeness, warmth, and emotional connection—

is ultimately the cornerstone of secure attachment. Some examples are as follows:

- **Dunstan baby language** is an effective method to decipher between your infant's different cries so that you can respond to his or her needs appropriately: NEH is hungry, OWH is sleepy, HEH is discomfort, EAIR is lower gas, and EH communicates a need to burp. Refer to www.dunstanbaby.com.

- **Connect** with play, quality time, physical closeness, and taking the time to listen. Babies are innately intelligent, and they may just surprise you with their attentiveness and willingness to cooperate in daily tasks at such a young age— e.g., a young baby may lift his or her hips up when having a diaper change, or might attempt to push their legs through pant holes when being dressed.

- **Tuning into a baby's hunger cues** will provide parents with the confidence that their baby is well fed and content. Common early cues include smacking or licking lips, opening and closing their mouth, sucking on fists, rooting around for the breast, fidgeting, squirming, and fussing. If a baby is crying inconsolably or arching their back, this may indicate that you have missed his or her early hunger cues.

- **Pay attention to a child's tired signs** for his or her optimal sleep window and to minimize overtiredness and overstimulation. Common cues include rubbing eyes, yawning, sharp jerky movements of limbs, increased fussiness, crying, losing interest in activities, red eyebrows, ear pulling, and staring into space. If a baby is crying inconsolably or arching their back, this may indicate that you have missed your child's optimal sleep window.

- **Remain physically close to your young baby.** Physical closeness helps a baby regulate physiologically and emotionally. Cosleeping and baby wearing are wonderful ways to honor a child's fourth trimester—and beyond.

- **Breastfeed if possible.** Breastfeeding promotes closeness, boosts a baby's immune system, provides optimal nutrition, and floods mother and baby with the feel-good hormone, oxytocin. *Feeding on demand in the first three months is recommended.*

Physical Health

If a child is unwell, injured, in pain or discomfort, sleep and behavior will naturally be affected. Nutrition, activity levels, and the opportunity for a child to practice his or her newfound skills by day will all dictate overall sleep ability and degree of sleep regression at times of change. The health of a parent is equally important. If parents' physical well-being and energy levels are compromised, they are less likely to be patient, calm, or accepting of their child's emotional experience and physical needs. Often this leads to a break in connection—hindering sleep ability and affecting behavior. *If you are concerned about your child's health at any time, please consult your health-care practitioner.*

ROUTINE

Routine provides children with predictability and security—essential to their ability to self-settle, fall asleep with limited resistance, and sleep for longer. Children feel more confident and secure when they know what they can expect—from having structure in their day (i.e., mealtimes, nap times, bedtimes, and playtimes) to our responses to them and the boundaries that we establish for their behavior, and at sleep times.

An age-appropriate routine can help minimize overtiredness, which is the predominant catalyst for bedtime resistance, catnapping, early rising, frequent night waking, and the habits that parents develop to counteract the overstimulation that occurs as a result (e.g., feeding, rocking, patting, or holding to sleep). When a child is overtired, that is, from lack of day sleep or inappropriate rest or wind-down time, his or her cortisol levels escalate (cortisol is a stress hormone, which has a far more potent stimulant effect than caffeine). Bedtime resistance and erratic behavior commonly ensues, making it extremely challenging for a child to fall asleep (and remain asleep) without parental intervention—and making any attempts to change sleep patterns unnecessarily arduous.

Other variables with a child's routine that may impact sleep ability include undertiredness (from too much day sleep), developmental stage, teething, a change to the sleep environment, lack of stimulation or physical activity, lack of connection (i.e., listening, play, and quality time), overstimulation or exhaustion, travel, holidays, a change in carers, and dropping naps.

Our current emotional state will also discern our level of responsiveness to our children and our commitment to any parenting or sleep method. When parents are confident in their decisions and follow through, our children feel safer and will naturally be more responsive to change. We all have our days, or times in life where things feel increasingly difficult or stressful, so it is important to remember to be kind and patient with yourself. Nobody is perfect, and "good enough parenting" is good enough.

The 80/20 Rule

"Consistency" is the most overrated (and overused) word in the world of baby sleep. Instead of asking parents to be *consistent*—which often elicits resistance to change—it's simply easier to refer to the 80/20 rule, which maintains that whatever we are *persistent* in doing 80 percent of the time establishes our habits and patterns—whether we are conscious of this or not. The remaining 20 percent affords families with some flexibility to accommodate for life's unexpected turn of events: illness, teething, developmental leaps, life transitions, travel, holidays, temporarily being out of routine, and missing the sleep window.

The 80/20 rule also applies to breaking habits. For example, if you can ensure that 80 percent of the time you are not feeding your child to sleep, if he or she happens to fall asleep on the breast every now and then, it's not the end of the world. Similarly, if your child can self-settle 80 percent of the time but occasionally requires some additional assistance to fall asleep (typically common during times of teething, illness, separation anxiety, and developmental milestones) you need not assume that you are creating long-term or "undesirable" sleep patterns.

The Rule of Three

When making any changes to a child's routine, persisting for a *minimum of three days*—ideally one to two weeks—will allow you to appropriately gauge the effectiveness of the change implemented, before pursuing alternative avenues. *I recommend focusing on one change at a time to avoid overwhelm and confusion.* A period of three days also seems to be the average time frame whereby a child may develop new sleep patterns—or crutches. Therefore, when changing habits that require a gradual withdrawal of intervention (e.g., rocking or feeding to sleep), ensure that you remove your intervention slightly every three days— refer to "The Sleep Play Love Method."

ENVIRONMENT

Light, noise, sound, temperature, smells, and toxins can impact a child's sleep ability. The optimal environment may also be influenced by the age and sensitivity of your child (e.g., babies under twelve months may require additional bedding layers as they are unable to effectively regulate their own body temperature, or a soft light at night may be necessary for older toddlers, as some may develop fear of the dark from two years of age).

Optimizing the Environment

- **Expose your child to natural, unfiltered sunlight every day.** This is essential for melatonin production (sleep hormone) and regulation of your child's circadian rhythm (internal body clock)—necessary for deciphering day from night and establishing regular sleep patterns.

- **Maintain a dark room for all sleeps.** A dark room encourages the release of melatonin. A dimmed salt lamp may be used in or outside your child's room if you need to navigate your way for overnight settling or feeds. *Red light is less disruptive (than white or blue light) to the circadian rhythm.*

- **Maintain a room temperature between 66°F and 72°F (19°C and 22°C).** Many children wake overnight or early in the morning because they are cold—especially in the cooler months. Maintaining warmth can be the key to helping a child sleep more soundly, and for longer. Refer to "The Sleep Play Love Bedding Guide" as follows.

- **Make your child's room a safe, cozy haven.** Think warmth, security, and comfort:

  · Rugs can add warmth to tiles, polished concrete or wooden surfaces.
  · A rocking or feeding chair can offer a resting place for weary parents when attending to unsettled children overnight.
  · Empower older children by allowing them to select their own bedding, wallpaper, or a special toy for their room.
  · Ensure a safe transition from a crib to toddler bed by using a foam, mesh, or wood safety guard (bed rail).

- **White noise** can promote sound, quality sleep for all ages because it helps to block out external and household noises that may otherwise wake your child during naps and overnight. Ensure that the volume is no louder than 50 dB (approximately the volume of somebody taking a shower). Position between your child and the greatest source of noise (e.g., a door or window) and ensure a distance of at least one to two meters from your child's head. *I recommend Sleepy Sounds (downloadable for free on iTunes) on a white noise or heavy-rain sound setting and playing indefinitely during sleep times—not on a timer.*

- **Reduce EMF exposure.** Electromagnetic frequency can interfere with a child's sensitive, developing brain. To minimize exposure, be sure to switch off Wi-Fi and all electrical appliances at the wall when not in use and overnight. Switch phones and iPads to airplane mode and position your child's head away from any power boards or electrical cables.

- **Avoid baby monitors.** Albeit a personal preference, be mindful that video and sound monitors can disrupt sleep for many reasons. Not only do they emit high levels of EMF but the camera light on video monitors can also distract babies at sleep times if positioned in their line of vision. Monitors can also impact the parent's ability to sleep soundly because of their sensitivity to movement (monitors will light up and make sounds multiple times throughout the night when intervention is unnecessary). If you decide to use a monitor for peace of mind, where possible, opt for a *wired baby monitor*.

- **Position your child's crib/bed away from windows.** Drafts from windows can make your child cold overnight.

- **Avoid toxins in your child's room and your house.** This includes wall paint, skincare products, carpet, bedding, mattress, clothing, and cleaning products. Opt for organic where possible.

- **Avoid blue and white light *at least* one hour preceding sleep times.** Blue light (emitted from electronics, computers, iPhones, iPads, and televisions) and white light (such as internal household lights and lamps) interfere with a child's circadian rhythm because it suppresses melatonin, compromising a child's ability to fall asleep and remain asleep.

- **Implement a relaxing bedtime routine.** Try reading books, singing a song, diffusing essential oils (e.g., lavender, frankincense, cedarwood, bergamot, valerian, chamomile, and orange) or a guided meditation. To avoid the infamous "second wind," ensure that the actual "good-night" routine (in the child's bedroom) is no longer than twenty minutes.

- **Swaddle your young baby.** Swaddling mimics the womb environment, encouraging security and sounder sleep in the initial three months of life (i.e., the fourth trimester). It also muffles the Moro or startle reflex, preventing your baby from startling themselves awake midsleep. Many children commence the transition out of the swaddle between four to six months when they begin to roll, which may pose a risk at sleep times—this is also the age when the Moro reflex commonly integrates (i.e., is no longer active). *Refrain from swaddling your child in a car seat or baby carrier.*

- **Install a safety gate.** A safety gate may be necessary for toddlers who are transitioning from a crib to a toddler bed—especially if they start resisting sleep times and venturing out of bed repetitively at bedtime and overnight.

- **Remove crib mobiles, wall decals, light-up sound machines, and toys** to avoid distraction and overstimulation.

- **Incorporate playtime in your child's room.** Playtime in a child's crib and room encourages safety, comfort, and familiarity and can aid better sleep during transitions (e.g., separation anxiety, milestones, and changes to routine).

THE SLEEP PLAY LOVE BEDDING GUIDE

Being warm is one of essential environmental sleep foundations that can greatly impact a child's sleep duration and quality. Until children are at least twelve months old, they are unable to regulate their own body temperature. If they are not warm enough, many babies will catnap, wake frequently overnight, or wake early in the morning—commonly from 4:00 a.m. onward, or approximately two hours before waking time—when their body temperature is naturally at its lowest. Following is a guide for appropriate clothing and bedding from birth to thirty-six months. I always recommend, where possible, to keep a steady room temperature, ideally between 66°F and 72°F (19°C and 22°C).

BABIES SWADDLED FOR SLEEP (Birth to Six Months)

ROOM TEMPERATURE	SINGLET	FULL-LENGTH BODYSUIT (ARMS AND LEGS)	SWADDLE/WRAP	COTTON BLANKETS (OPTIONAL)
66°F—72°F or 19°C—23°C	✓	✓	✓	4—6
73°F—79°F or 24°C—26°C	✗	✓	✓	2—4
80°F—86°F or 27°C—30°C	✓	✗	✓	1—2
87°F or 31°C and over	✗	✗	✓	NIL

For temperatures of 87°F or 30°C and over, a pedestal or ceiling fan can be used.

BABIES NOT SWADDLED FOR SLEEP (Four to Twelve Months)

ROOM TEMPERATURE	SINGLET	FULL-LENGTH BODYSUIT (ARMS AND LEGS)	SLEEPING BAG (TOG)	COTTON BLANKETS (OPTIONAL)
66°F—72°F or 19°C—23°C	✓	✓	2.5	4—6
73°F—79°F or 24°C—26°C	✗	✓	1.0	2—4
80°F—86°F or 27°C—30°C	✓	✗	0.5	1—2
87°F or 31°C and over	✗	✗	0.3	NIL

For temperatures of 87°F or 30°C and over, a pedestal or ceiling fan can be used. Where the temperature is maintained at 68°F or 20°C, some babies (especially twelve months and over) may not need blankets in addition to a sleeping bag.

BABIES NOT SWADDLED FOR SLEEP (Twelve to Thirty-Six Months)

ROOM TEMPERATURE	SINGLET	FULL-LENGTH BODYSUIT (ARMS AND LEGS)	SLEEPING BAG (TOG)	COTTON BLANKETS (OPTIONAL)
66°F—72°F or 19°C—23°C	✓	✓	2.5	4—6
73°F—79°F or 24°C—26°C	✗	✓	1.0	2—4
80°F—86°F or 27°C—30°C	✓	✗	0.5	NIL
87°F or 31°C and over	✗	✗	0.3	NIL

For temperatures of 87°F or 30°C and over, a pedestal or ceiling fan can be used. Where the temperature is maintained at 68°F or 20°C, some babies may not need blankets in addition to a sleeping bag. If your child is no longer in a sleeping bag (i.e., between two and two and a half years old), use a bed sheet in place of a 0.3 or 0.5 tog sleeping bag, and a warm blanket/quilt in place of a 1.0 or 2.5 tog.

Bedding and Clothing Tips

- **Always use your discretion when dressing your baby for sleep.** You may need to adjust his or her clothing or bedding layers if you live in a more humid climate, or if your baby is naturally a "hot-bod."

- **If your baby has a temperature and is unwell or sweating, remove bedding layers accordingly.** Reduce the thickness (tog) of your child's sleeping bag and dress your baby lightly—it is better to underdress in these circumstances.

- **Your baby's hands and feet will always feel colder than the rest of his or her body, so don't use these body parts as a guide to how hot or cold your baby feels.** Feel your baby's chest, back of the neck, and ears. If these feel hot to the touch, then begin by removing bedding layers and then clothing—and lastly adjust the room temperature.

- **Blankets are optional, and are to be used at the parent's discretion.** Current safety guidelines stipulate that blankets pose a safety hazard for infants under twelve months old.

- **Certain skin conditions such as eczema may call for less bedding.** Heat can exacerbate symptoms. Consult with your health-care professional where necessary.

- **Avoid sleeping your baby in a hat or a beanie** as this can cause overheating.

- **Familiarize yourself with safe sleeping practices to prevent SIDS.** Sleep your baby on his or her back, maintain a smoke-free household, do not overbundle your baby, and keep the sleep space free from toys, excess bedding, and pillows. *Refrain from using a pillow for sleep times until your child is at least two years old (or has moved out of the crib and into a bed).*

- **One hundred percent cotton, bamboo, or organic nontoxic sheets, mattress, and clothing are preferable.** Synthetic fibers such as polyester, fleece, and flannel can overheat children, causing them to sweat and consequently make them cold—not to mention are toxic to the environment!

- **Crib bumpers of any kind are generally not encouraged** for safety reasons.

- **An organic, firm mattress is preferable.** Most mattresses are treated with fire retardants and a host of other chemicals during the manufacturing process. Alternatively, use a wool or cotton mattress topper coupled with a pure cotton mattress protector—plastic does not breathe, so may contribute to sweating overnight. A topper may also help make the mattress slightly softer and more comfortable for your child to sleep on.

- **Avoid purchasing a mattress secondhand where you don't know the history.** A secondhand crib is acceptable— provided it meets the safety standards. You can easily search for your country's relevant standards online.

- **Weighted blankets** help to calm the nervous system; encouraging relaxation and deeper sleep for children with sensory processing sensitivity, and/or those who experience anxiety.

- **Where possible, use a bar or oil heater instead of ducted or reverse-cycle heating.** Ducted heating can circulate dust and toxins, and when set to a specific temperature overnight, the noise of the heater turning on and off intermittently can disturb sleeping babies.

- **Sleep positioners are generally not recommended for safety reasons.** Most babies begin to roll between four and six months, and therefore, it is common for them to roll onto their tummy (and/or around the crib) during sleep times. Cease swaddling and ensure that your baby is warm enough. *Some babies will move around in their sleep if they are cold. Refer to the Sleep Play Love Bedding Guide.*

- **A ceiling or manual/pedestal fan is preferable to ducted or reverse-cycle air conditioning.** Air conditioning can make children too cold, potentially leading to illness. Cool air blowing directly on a child may also be distracting and uncomfortable.

- **For unsettled babies or those with colic or reflux, occasional day sleeps in a baby carrier, swing, hammock, stroller, capsule, or car seat (if in transit) is acceptable—** just ensure that you follow the appropriate safety guidelines and supervise your child *at all times.* Do not sleep your baby in these apparatuses overnight.

Sleep Play Love **Recommended Brands***

Love to Dream: swaddles and sleep bags.
Baby Loves Sleep: Sleepy Hugs sleep suit/transitional swaddle. Use code SLEEPPLAYLOVE15 at checkout for a 15 percent discount.
Hello Night: Wearable Blankets and layer sets—an innovative sleeping bag alternative.
Pure Baby: sleepwear.
The Gro Company: grobag sleep bags and groclock.

ergoPouch: swaddles and sleep bags.

Aden + Anais: swaddles, loveys, sleep bags, and bedding.

One hundred percent cotton Bambi Mattress Protector: alternatively, you may layer cotton towels.

*My recommendations, suggestions, and guidance are based solely upon my own personal experience, education, and knowledge. When selecting appropriate bedding (i.e., brands, clothing, layers, and materials), every child will have individual requirements, which must be considered—together with any pre-existing medical conditions, allergies, and/or illness (and at the parent's discretion). Accordingly, Sleep Play Love expressly disclaims any liability, loss, damage, or injury caused by information provided.

NUTRITION

Inadequate nutrition and/or hunger can lead to catnapping, bedtime resistance, frequent night waking, and persistent crying.

In the early months, many parents struggle to know if their baby has fed substantially. Tight, clenched fists, and a sunken fontanelle may be an indication that an infant is hungry or dehydrated. If a baby is crying from hunger prior to falling asleep, his or her fists will remain clenched long after they have fallen asleep. A satisfied baby may still clench his or her fists while crying—but once asleep, their hands will soften and his or her palms will remain open.

Feeding alone won't prevent a child from waking overnight, and it is important that other areas such as emotional well-being, sleeping environment, and routine have been addressed.

Growth spurts, developmental milestones, varying activity levels, illness, and teething can influence appetite, nutritional needs, and sleeping ability. Similarly, if your child is underweight or was born prematurely, he or she may have additional requirements for daytime and overnight feeds in the initial twelve to twenty-four months. Prior to dropping feeds, or night weaning, your child's readiness, such as age and daily nutritional intake, must be considered.

There are various foods that can promote sleep, and there are a host of foods and food ingredients that can wreak havoc on sleep, behavior, health, and allergies. Frequent water intake and snacks throughout the day can also help to minimize behavioral difficulties in toddlers that may be exacerbated by low blood sugar or dehydration—which can consequently lead to bedtime challenges.

Below is a list of the most common prosleep and antisleep foods. You don't have to avoid everything on the antisleep list; however, it may be a good idea to steer clear of these foods in the hours preceding bedtime—especially for children who may be particularly sensitive, and those with food allergies or intolerances.

Prosleep Foods

- **Dairy, almonds, sesame seeds, leafy greens, oranges, and sardines** contain calcium, which works to calm the nervous system and can help children fall asleep and stay asleep.

- **Beets, pork, poultry, and peanuts:** foods high in B3 (niacin) can extend the REM cycle and reduce middle of the night waking.

- **Oily fish, such as salmon and tuna, avocado, nuts, seeds, and cold-pressed vegetable oils** are rich in omega essential fatty acids, which can enhance the brain's secretion of melatonin (sleep hormone).

- **Seeds, nuts, and green vegetables** contain magnesium, which relaxes the muscles and calms the nervous system to encourage a sleepy state.

- **Meats, leafy greens, and legumes** contain ferritin, which is responsible for storing iron in the body. Low iron, specifically low ferritin, may result in a weakened immune system, disturbed sleep, difficulty linking sleep cycles, and in extreme cases, sleep disorders. Best sources are liver, poultry, red meat (preferably organic or grass fed), and seafood. Vegetarian sources include soybeans, lentils, lima beans, kidney beans, navy beans, peas, spinach, molasses, and fortified breakfast cereals.

- **Meats, fish, poultry eggs, legumes, peanut butter, tofu, and dairy** are high in protein, which assists in stabilizing blood sugar—keeping babies and children satisfied for longer. These foods are most beneficial to sleep when consumed in combination with carbohydrates and healthy fats (such as brown rice and avocado) and cold-pressed oils, such as coconut and flax. *Opt for grass fed, organic, and non-GMO where possible.*

- **Honey** contains glucose, which instructs the brain to shut off orexin, the chemical known to trigger alertness. Some children are sensitive to sugar—irrespective of the source— so this can also be one to potentially avoid. *Honey is not recommended until at least twelve months of age.*

- **Cherries** are a natural source of melatonin. When eaten regularly, they may help regulate the sleep cycle.

- **Almonds, turkey, hummus, and milk** contain tryptophan, which is metabolized into serotonin and melatonin, two of the main chemicals responsible for sleep.

- **Oatmeal, whole-grain or whole-meal bread, rice, pasta, and crackers:** foods that are high in carbohydrates boost serotonin and increase tryptophan absorption—both essential chemicals for sleep. *Some children may be sensitive to gluten found in wheat, so gluten-free options may be preferable.*

- **Bananas** are rich in magnesium and potassium which serve as muscle and nerve relaxants. The carbohydrates and vitamin B6 found in the fruit also converts tryptophan into serotonin, increasing relaxation even more.

Antisleep Foods

- **Chocolate** contains tyrosine, which is converted into dopamine, a stimulant. This causes alertness and restlessness. Chocolate also contains caffeine and is high in sugar.

- **Excess salt** in processed foods, cheeses, and snacks can exacerbate thirst, resulting in increased water consumption before bed and during the night. This often leads to leaky diapers and more frequent night waking—either to consume water or to use the bathroom.

- **Popcorn, red meat, beans, and legumes** can be difficult to digest and may cause bloating and gas discomfort.

- **Processed sugars** cause blood sugar levels to rise and fall dramatically. In its attempt to stabilize blood sugar levels, the body will force the adrenal glands to release adrenaline (stress hormone), which can lead to difficulty falling asleep and remaining asleep. Some children are also sensitive to the natural sugars in fruit and honey, so it may be best to avoid these before sleep.

- **Spicy or fried foods** can cause heartburn, which is often exacerbated when lying down. They may also cause stomach discomfort such as gas, bloating, and cramps.

- **Processed meats, soy products, and some hard cheeses** contain high levels of tyramine, which causes the brain to release a chemical that makes us feel alert. Fermented soy products have some of the highest amount of tyramine. Limit your child's intake of miso, tempeh, tofu, soy milk— and even teriyaki sauce. Parmesan, romano, and asiago are among the cheeses to avoid.

- **Tomatoes and tomato-based sauces** tend to cause acid reflux and heartburn.

Refer to "Routines and Recommendations" for the average recommended requirements for milk and solids by age.

POSITIVE SLEEP ASSOCIATIONS

Positive sleep associations (or cues) are key to establishing sustainable sleep patterns. This involves implementing a predictable nap and bedtime routine, which can be replicated by anyone, anywhere, at any time. Positive sleep associations day and night provide children with predictability, security, and the necessary wind-down time before bed, which can help to promote self-settling and minimize bedtime resistance and night waking.

Some Examples Include the Following:

- Bath
- Massage. *Deep pressure massage calms the nervous system and is especially beneficial for overstimulated infants or overtired babies and toddlers.*
- Swaddle and/or sleeping bag
- White noise
- Draw blinds
- Read a book
- Sing a song
- Cuddle-and-kiss good-night

Tips

- Although white noise is considered a "positive" sleep association, you may remove this from your child's routine simply by reducing the volume slightly over three to seven days.

- A safety-approved lovey may help children adapt to change with greater ease. To increase the comfort factor, express some breastmilk on the object and/or have mom wear it close to her skin for a day or so before giving it to the child. *Use strictly for bedtimes—and with awareness—to avoid the lovey developing into a control pattern and/or sleep need.*

- For children who are transitioning into a new sleep space e.g., from bassinet to crib, crib to bed, or when ceasing cosleeping; an old T-shirt of moms (worn for one to two days prior to infuse mom's scent) can encourage security and comfort at times of change. An older child may like to snuggle with the shirt at sleep times—or for younger babies, you can experiment with applying the shirt like a fitted sheet over the top of the crib mattress (so the baby's head would rest on the chest of the shirt at sleep times).

- Sleep associations such as rocking, feeding, or holding to sleep, the car, carrier, swing, stroller, and the pacifier often develop into unsustainable sleep needs or control patterns and impact a child's ability to self-settle, fall asleep, and remain asleep without repetitive parental intervention. Where possible (or at least 80 percent of the time) avoid such sleep associations immediately preceding sleep times if you wish to encourage independent sleep in the long term.

- Children don't necessarily have to bath every day—in fact scheduling bath time every second or third day may be beneficial for their gut health and overall immunity. For some children, bath time is a calming experience that helps them relax before bed. For others, it can be overstimulating, which has an adverse result. In such instance, I recommend scheduling bath times *before* mealtimes and not immediately preceding bedtime.

DEVELOPMENTAL STAGES, MILESTONES, AND TRANSITIONS

Parents should relax in the knowledge that each infant's development is directed by his unique inborn timetable. Infants will always do what they are capable of doing and are naturally wired to advance their physical abilities independently. They never hold back. An infant who is given ample opportunity to move freely on his back will discover "tummy time" on his own. Eventually, he learns to roll to his back again. He then progresses to crawling, creeping, sitting, standing, climbing, walking, running and jumping, all without the need for parental prompting, propping or other intrusions. As Magda Gerber said, readiness is when they do it.

    —Janet Lansbury

Developmental milestones and leaps are a constant in the first three years. Even the slightest change in development, such as learning a new skill, can cause sleep to regress either a little, or a lot—the degree of which will depend on a child's temperament (or sensitivity), age, parental responsiveness, and the parent-child connection, among other sleep foundations.

The reason why a child's sleep may regress during such times is because, like adults, children process information in their sleep. Their little brains are so busy practicing new skills, perceiving, exploring, and experiencing during their waking hours, that they often have difficulty "switching off" when it is time to sleep.

When experiencing developmental change, it is common for children to become progressively overstimulated and overtired throughout the day. And because children's cognitive ability often exceeds their physical capabilities, frustration and consequently crying, clinginess, and tantrums are inescapable. At such times, many children may wake more frequently overnight—sometimes between one to three hours at a time—or take longer than usual to fall asleep, practicing their newfound skills in their crib (e.g., rolling, rocking on all fours, standing, babbling, or talking). This is widely prevalent and may continue from a few days to a few weeks.

Although sometimes unavoidable, you may be able to minimize the impact of developmental change on your child's sleep by utilizing the key connection tools as prefaced in "Emotional and Physical Well-Being." Not all protests or crying warrants the need for the breast or pacifier, nor does it signal an urgent desire to be rocked, shushed, or bounced. Supporting children to *release* their tensions and frustrations through regular quality time, play, and listening—*rather than using distraction*—is effective to counteract the feelings of overwhelm and insecurity that peak during times of change and transition.

Avoid your impulse to "rescue" your child by picking them up at the first sign of a grizzle—they may simply just be expressing their frustration of being unable to effectively grasp an object, roll over, or crawl. Instead, move in close, use plenty of eye contact, listen, and warmly validate your child's emotional experience (e.g., "I can see you are trying really hard to roll over/crawl/touch that toy. You are doing great. I am right here for you darling").

Just as it is not your responsibility to stop your child from crying, it is also not your role to "fix" their problems—doing so (continuously) can rob them of vital problem-solving opportunities and inhibit their physical and/or cognitive developmental progression.

If your child can transition from standing to lying, or rolling from back to front—and vice versa—unassisted during the day, afforded the opportunity and encouragement, they *should* be able to do this by themselves overnight too.

If your child is standing in their crib, try kneeling beside him or her and pat the mattress to encourage them to lie back down. If your child is rocking on all fours or is attempting to roll without success, reassure him or her that they are safe and loved and that you will stay with them for as long as they need you to. Warm validation can make a child feel safe and understood—for example, "I can see you are having a hard time getting to sleep" or "I can see you're very busy practicing your new skills!" or "you really want to crawl, don't you?"

If you have addressed your child's primary needs (e.g., a clean diaper, hunger, temperature, and closeness) and your child continues to cry or fuss, it is possible that he or she may be doing so in an attempt to recover from a buildup of stored or present emotions, stress, or tension. When children are listened to and supported through their emotional release in a parents' loving presence, it is common to witness a dramatic progression in developmental skills (both cognitive and physical), language capabilities, and improvement in sleep and behavior. *I have witnessed children who, following a prolonged period of active listening, have started walking, talking, or using the potty–when previously they were unable (or afraid) to do so.*

Developmental Effects on Sleep

- Catnapping or shorter naps than usual
- Difficulty resettling at naps and bedtime
- Heightened irritability, fussiness, or crying
- Increased behavioral difficulties: tantrums, off-track behavior, and aggression
- General unsettledness or wakefulness at sleep times
- Bedtime resistance
- Waking themselves up rolling in the crib (four to seven months)

- Standing up, sitting, or kneeling in their crib or jumping up and down (eight months onward)
- Babbling, talking, and/or calling out at sleep times– or when they wake midnap, or overnight
- Increased intervention required from a caregiver to fall asleep, or back to sleep
- Separation anxiety
- Frequent night waking—specifically after midnight
- Wakefulness, unsettledness, or hyperactivity in the early hours of the morning—commonly between 1:00 a.m. and 5:00 a.m.
- Early rising

Solutions

- **Optimize the sleep environment**, particularly a warm-and-dark room that is free from distractions. White noise can also muffle any outside or household noises—which may otherwise keep your child awake or wake them prematurely during naps or overnight. Refer to "The Seven Sleep Foundations: Environment."

- **Swaddle young babies for sleep times**, especially four months and under.

- **Implement an age-appropriate routine** to minimize overtiredness. Refer to chapter "Routines and Recommendations."

- **Be responsive to your child's sleep cues.** Because children are more susceptible to overstimulation during times of developmental change, you may temporarily schedule their awake time slightly earlier (e.g., by ten to fifteen minutes).

- **Refer to the Wonder Weeks** for further insight into your child's current developmental stage and how you can best support them during these times of growth (www.thewonderweeks.com).

- **Encourage wind-down time and positive sleep associations before sleep times**—that is, ten to fifteen minutes before naps and thirty to sixty minutes before bedtime at the end of the day.

- **Quality one-on-one time and promoting laughter through play** builds connection and safety, and encourages the release of tension and frustrations. This is essential for sound sleep at times of change and unfamiliarity. If quality time is currently a part of your daily routine, you may experiment with temporarily increasing the length of time spent to help your child adjust to any change with greater ease (e.g., from ten minutes to fifteen or twenty minutes).

- **Listen** lovingly as your child offloads his or her all-consuming feelings of frustration and exhaustion momentarily throughout the day. In doing so, it is not uncommon to experience improved sleep and considerable progress in developmental ability. *Remember, what goes in (e.g., frustrations, hurts, and disappointments experienced in the present moment) must go out (i.e., emotional release such as crying, trembling, and tantrums). Helping children to release their feelings by day is preferable to most parents than assisting them to do so overnight (i.e., night terrors, disturbed sleep, screaming, nightmares, and an increased need for parental intervention/comfort).*

Milestones and Transitions

When experiencing developmental milestones, life transitions, or a change to a child's sleep routine, insecurity (or fear) is inextricable. Consequently, many children experience sleep regression, separation anxiety, withdrawal, increased clinginess, crying, and tantrums. Aggression is also a common by-product of fear, so behavior such as biting, pinching hitting, pulling hair, and pushing can be intensified during these times.

Where possible, avoid too much change at once. Plan ahead and focus on the transition at hand to avoid overwhelming your child. Because children thrive on connection and predictability, it is essential to *communicate any change in advance* if we intend to prepare them adequately. Although a baby or younger child may not understand each and every word spoken, he or she can comprehend the overall intention and/or the tone communicated.

Validate and acknowledge any feelings that may arise as your child attempts to process change, or the idea of it—tantrums, crying, resistance, overnight waking, and screaming can be expected. Support your child to offload their feelings frequently throughout the day by listening lovingly rather than scolding, using punishments, or the use of control patterns to stop the crying. Releasing emotions by day will reduce the need for children to wake overnight to do so.

As parents, we can minimize sleep regression and ensure a smoother transition for all involved when we make safety, security, and connection a priority. Regular quality time, listening, role-playing, and roughhousing play can be effective in offloading tensions and fostering safety and security at these times. Refer to the connection tools as prefaced in "The Seven Sleep Foundations: Emotional and Physical Well-Being."

Examples of Common Milestones and Transitions

- Transitioning from a crib to a toddler bed

- Transitioning from cosleeping to own crib and/or room
- Introducing a new sibling to the family
- Potty training
- Transitioning out of the swaddle
- Weaning from breastfeeding, the bottle, or pacifier
- Introducing the bottle
- Night weaning
- Starting childcare
- Moving house
- Daylight savings and standard time conversion
- Travel or holidays

The above transitions are covered in further detail in "The Sleep Play Love Method" and "Managing Transitions."

TEMPERAMENT AND GENETICS

Temperament and genetics influence the way that a child interacts with his or her environment and determine a child's responsiveness, sensitivity, adaptability, ability to self-soothe, and how well they can sleep. For example, a sensitive, anxious, "high-needs," or spirited child may experience greater regression and require more parental intervention at times of teething, illness, transition, and developmental change. To the contrary, a child with a calm or easygoing temperament is often more adaptable and, therefore, may rely less on a caregiver at sleep times and/or experience less regression during change and transition. There is no one-size-fits-all approach, and the temperament and genes—of parent and child alike—must be considered when deciding upon routine and parenting approach, and the most effective sleep improvement strategy.

According to the field of epigenetics—and contrary to existing belief systems—*we are not victims of our genetics*. In fact, approximately 95 percent of our genetic expression is determined by our perception of our environment. A child's prenatal and birth experience, together with the parent's emotional disposition, will discern a child's genetic expression and temperamental variation. The apple rarely falls far from the tree. Safe to say, if you or your partner is an early riser, night owl, good or not-so-good sleeper, anxious, or relaxed, your child will be likely to display these characteristics also. Other traits may include activity level, distractibility, persistence, approach-withdrawal, intensity, regularity, sensory threshold, and mood. The impact on sleep can therefore be profound. Conditions such as colic, allergies, and night terrors are also said to have some genetic influence—so if your child displays these patterns, it is likely that either a parent or close relative shares these attributes.

SECTION III
COMMON SLEEP DIFFICULTIES AND SOLUTIONS

CATNAPPING

Catnapping refers to regular short naps in the first six months—on average between twenty to forty minutes in length. Albeit developmentally normal, catnapping can be extremely frustrating for parents, who often recall that they spend their entire day settling and resettling their babies for sleep—usually unsuccessfully. These short naps are in fact, a natural daytime sleep pattern from birth to six months as a baby is establishing his or her circadian rhythm (internal body clock). This can also be attributed to the fact that young babies are biologically programmed to wake easily, and more often for survival. Infants spend 50 percent of their time in REM sleep (active/light sleep), so are more easily disturbed by changes in their environment such as noise, light, temperature, and smells—this is a primal survival instinct. When babies reach six months, they spend increasingly more time in a deeper sleep (non-REM), with REM sleep dropping to 30 percent.

While most catnapping in the early months is biological, catnapping in older babies (i.e., seven months onward) may highlight a need for a change to your routine or environment—commonly a reflection of habit, lack of routine, hunger, overtiredness, undertiredness, being too cold, illness, teething, developmental change, leaps, or sleeping in a room that is not dark enough.

Not all catnapping is a cause for concern, and in many cases, with consideration to the seven sleep foundations (as prefaced in the previous chapter), it should correct itself over time as your children become older and their awake window increases.

A common pattern I have noticed is that: babies six months and under who are sleeping through the night—or with the exception of one to two overnight feeds—often have shorter day naps in general (forty-five minutes or less), whereas babies who wake more often overnight are overall better day sleepers.

Where there may be cause for concern with prolonged catnapping is if your baby is waking upset or tired after a short nap, he or she is unable to make it through to his or her next scheduled nap time without becoming upset or irritable, and/or is waking frequently overnight because of overstimulation/overtirednessness attributed to the lack of day sleep.

Solutions

- **Connect.** Quality time, listening, and play are vital to children's confidence and sense of security. When children feel safe, they often sleep sounder and for longer—and have less need for parental intervention at sleep times. Refer to the connection tools as outlined in "The Seven Sleep Foundations: Emotional and Physical Well-Being."

- **Implement an age-appropriate routine.** Being overtired is the main cause for catnapping. Adhering to age-appropriate awake times will help you to avoid missing the sleep window. Refer to age-specific routines in "Routines and Recommendations."

- **Nap at home where possible** instead of in the car, stroller, carrier, or in transit. If you must travel out in the car, where possible, plan trips once your child has woken from the nap. *Remember the 80/20 rule, although this may resemble 50/50 with babies under three months!*

- **Optimize the sleep environment.** The key foundations to counteract the catnap are a dark room, white noise, and warmth. Refer to recommendations as per "The Seven Sleep Foundations: Environment."

- **Place your baby in the crib awake.** Avoid using your intervention at *every* sleep time such as rocking, feeding, or holding. Refer to "The Sleep Play Love Method" for assistance with how to gradually remove your intervention and transition your child to independent sleep.

- **Keep young babies swaddled for sleep.** This helps to muffle their Moro reflex, preventing them from startling themselves awake midnap. Most will transition out of the swaddle between four and six months.

- **Rule out hunger.** You can experiment with scheduling feeds *before* sleep times instead of upon waking to rule out hunger as a cause for your child waking prematurely. *The exception to this is babies with reflux.*

- **Where possible, resettle your baby when he or she wakes under forty-five minutes.** Between three to four months, forty-five to sixty minutes is a realistic expectation for nap length. If your baby sleeps for less than forty-five minutes, attempt to help him or her fall back to sleep (for a maximum of twenty minutes). You may choose to hold your baby and listen as he or she cries or fusses, or use your presence and warm validation as the baby remains in their sleep space. Your chosen method of helping your baby feel safe will depend heavily on the baby's needs in the moment (i.e., a grizzle or protest versus an emotional cry).

- **Get out in the sunshine every day.** Natural sunlight exposure stimulates melatonin production (sleep hormone) and is essential for regulating sleep patterns.

- **Reset your child's body clock.** This is most effective for children under twelve months, and who habitually wake at the same time into their nap/s. Depending on the length of your child's nap, enter their room approximately thirty minutes into the nap—or five minutes before their usual wake-up time for children who habitually wake under thirty minutes; *this is shortly before they transition from a deep sleep to lighter sleep.* Rouse your child gently—without waking them completely. Once they begin to stir, soothe them back to sleep using reassuring words such as "Sleep time now, sweetie" or a gentle touch or rock from side to side while they remain in their crib. If your young baby has taken to a pacifier, you can replace this into his or her mouth if it helps prolong the nap temporarily. The aim of this process is to extend the nap by assisting your child to transition into the next sleep cycle without waking him or her completely. *You may have to employ trial and error with timings and be persistent with this technique for three to seven days to gauge effectiveness. Long-term improvements to nap length cannot be guaranteed.*

FEEDING, ROCKING, PATTING, OR HOLDING TO SLEEP

Children of all ages seek comfort in movement (rocking, car, or carrier), sucking (breast, bottle, or the pacifier) and closeness (touch, holding, or parental presence) to fall asleep and back to sleep when they wake from a nap or overnight. Although these actions are helpful when satisfying neonatal reflexes during the fourth trimester, a child's ability to sleep independently can be compromised when these actions become *needs* for sleep, or for comfort ongoing—commonly presenting as long-term sleep and behavioral challenges.

To understand *why* babies experience difficulty linking sleep cycles unassisted when they are reliant on *something* to fall asleep, it is important to first understand their sleep cycle. Babies have a shorter sleep cycle and spend more time in a lighter stage of sleep (REM) than older children or adults. On average, a baby's sleep cycle is forty-five to fifty minutes in length, and they cycle through stages of light and deep sleep throughout this time—refer to Figure 2.

Baby's Sleep Cycle
Every 45 Minutes

40-50 min
Light sleep, easy
to wake up

0-10 min
Starting to fall
asleep

30-40 min
Coming out of
heavy sleep

10-20 min
Getting deeper
into sleep

20-30 min
Heavily
asleep

Figure 2: A Baby's Sleep Cycle

Stage one (non-REM): The first ten minutes of babies' sleep cycle is typically when they would be held, rocked, or fed into a drowsy state. Their eyes may be closed, and they appear relaxed; however, they may occasionally twitch and easily awaken with noise—or if transferred from a parent's arms into their crib.

Stage two (non-REM): After ten to twenty minutes, babies transition into a deeper sleep. Their heart rate, blood pressure, and temperature drop. Although still considered a light stage of sleep, it becomes much harder to wake children during this stage. This is often when a breastfed child will fall off the breast or otherwise appear still and relaxed, and parents will try to transfer their sleeping baby from their arms to the crib. *This stage of sleep typically lasts between fifteen to twenty minutes.*

Stage three (non-REM): This stage begins twenty to thirty minutes after falling asleep. A child will be in the deepest sleep at this point in the cycle and be most difficult to awaken.

Stage four (REM): Approximately thirty minutes after falling asleep, children will cycle into a lighter stage of sleep again and will either (a) transition into another sleep cycle on their own (provided they have the ability and opportunity to do so and there has been no immediate change to their environment since they fell asleep) or (b) they will wake up completely and call out for a parent to comfort them back to sleep or bring them out of bed.

There are usually two reasons that children will wake and be unable to settle back to sleep once they awaken from this light stage of sleep: (1) environmental changes such as temperature, noise, and light, or (2) they did not self-settle at the beginning of the sleep time —that is, they were fed, rocked, held, or patted to sleep—or fell asleep with a pacifier. If children are reliant on a certain action (movement or sucking) or object (pacifier or lovey), it is highly likely that they will seek this same action (or "thing") repetitively to fall back to sleep day and night. Consequently, frequent overnight waking and catnapping often ensue.

Solutions

- **Connect.** Incorporating some quality one-on-one time, encouraging laughter through play (e.g., role-playing and roughhousing), and listening to your children as they release their emotions in the moment (through tears and tantrums) fosters safety and security and can ensure your child makes the transition to independent sleep with greater ease and cooperation. Refer to the connection tools as outlined in "The Seven Sleep Foundations: Emotional and Physical Well-Being."

- **Follow an age-appropriate routine to avoid overtiredness.** Any settling attempts will be futile with an overtired child, especially toward the end of the day. The same applies if your child is not tired enough. At either end of the spectrum, a child will require more intervention from a parent to fall asleep and back to sleep. A well-rested child is less likely to fall asleep on the breast or bottle and in fact may become more overstimulated or irritated if he or she is rocked, patted, or held. Refer to "Routines and Recommendations."

- **Try an earlier bedtime.** A bedtime between 6:30 p.m. and 7:30 p.m. is ideal for most ages. Scheduling feed times earlier (ideally twenty to thirty minutes before bedtime) can also help to alleviate the feed-to-sleep association.

- **Introduce positive sleep associations.** Wind-down time with sleep cues such as a dark room, swaddle/sleeping bag, and white noise will help replace *you* as the main sleep association. Refer to "The Seven Sleep Foundations: Positive Sleep Associations."

- **Optimize the sleep environment.** This can work wonders for sleep by making your child feel comfortable, safe, and secure. Refer to "The Seven Sleep Foundations: Environment."

- **Place your baby down awake to encourage self-settling.** All babies wake overnight; however, not all have the skills to fall back to sleep on their own. Refer to "The Sleep Play Love Method" for assistance with breaking habits and transitioning your child gently and respectfully to independent sleep.

- **Choose your timing wisely.** Commit to changing this

pattern when you have support from your partner/friends/family, your calendar is relatively free of social engagements, and you and your child are in a good space physically and emotionally. Avoid making these changes when your child is unwell or when he or she is already feeling insecure as an outcome of other life transitions (e.g., starting childcare, introducing a new sibling, or potty training).

- **Communicate all changes with your child in advance to gain their cooperation.** Communicate precisely what you will be doing on that day—or night—and how their routine will be different. Acknowledge any feelings of uncertainty that your child may have as they arise, and support the release of any fear, sadness, frustration, dependency, and/or grief they may experience during this transition by listening lovingly.

- **Try gradual withdrawal.** You don't need to stop feeding, rocking, or patting altogether; these can be great comforting tools at times. But if you wish to encourage self-settling, try to gradually reduce the degree to which you assist your child to fall asleep and be sure to revoke your intervention slightly every three days. Refer to "The Sleep Play Love Method" for options dependent on your child's individual sleep pattern/needs.

- **Persistence pays.** Babies are fast learners and more adaptable than we give them credit for—you may just be surprised at how uncomplicated this process can be. In my experience, it is usually the parents who are more attached to the behavior than the children!

EARLY RISING

Early rising is common for babies and toddlers. Being out of routine, developmental milestones, leaps, teething, illness, environment, and routine can all contribute to early morning waking—and too often, this may become a withstanding habit. While 6:00 a.m. is considered a "reasonable" time for a child to wake for the day, early rising specifically refers to habitual waking prior to 6:00 a.m. Because children transition into a lighter stage of sleep from 4:00 a.m., they are more susceptible to early rising due to pain, discomfort, hunger, illness, or a change in their environment such as light, noise, or temperature.

Solutions

• **Opt for an earlier bedtime.** Contrary to logic, a later bedtime does not equal a later wake-up time; in fact, quite the opposite. If children are going to bed late, being overtired can cause them to continue to wake earlier each day. A regular bedtime between 6:30 p.m. and 7:30 p.m. is ideal for most age groups.

• **White noise.** Birds, garbage trucks, traffic, and household noises (such as plumbing, creaky floorboards, and siblings) can cause your child to wake prematurely in the morning. Looped white noise playing overnight can encourage sounder and longer sleep.

• **Choose an appropriate nap time.** The timing and length of a daytime nap can have a significant impact on the time your child wakes in the morning:

  · Experiment with moving the first nap a little later (e.g., by fifteen to thirty minutes). Assure consistency for a minimum of three days to determine whether there is any change to the wake-up time. Adjust any subsequent naps out (later) accordingly.
  · If your child is two years and over, ensure that he or she has at least four hours of awake time between waking from their day nap and bedtime at the end of the day to avoid undertiredness (and, therefore, resisting bedtime for an hour or more). You may need to experiment with your child's optimal awake window as capabilities can differ between children.
  · Don't let your child nap for too long during the day, as this can reduce the overall night sleep duration and cause him or her to rise early. Refer to "Routines and Recommendations" for the average sleep requirements by age.

• **Darken the room.** Children often rise with the sun. A dark environment signals to the brain that it is time for sleep and encourages the release of melatonin (sleep hormone). Try blackout blinds, foil, garbage bags, black contact sheets, or cardboard on the windows to keep the room dark.

• **Be sensitive to your child's developmental stage.** Early rising often starts at times of developmental change, illness, or when children are teething. Allow plenty of time and space for your child to practice their newfound skills during their waking hours to reduce their inclination to wake overnight or early in the morning to explore and release the associated physical tension. Quality one-on-one time, encouraging laughter through play (i.e., roughhousing and role- playing), and appropriate wind-down time with positive sleep associations can also help. Refer to "The Seven Sleep Foundations: Developmental Stages, Milestones, and Transitions."

- **Rule out hunger.** Many children wake hungry in the early hours—especially when their last meal or milk feed was at, or before bedtime the night before. Between 4:00 a.m. and 5:00 a.m. is also when blood sugar levels are at their lowest, which can trigger a hunger response. If your child is six months and older, ensure that he or she is consuming *at least* three solid meals per day, plus scheduled milk feeds and water. Babies under nine months may still benefit from one milk feed overnight, or you can experiment with a dream feed (detailed in "Routines and Recommendations") for babies six months and under. Meals that combine complex carbohydrates, healthy fat and protein help to sustain blood sugar levels overnight and may minimize early rising—refer to "The Seven Sleep Foundations: Nutrition."

- **Turn up the heat.** Between 4:00 a.m. and 5:00 a.m. is the coldest time of the day, and therefore, there's little surprise that children commonly wake during this time. A safe oil (or bar) heater or added blankets will prevent your child waking up cold in the early hours. An environment between 66°F to 72°F (19°C to 22°C) is optimal, plus appropriate bedding and clothing. Refer to the "The Sleep Play Love Bedding Guide."

- **Use a Gro-Clock or Ooly.** If your child is sleeping in a toddler bed and at least two years old, a Gro-Clock or Ooly can be a great investment; however, they must be old enough to comprehend the concept of staying in bed until the "sun comes up" or the color changes.

• **Treat early morning waking (prior to 6:00 a.m.) as a night waking.** If you continue to bring your child out of bed at 5:00 a.m. to watch television, play, or come into your bed for snuggles, they will continue to habitually wake at that time to start the day—and may start waking more often overnight, expecting the same outcome. Be persistent with resettling, and ensure the child remains in their room until *at least* 6:00 a.m. If you wish to cuddle with your child in your bed upon waking at 6:00 a.m., then be sure to establish a clear differentiation between night and day—for example, open the blinds and say, "Good morning, darling."

• **Reset your child's body clock.** Fresh air and plenty of natural, unfiltered sunlight during the day helps to keep your child's internal body clock ticking. If your child has habitually been waking at the same time each morning (i.e., for a week or more), go into your child's room *one hour before* his or her usual waking time (e.g., 4:00 a.m. for 5:00 a.m. risers). Rouse your child gently, without waking him or her completely. Once he or she begins to stir, soothe them back to sleep using reassuring words such as "Sleep time now, sweetie" or a gentle rock from side to side while your child remains in their crib. For children twelve months and under, you may also experiment with introducing a dream feed temporarily, one hour before the child's usual wake time. *You may have to be persistent with this technique for three to seven days to gauge effectiveness, and long-term improvements to the child's wake-up time cannot be guaranteed.*

COLIC

Although there is no official medical diagnosis for colic, it is usually defined by the *rule of three*—symptoms start roughly at three weeks of age, and the baby will be crying for more than three hours per day, for more than three days per week, and for longer than three weeks (in an infant who is well-fed and otherwise healthy). More often, persistent crying will occur in the evenings from 5:00 p.m. onward (otherwise known as *witching hour*). Symptoms usually peak at six weeks and subside between three to four months.

As we know, there are many variables to crying in the early weeks: prenatal stress, birth trauma, unfilled needs, overstimulation, developmental frustrations, and frightening events such as loud noises or parental separation. Colic also seems to be more prevalent in babies who have more sensitive or emotional temperaments.

There is no quick fix for colic symptoms. Pediatrician Harvey Karp (Happiest Baby on the Block) promotes the five *S*s: swaddling, side/stomach (i.e., holding position), shushing (or white noise), sucking (on breast or pacifier), and swinging (or movement) as a safe and effective settling tool to "switch on" a baby's calming reflex and stop children crying. While this method can be successful, it is important that we address the core reason for the crying, and afford children the opportunity to heal and recover from any momentary or stored stress, trauma, or tension as necessary. Any settling attempts such as rocking, shushing, the breast, or pacifier may be effective at stopping the crying temporarily; however, it can often develop into a control pattern if parents habitually use such methods to repress a child's emotional release. *Common issues include feeding for comfort, pacifier reliance, and patterns such as holding or rocking to sleep.*

Solutions

- **Encourage stress-relief crying** as often as possible, after ensuring your child's primary needs have been satisfied.

- **Expose your baby to plenty of direct sunlight.** This encourages melatonin production, which in addition to regulating the circadian rhythm, can suppress intestinal cramps (one of the suspected causes for persistent crying in the first three months).

- **Try a pacifier.** Albeit a personal choice, a pacifier may help to satisfy your baby's sucking reflex in between feeds in the early weeks and prevent overfeeding—which can exacerbate colic symptoms. *Do not use a pacifier as a replacement for milk. To avoid the pacifier developing into a control pattern, use only in moderation and not with the intention to stop your child from crying or fussing. Encourage emotional release by listening where possible.*

- **Minimize upset from digestion and gas discomfort** by block feeding (i.e., feeding from one breast per feed), regular burping in between and after feeds, and eliminating any suspected allergy-inducing foods from your diet if breastfeeding—the main offenders include dairy, soy, wheat, gluten, nuts, citrus, and seafood.

- **Slightly elevate your baby's crib mattress** so that he or she is not lying flat. Colicky babies also love being on their tummy or side for sleeping as this seems to ease their discomfort. If you opt for these sleeping positions, ensure your child remains supervised at all times.

- **Keep stimulation to a minimum** especially in the first month. Avoid light-up toys, television, rattles, loud environments, or too many visitors. Babies will be stimulated enough simply by interacting with their parents or observing their immediate environment. Excess stimulation only overwhelms their central nervous system causing stress—which must be offloaded through (lots of) crying.

- **Incorporate ten to fifteen minutes of wind-down time before bed.** Positive sleep associations such as a swaddle, a dark room, and white noise can help.

- **Cosleeping and baby wearing can be beneficial in the early months.** Babies thrive on physical closeness, warmth, and movement and rely on their parents for coregulation of their physical and emotional state.

- **Try a slightly shorter awake window (e.g., by ten to fifteen minutes).** This may be especially beneficial for sensitive temperaments.

- **A warm bath** may help to relax babies and ease any associated tension in their stomach.

- **Swaddle for sleep until three to four months of age.** Swaddling restricts children's startle (Moro) reflex and makes them feel safe and secure—replicating the womb environment throughout the fourth trimester. Swaddling also helps to calm babies' nervous system, which may counteract the unsettledness associated with colic.

- **Try natural or holistic therapy.** Massage, cranial sacral therapy, reiki, chiropractic, osteopathy, and kinesiology can help; select a practitioner with experience in treating infants.

- **Focus on rebuilding the mother's gut health.** There can sometimes be a correlation between the mother's digestive health and that of her baby. And because colic symptoms *may* present because of intestinal cramps, it can be beneficial for a breastfeeding mother—and also the baby—to take a daily probiotic. Fermented foods such as sauerkraut, kefir, and kombucha can also help.

- **Natural or pharmaceutical remedies** such as Infacol, Wrenn and Co., Infants Friend, Hyland's Baby Colic Tablets, Colic Calm, and Young Living essential oils (such as Gentle Baby, peppermint, fennel, ginger, and DiGize) can help to ease symptoms.[*]

- **Specialized products such as Babocush, SNOO, and the Tranquilo Mat** have been designed to alleviate the unsettledness, which often accompanies colic and reflux.

[*]*It is always best to consult your health-care professional before administering any medication, homeopathic or natural remedies. Always seek professional advice regarding the appropriate remedy and dosage for your child's age and symptoms. A lactation consultant may be able to diagnose a lip- or tongue-tie, which commonly presents as a colic symptom and unsettledness in the early weeks.*

REFLUX

Reflux is commonly experienced in the first three to four months. Most symptoms subside after four months; however, more extreme cases of reflux (i.e., gastro-oesophageal reflux disease—or GORD) can persist for up to twelve months or longer. While all babies have some degree of reflux owing to their immature digestive systems, the symptoms to look out for (of which some may require medical treatment) are as follows:

- crying or uncomfortable after eating
- coughing or choking regularly
- refusing the breast or bottle
- arching back after eating
- resistance to lying on their back
- gassy and/or foamy bowel movements
- colicky, unhappy, or seemingly uncomfortable in their body
- wheezing, apnea, or breathing difficulties (respiratory infections)
- sour breath, burps, and hiccups
- throwing up, usually projectile vomiting (except with silent reflux)

- failure to gain weight
- expressing a dislike for being in the car—if their posture is slumped, the increased pressure in their stomachs can exacerbate the reflux

Solutions

- **Feed your baby upon waking** rather than before sleep.

- **Encourage stress-relief crying.** Provided that the child's primary needs have been addressed, crying is a safe and effective medium to reduce pain and to aid the relief of stress and tension.

- **Keep your baby upright for at least thirty minutes after a feed.** Avoid laying your child on their back, or changing their diaper immediately following a feed, as this may exacerbate symptoms. You may even try feeding your baby in an upright position if this helps.

- **A pacifier may be useful in between feeds** to satisfy a baby's neonatal sucking reflex.

- **Keep stimulation to a minimum.** Avoid television, visitors, loud music, light-up toys, blue and white lights, and constantly rotating a child from one apparatus to the next (e.g., swing, play mat, bouncer, carrier, and car).

- **Keep your baby swaddled** for sleep times until three to four months of age—this may help calm their nervous system and encourage them to sleep longer.

- **Try a shorter awake window in between sleeps.** This may help to minimize overtiredness and overstimulation, which leads to unsettled behavior and sleeping difficulties.

- **Wear your baby for naps.** Any position whereby your baby remains upright will alleviate discomfort.

- **Slightly elevate the mattress** so that your baby is not lying flat.

- **Incorporate wind-down time before sleep** and positive sleep associations.

- **If you are breastfeeding, try limiting or eliminating dairy products from your diet (for at least one month).** Dairy can cause problems because the proteins found in this food can irritate a baby's immature digestive tract. Other common allergens include wheat, gluten, citrus, coffee, nuts, eggs, and soy.

- **Try natural or holistic therapy.** Massage, cranial sacral therapy, reiki, chiropractic, osteopathy, and kinesiology can help; choose a practitioner with experience in treating infants.

- **Natural remedies may ease symptoms.** Some natural remedies include probiotics, gripe water, Hyland's cell salts (natrum phosphoricum), and Young Living essential oils (such as Gentle Baby, peppermint, fennel, ginger, and DiGize).[*]

- **Specialized products such as Babocush, SNOO, and the Tranquilo Mat** have been designed to alleviate the unsettledness, which often accompanies colic and reflux.

*It is always best to consult your health-care professional to obtain an official reflux diagnosis rather than self-diagnosing or before administering any medication, homeopathic or natural remedies. Always seek professional advice regarding the appropriate remedy and dosage for your child's age and symptoms. A lactation consultant may be able to diagnose or rule out a lip- or tongue-tie, which could be contributing toward the reflux symptoms.

NIGHTMARES

Nightmares are a normal part of children's development and a way for them to process the events from their day. Although nightmares may be experienced in children as young as nine months, they occur more frequently in children two years and older. The main triggers for nightmares include being overtired or overstimulated, scary movies/books/events/video games, increased body temperature (prevalent during illness), and anxiety.

Signs of Nightmares

- The child awakens completely following a nightmare, and may appear frightened for some time afterward.
- Most children will seek out comfort after they wake—either by calling out from their bedroom or venturing into their parent's room in the early hours.
- Nightmares occur most frequently from 4:00 a.m. onward—during REM sleep, where dreaming is most prevalent.
- Children are likely to recall their bad dream in vivid detail.

Solutions

- **Connect.** Incorporate some quality one-on-one time. Children are extremely resourceful and will often literally act out their fears when they feel safe and supported to do so. You may choose to incorporate some role-playing or role reversal whereby you pretend that you are the one who is afraid of something and call upon your child's courage to help ease your anxiety. *A common fear among children from two years of age is the dark (e.g., shadows, animals, and monsters).* Be prepared to listen and encourage laughter or tears where appropriate, so that your child may recover from any fear or insecurity that may be triggering the nightmares. If you are already implementing quality time daily, try increasing the length of time spent (even if only temporarily); this can have a profound impact on children's security and confidence—helping them to overcome their fears, and avoid "bad" dreams.

- **Talk to your children openly about their fears.** Addressing your child's fears and asking them what their dream was about can help them process the experience and may ascertain the catalyst for the nightmare so that the trigger/s may be avoided (or minimized) in the future.

- **Listen.** Encourage your child's full spectrum of emotional expression by day to support their efforts to emotionally self-regulate. Laughter and crying effectively releases fears and tensions, which if unreleased by day, may otherwise surface as nightmares or regular overnight waking.

- **Roughhousing play** promotes safety and encourages laughter (the essential ingredient for healing fears). After the bath or before bedtime is a perfect time to engage in some play such as rough-and-tumble, horseback rides, or "play fighting." This rigorous play helps to burn any stored/stagnant energy and affords children the opportunity to laugh away any built-up stresses or tensions from their day—which may otherwise surface as nightmares or disturbed sleep.

- **Implement a relaxing bedtime routine** free from screen time, television, bright lights, and loud noises. Suggested activities include building blocks, reading, singing songs, a massage, and debriefing/talking about their day—for older children.

- **Schedule an earlier bedtime (ideally between 6:30 p.m. and 7:30 p.m.) and regular naps or downtime during the day.** Overtiredness from lack of day sleep (or rest), or a bedtime that is too late can contribute to the frequency of nightmares.

- **Ensure your child remains well hydrated and has a healthy, balanced diet.** Certain additives can wreak havoc on a child's nervous system and sleep ability, therefore, a well-balanced diet free from processed foods, refined sugar, and artificial colors, sweeteners, and preservatives is recommended. Low blood sugar, dehydration, and magnesium deficiency can also contribute to nightmares and disturbed sleep. Frequent water consumption and magnesium-rich foods such as bananas, almond butter, and yogurt consumed before bedtime may help.

- **Avoid inappropriate or scary movies, books, or games.** Ensure that all screen time is supervised and age-appropriate.

- **Dress your child appropriately.** Increased body temperature can be attributed to the frequency of nightmares—this may explain why children and adults often experience nightmares when they are ill or have a fever. Opt for pure cotton, organic bedclothes and bedding where possible—avoiding synthetic fibers such as polyester, spandex, and nylon, as these can restrict airflow and cause overheating. Refer to "The Sleep Play Love Bedding Guide."

- **Limit screen time,** particularly after 3:00 p.m. Blue light (emitted from electronics) suppresses the sleep hormone melatonin and can cause overstimulation.

- **Essential oils** such as chamomile, lavender, geranium, marjoram, bergamot, frankincense, neroli, rose, frankincense, sandalwood, and vetiver, and Young Living's Northern Lights Black Spruce (in a burner or diluted in oil for a body massage) may be helpful for a child who is feeling afraid or anxious.

- **Ensure your child's room is free from clutter.** Limit accessories and decorations and keep cupboard doors closed —these can cast shadows in the dark. Some children may feel safer to sleep with their bedroom door slightly ajar, rather than closed.

- **Some children may prefer to sleep with a soft night light.** Opt for a salt lamp as red light is less disruptive to the circadian rhythm.

NIGHT TERRORS

The most significant difference between a nightmare and a night terror is the child's recollection of the event. Night terrors appear to run in families, and affect an estimated one to six percent of children. Although usually experienced by children between four to six years of age, they can start as early as nine months. Night terrors are defined as a partial arousal during non-REM (deep sleep) and commonly occur at the same time each night, during the first few hours following bedtime—typically between 10:00 p.m. and 11:00 p.m. Night terrors are usually more distressing for the parent than the child, as the child will not have any recollection of the episode in the morning and is most likely unaware of the presence of a parent in the room because he or she is only partially awake.

Signs of Night Terrors

- Children appear distraught, terrified, or confused
- They are sitting up in their bed (eyes open or closed)
- Screaming or crying inconsolably
- Thrashing

Solutions

Refer to aforementioned solutions in "Nightmares" in addition to the following:

- **Ensure that the child's environment is safe** and that they can't hurt themselves if they're moving or thrashing about during an episode.

- **Try not to move your child or try to wake them midepisode.** It's best to "wait it out." *The average night terror episode lasts less than fifteen minutes.*

- **Once the episode has finished, try keeping the child up for a while.** If they fall straight back to sleep, they may have a higher chance of having another night terror.

- **Reset your child's body clock.** Rouse your child gently from sleep *one hour before* their usual waking time (making sure not to wake him or her completely). When your child begins to stir, you may comfort them back to sleep using loving words and a gentle rub on the back.

- **Lully is a proven solution** to prevent night terrors from reoccurring (within four weeks) in children who experience these episodes regularly. Refer to www.lullysleep.com.

Nightmares and night terrors rarely have long-lasting psychological effects on children. If you are concerned about how often your child is having nightmares or experiencing night terrors, please seek professional advice.

BEDTIME RESISTANCE AND
FREQUENT NIGHT WAKING

Although there may be countless variables to bedtime resistance and night waking, in my years of working with hundreds of families, and from personal experience with my own children, I have identified various patterns, potential catalysts, and solutions.

This is a guide only. There can be many other reasons specific to your individual family circumstance, such as allergies, genetics, environment, medical conditions, sleep disorders, stimulants or food sensitivities, nutrition, fears, habits, and routine (among many others), that must be considered.

If you are experiencing bedtime resistance or frequent wake-ups between 7:00 p.m. and 11:00 p.m., common reasons include the following:

- **Teething, illness, or on the verge of illness.** Seek medical advice where necessary. For further information, refer to "Common Sleep Difficulties and Solutions: Teething and Illness."

- **Environmental: temperature, light, and noise.** Follow the "The Sleep Play Love Bedding Guide" and recommendations in "The Seven Sleep Foundations: Environment."

- **Lack of boundaries around sleep.** If a child is refusing to sleep or continues to get out of bed multiple times (at the beginning of—or during—the night), this may present an opportunity for the parent to set some firm, yet loving, limits surrounding sleep times. Some alternatives to simply returning your child to bed repeatedly (while trying to remain calm) may include installing a safety gate at the child's bedroom door, employing "check-ins" (i.e., leaving the child's room for one to two minutes to wash the dishes before returning to tuck him or her in once more), or gradually removing the parent's degree of intervention (closeness) over time (e.g., instead of lying with the child in his or her bed until they fall asleep, kneel beside the bed with a hand on their chest). Refer to "The Sleep Play Love Method" for gradual withdrawal options.

- **Distractions: crib mobiles, baby monitor light, toys, wall decals.** Remove all distractions from your child's direct line of vision and ensure the child's sleep environment is dark. If you are using a light or sound baby monitor, position this away from your child's head and out of sight (monitor lights can distract children).

- **Separation anxiety or lack of connection time.** Focus on plenty of connection during the day (i.e., quality one-on-one time, roughhousing, and role-playing), listening (to tears and tantrums), and encourage crib/bedroom play to build safety and security. If not released by day, unresolved feelings can bother children at night. Roughhousing is especially effective before bedtime to release built-up tension, stress, and anxiety. You may also try having a heart-to-heart with your child before bedtime. It may help for them to talk about their day, and/or all the things that you plan to do together the following day (e.g., having breakfast, going for a play at the park, picking up their older sibling(s) from school, or baking a cake). This works as an attachment bridge to help ease anxiety.

- **Lack of day sleep or being out of routine.** Follow an age-appropriate routine and stay at home for day naps where possible. Refer to age-specific routines in "Routines and Recommendations."

- **Insufficient awake window preceding bedtime (undertired).** Follow an age-appropriate routine and tune into your child's tired cues (where possible) for their optimal sleep window. Refer to age-specific routines in "Routines and Recommendations."

- **Excessive awake window preceding bedtime (overtired).** Refer to age-specific routines in "Routines and Recommendations."

- **Too much day sleep or sleeping too late in the afternoon.** Follow an age-appropriate routine and try not to exceed the average recommended nap hours per twenty-four hours (according to age)—especially important for children seven months and over. Refer to age-specific routines in "Routines and Recommendations."

- **Actions or objects that interfere with a child's ability to self-settle (e.g., rocking, holding, patting, or feeding to sleep, pacifier, or lovey).** Some children will continue to wake every twenty to forty minutes after falling asleep (for two to three cycles or more) when they are reliant on something or someone to help them fall asleep at the beginning of the night. Refer to "The Sleep Play Love Method" for how to gently and respectfully transition your child to independent sleep.

- **Overstimulation from the day or preceding bedtime.** Follow an age-appropriate routine, swaddle young babies, avoid screen time and blue light (from electronics) in the late afternoon and early evening, and ensure appropriate wind-down time prior to sleep times with positive sleep associations. Stress-relief crying can help a child offload any stresses or tensions from the day that may otherwise contribute to bedtime resistance and overnight waking.

- **Not being swaddled.** Swaddle your baby until he or she is at least four months.

- **Night terrors.** Commonly occur at the same time each night (between 10:00 p.m. and 11:00 p.m.). Follow an age-appropriate routine to avoid overtiredness, avoid excess stimulation and blue light prior to sleep times, encourage wind-down time before bed with positive sleep associations, and ensure a regular bedtime that is not too late. Refer to "Common Sleep Difficulties and Solutions: Night Terrors" for triggers, signs, and solutions.

- **Hunger.** Most prevalent in babies under twelve months, and particularly breastfed babies. If your child is younger than six months, try introducing a dream feed between 10:00 p.m. and 11:00 p.m. For babies six months and over, ensure adequate solids and milk consumption during the day (three meals plus snacks, water, and milk). Refer to the average feeding guidelines by age in "Routines and Recommendations."

If you are experiencing frequent wake-ups between 12:00 a.m. and 4:00 a.m., common reasons include the following:

- **Teething or illness.** Seek medical advice where necessary. Refer to "Common Sleep Difficulties and Solutions: Teething and Illness."

- **Hunger.** Most prevalent in babies under twelve months, and particularly breastfed babies. If your child is younger than six months, try introducing a dream feed between 10:00 p.m. and 11:00 p.m. For babies six months and over, ensure adequate solids and milk consumption during the day (three meals plus snacks, water, and milk). Refer to the average feeding guidelines by age in "Routines and Recommendations."

- **Developmental milestones and leaps.** At times of developmental change, children may wake unsettled and have difficulty falling back to sleep—sometimes anywhere between one and three hours (usually after midnight). This is often due to insufficient wind-down time, overstimulation, and their inability to switch off from their day and all that they are learning. Adhere to an age-appropriate routine, implement positive sleep associations, and schedule appropriate wind-down time preceding sleep times. Allow children the time and space during the day to practice their newfound skills and support them to offload any developmental frustrations through stress-relief crying (while listening lovingly); this will reduce the need for them to wake overnight to "let off steam" either emotionally or physically. Refer to further tips in "The Seven Sleep Foundations: Developmental Stages, Milestones, and Life Transitions."

- **Too much sleep overall during the day (i.e., too many

hours napping). Be mindful not to exceed the average recommended nap hours per twenty-four hours (according to age). You may need to experiment with capping day naps from ten months as necessary (e.g., from ninety minutes or two hours, to one hour). Refer to age-specific routines in "Routines and Recommendations."

- **Allergies.** Allergies such as hay fever often peak between 1:00 a.m. and 4:00 a.m. Seek medical attention where necessary, and prior to administering medication.

If you are experiencing frequent wake-ups between 4:00 a.m. and 6:00 a.m., common reasons include the following:

- **The first nap was scheduled too early and/or the child napped for too long, or too much day sleep was taken during the previous day(s).** Follow an age-appropriate routine and don't exceed the total recommended hours for naps as outlined in the routines within this book. Experiment with gradually scheduling the first nap later by fifteen to thirty minutes over three to seven days and cap the nap to a maximum of two hours.

- **Overtired from lack of sleep the previous day, bedtime was too late, bedtime was too early (e.g., 6:00 p.m. or earlier), or excessive awake time at the end of the day.** Follow an age-appropriate routine and opt for a bedtime between 6:30 p.m. and 7:30 p.m.

- **Nightmares.** Most commonly occur in the early hours of the morning when a child transitions into a lighter stage of sleep. Refer to triggers, signs, and solutions in "Common Sleep Difficulties and Solutions: Nightmares."

- **Developmental leaps and milestones.** It can be common

for children to start rising early at times of developmental change. Avoid overtiredness by adhering to an age-appropriate routine and implementing positive sleep associations and appropriate wind-down time preceding sleep times. Allow your children the space and time to practice their newfound skills during the day and support them to offload developmental frustrations through crying (while listening lovingly); this will reduce the need for them to wake overnight to do so. Refer to further tips in "The Seven Sleep Foundations: Developmental Stages, Milestones, and Life Transitions."

- **Environment: noises, temperature, and light.** Optimize the sleep environment. Refer to "The Seven Sleep Foundations: Environment."

- **Too cold.** Between 4:00 a.m. and 5:00 a.m. is the coldest time of the morning. Refer to the "The Sleep Play Love Bedding Guide."

- **Teething, illness, or on the verge of illness.** Seek medical advice where necessary. Refer to "Common Sleep Difficulties and Solutions: Teething and Illness" for symptoms, common effects on sleep, and solutions.

- **Hunger.** Most prevalent in babies under twelve months and particularly breastfed babies. If your child is younger than six months, try introducing a dream feed between 10:00 p.m. and 11:00 p.m. For babies six months and over, ensure adequate solids and milk consumption during the day (three meals plus snacks, water, and milk). Refer to the average feeding guidelines by age in "Routines and Recommendations."

- **Habit.** Habitual early rising can occur following a leap, illness, teething, or when a child has been out of his or her usual routine for a prolonged period (e.g., holidays or travel). Some children will continue to wake early because their parents regularly bring them into the family bed from 5:00 a.m. or cosleep from the early hours, which further fuels early rising. Refer to "Common Sleep Difficulties and Solutions: Early Rising."

SEPARATION ANXIETY

"Most of us have the strong temptation to distract a crying child with games, songs, or toys, to discount her feelings by telling her it's okay and that she shouldn't cry. But to ensure healthy emotional development, a child's feelings of fear and loss during separation need to be expressed and heard, not erased or invalidated."
—Janet Lansbury

Separation anxiety commonly peaks between ten to eighteen months and usually subsides around two to three years of age; however, some children may show signs of this as early as six months when they begin to develop object permanence.

"Unresolved fears about separation are often at the root of difficult behaviors."
—Patty Wipfler, Hand in Hand Parenting

Children of all ages thrive on love and connection. When this connection is temporarily lost (e.g., a parent leaves the family home for work or travel, the child attends daycare, a parent is distracted, a new sibling is introduced to the family, or other routine changes that may bring about uncertainty and insecurity), children are likely to exert some of the following behaviors to show that they are feeling "off track":

- Aggressive behavior such as biting, pinching, hitting (stemming from fear).
- Forcefully affectionate.
- Withdrawal from others.
- Limited attention span—changing from one activity to another.
- Clingy, whiny, picky, sensitive, high needs.
- Needs a special object (e.g., lovey or pacifier) to keep him or her from feeling upset.

Solutions

- **Plan in advance and say your good-byes.** Prior warning may be necessary to allow a long, tearful good-bye and relieve children of any pain and fear surrounding the separation. Keep in mind that children may have accumulated feelings from previous separations, which may or may not have been acknowledged at the time. Initially, a child may need to offload feelings (by crying) for thirty to sixty minutes (or longer). The longer they are supported to do this, the easier these separations will be in future. If you are unable to sit with your child for this amount of time, then you can employ "check-ins" such as "I need to go and water the garden now, but I'll come back in a couple of minutes to check on you." *Repeated cries over several days or weeks may be necessary to relieve children's fears.*

- **Connect.** When your child feels close to you, he or she will feel safe to cry and express their feelings around the impending separation. Encourage your child to cry as hard, and for as long as necessary. Schedule some quality one-on-one time in advance, and use plenty of eye contact, cuddles, and physical closeness. Listen lovingly if your child begins to cry or tantrum—avoiding time-outs, scolding, shaming, or punishments.

- **Encourage laughter** through roughhousing or role-playing. Laughter heals fears and can make separations and transitions easier. For example, the next time you hug your child, refuse to let him or her go—squeezing them tighter or tugging him or her playfully as they attempt to break free, saying, "No! Don't leave me!" or "Come back! I don't want you to go!" Watch as your child giggles and rejoices in all the love and attention he or she is receiving. This type of role-playing empowers children and is effective for restoring their confidence and security.

- **Avoid distraction.** Some parents feel it will be easier to sneak out without saying good-bye for the fear of conflict/upset/tantrums/crying. This often only makes things worse, adding to a child's fears and insecurities—that is, your child might feel confused or upset when he or she realizes that you're not around and might be more difficult to settle the next time that you leave him or her. Always tell your child *when and where* you are going, and *when you will be back*—some (young) children may need this forewarning, even at times when you are simply leaving the room.

- **Use an attachment bridge.** Psychotherapist and parenting educator Andrea Nair suggests the use of an attachment bridge to help ease anxiety around separation. An attachment bridge refers to using some form of object or words to connect the time that you are together, over the time you are apart, and to the next time that you are together again. This may be comforting for children and help to ease any anxiety that they may be feeling. Examples may include giving them a belonging of yours to keep until you return, leaving little notes or cards in their lunchbox, video calls, or reassurance such as "When I come back after work, I am going to give you three big hugs and check that your eyes are still blue." The key to an attachment bridge is ensuring that children know when they will see you again.

- **Ensure safety and familiarity.** It helps if children are familiar with the place that they will be staying, and that they have a solid connection with the person(s) who will be caring for them. When you say good-bye to your child, reassure them that they will be safe—for example, "Grandma will take good care of you. I'll be back before dinner time. I'll always come back for you."

- **Acknowledge your child's feelings.** We are conditioned to want to avoid crying, conflict, and upset by dismissing our children's uncomfortable feelings—for example, "Don't be silly" or "I am only going for a little while" or "It's alright—don't cry." Instead, acknowledge how difficult this situation is for your child and validate his or her feelings of sadness: "I know you don't want Mommy to leave. I am sorry that I can't stay and play here with you. I am here now." Allow for some listening time, as your child will undoubtedly express his or her difficult feelings through tears and tantrums.

TEETHING AND ILLNESS

Many sleeping difficulties and undesirable sleep habits commonly develop when a child is teething or unwell. Try not to become too disheartened if you experience that your routine, consistency, and resolve seem to navigate south at these times. You can help to minimize the impact of these "teething pains" on your child's sleep—and yours—by taking the following into consideration.

How Long Does Teething Take?

While babies can grow their first tooth as early as three months, and some as late as twelve months, the average age to cut their first tooth is between six and seven months. Most children will have all their milk (baby) teeth by two and a half years.

Depending on the individual; their age, which teeth, and how many are coming through at the one time, the pain and effect on sleep and behavior may be experienced for one day to a week, or more. Refer to the chart in figure 3 for an average timeline of which teeth and when.

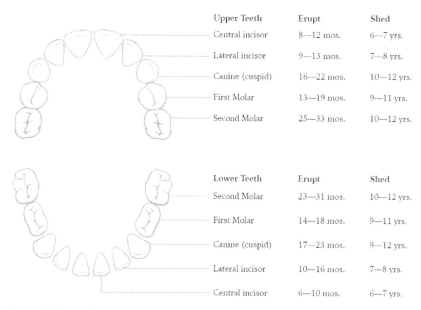

Upper Teeth	Erupt	Shed
Central incisor	8—12 mos.	6—7 yrs.
Lateral incisor	9—13 mos.	7—8 yrs.
Canine (cuspid)	16—22 mos.	10—12 yrs.
First Molar	13—19 mos.	9—11 yrs.
Second Molar	25—33 mos.	10—12 yrs.

Lower Teeth	Erupt	Shed
Second Molar	23—31 mos.	10—12 yrs.
First Molar	14—18 mos.	9—11 yrs.
Canine (cuspid)	17—23 mos.	9—12 yrs.
Lateral incisor	10—16 mos.	7—8 yrs.
Central incisor	6—10 mos.	6—7 yrs.

Figure 3. Baby Teeth Chart

Signs and Symptoms

- Red swollen gums
- Congestion and cold-like symptoms
- Red cheeks
- Dribbling or drooling
- Chewing or biting—on everything
- White buds visible in gums
- Rash on face and/or chin
- Nappy rash
- Runny stools
- More frequent bowel movements at all different times of the day (including nap times and in the middle of the night)
- Increased clinginess, irritability, and crying
- Loss of appetite
- Slight temperature
- Pulling at ears

The above signs and symptoms can also represent more serious illness. If you are concerned about the health of your child, always seek medical advice.

Effects on Sleep

- Catnapping or shorter sleeps than usual
- General unsettledness or wakefulness at sleep times
- Difficulty resettling at naps and bedtime
- Frequent waking in the hours immediately following bedtime (e.g., every thirty to sixty minutes)
- Waking in the early hours (specifically after midnight) and difficulty settling back to sleep
- Early rising
- Increased overnight waking—symptoms of teething and illness are usually intensified toward the end of the day and overnight

Solutions

- **Tune into your child's tired cues and maintain a regular day-and-night routine.** Overtiredness and overstimulation can further exacerbate discomfort—leading to irritability, bedtime resistance, and frequent waking.

- **Optimize the sleep environment.** Refer to "The Seven Sleep Foundations: Environment."

- **Elevate the mattress head slightly.** This can help to relieve the pressure and discomfort from teething, and the congestion associated with colds—as this can aid sinus drainage.

- **Administer pain relief where necessary,** and upon advice of your health-care provider. *Most effective when given thirty minutes before sleep times.*

- **Encourage wind-down time with positive sleep associations before bed.** Aim for ten to fifteen minutes before naps and thirty to sixty minutes at the end of the day. This can minimize overtiredness and ensure your child is as relaxed as possible for sleep times.

- **Be prepared to spend extra time sitting beside your child's bed** to help them to fall asleep or back to sleep when they may wake from naps or during the night—*many children will have an increased desire for comfort and closeness when in pain or discomfort.*

- **Teething rings and toys.** Chewing may temporarily relieve the pressure and pain caused by teething.

- **Baltic amber teething necklaces.** The anti-inflammatory properties in amber may help soothe swollen gums and reduce pain.

- **A humidifier** in the child's room may help to alleviate any associated congestion with teething or colds. Add some essential oils such as eucalyptus, tea tree, vetiver, or lavender.

- **Edible teething rusks.** Only recommended from six months of age, or after solids have been introduced.

- **Cold fruit, frozen fruit popsicles, or a cold face washer** to suck on can help reduce swelling and numb the pain.

- **Children may prefer soft or pureed foods to solids.** Chewing food can exacerbate teething discomfort, and some children lose their appetite when they are teething or ill. Opt for foods that are easily consumed and digested such as smoothies, freshly squeezed fruit or vegetable juices, mashed vegetables, pureed fruit, and yogurt.

- **Breastfeeding** is a natural pain relief and immunity booster. Breastmilk can also provide children with the nutrition and hydration that they may be lacking—especially if their appetite is suppressed—when teething or unwell.

- **Try holistic remedies.** Certain homeopathic teething remedies such as gels, tablets, drops, and essential oils can be effective for relieving pain and irritability. Pure clove essential oil (diluted with a carrier oil and applied to the gums) may be a natural alternative to pharmaceutical gels for teething. The following essential oils—either applied topically to the neck, chest, and feet, or in a diffuser—are said to have immune-boosting properties and can be beneficial in relieving common cold and flu symptoms; frankincense, oregano, eucalyptus, tea tree, lemon, rosemary, ginger, lemongrass, peppermint, cinnamon, copaiba, and Young Living's "Thieves" blend.

- **Delay any sleep training or other transitions** such as night weaning or weaning from the pacifier until your child has recovered completely.

- **Don't wake a sleeping baby.** When children are unwell they often need to sleep more to heal and recover. Avoid waking them for naps or if they are still sleeping in the morning.

- **Wear your baby.** Babywearing may offer comfort to unsettled (teething and unwell) babies, and help to encourage—or prolong—day naps. Holding babies close also helps to regulate temperature, and boost their immune system.

- **Be patient**. Respond to your child's needs appropriately and with love and compassion. Albeit exhausting and frustrating for parents, teething and illness is only temporary. You can proceed with your usual routine once your child has recovered. Refer to "The Sleep Play Love Method" as necessary for assistance with changing undesirable sleep patterns and encouraging independent sleep.

Illness symptoms and solutions can vary greatly. Never self-diagnose; always seek professional advice at times when you are uncertain of your child's symptoms or if your child requires assistance (medical and/or natural) to ease pain or accelerate the recovery process.

SECTION IV
ROUTINES AND
RECOMMENDATIONS

WHEN WILL MY BABY LEARN TO SELF-SETTLE?

Self-settling (or self-soothing), is often confused with sleep-training methodologies such as cry it out, controlled crying, responsive settling —or at worst, neglect. However, nothing could be farther from the truth.

True self-settling empowers children by enabling them to develop their own individual coping strategies naturally, without the dependence on a caregiver.

As parents, we cannot force self-setting through sleep training. Children will learn to self-settle according to their own inborn timeline when we provide a loving, supportive, and responsive presence for them to do so.

Babies' ability to self-settle depends on a few factors: their temperament, age, and the parent's level of involvement when putting them to sleep. While some babies can self-settle from birth, for others, this is an acquired skill that they become more competent at doing the older they become—usually after four months of age.

How Can I Encourage My Child to Fall Asleep Independently?

- **Establish positive sleep associations.** Incorporate a relaxing and predictable bedtime routine, which signals to your child that it is time for sleep (e.g., massage, swaddle/sleeping bag, white noise, dark room, or reading a book).

- **Tune into your baby's unique temperament, needs, and capabilities.** For example, sensitive or high-needs children may require increased parental intervention at sleep times (*especially* in the first three months), therefore making their ability to fall asleep independently more challenging.

- **Trust in your child's natural ability to develop their own coping strategies** at times of frustration, upset, or when overwhelmed. This may mean affording them one to two minutes of space at sleep times for them to locate their thumb or other comfort source—without intervening immediately to offer the breast or pacifier.

- **Acknowledge the role of crying as a natural stress relief and healing process for children.** Young babies often grizzle or cry at bedtimes in their attempt to release stored stress or emotion from their day so that they can sleep (well). If children's primary needs have been met, the kindest thing we can do is to hold them in our loving arms and support them to release their big feelings—so that naturally they can sleep better (with less intervention from us over time). The more often we can encourage our children to release their emotions throughout the day (without distraction), the less resistance we will experience at bedtimes, and the easier it will be for them to transition to independent sleep because they will feel safer, emotionally "lighter," and more confident.

- Become aware of *how often* you soothe your child through methods such as rocking, feeding, patting, holding, or offering the pacifier. These actions—when exercised routinely after three months of age—quickly become *our* habits and *our children's* sleep needs. Repressed emotions often become the catalyst for a host of sleep-related challenges, not to mention habits that become increasingly challenging to break as time progresses.

FINDING YOUR CHILD'S OPTIMAL AWAKE WINDOW

Finding the optimal awake window for each individual child can be nothing short of a science. That "magical window" where you optimize your child's ability to fall asleep independently—with minimal fuss or intervention—can be a matter of less than five minutes. Ideally, placing children to sleep when you observe their initial tired cues can ensure he or she falls asleep more easily and for longer. If you are observing a child's secondary tired cues, this may suggest you have missed the sleep window—often presenting challenges with settling and sleep.

How Can I Tell If My Child Is Undertired or Overtired?

Unfortunately, the boundaries between undertiredness and overtiredness are often inextricable. However, an undertired child is more likely to be of a relaxed or playful disposition. They may babble, call out, laugh, or have an increased desire to engage and play at bedtimes or when left in his or her crib. Although children may become progressively upset or frustrated, an undertired child is not likely to become immediately upset or hysterical when placed to bed. To the contrary, an overtired child will either display erratic or hyperactive behavior (i.e., the infamous "second wind") or may become very upset (e.g., crying, tantrums, or thrashing) at bedtimes. At either end of the spectrum, children will require more parental intervention and will often take anywhere between twenty minutes to two hours (on average) to fall asleep.

How Do I Know If I Have Missed the Sleep Window?

- Your child takes longer than twenty minutes to fall asleep.
- Your child frequently resists bedtime (anywhere from twenty minutes to two hours).
- Your child frequently catnaps during the day (and is six months or over).
- Your child requires more intervention from you to fall asleep—such as feeding, rocking, patting, or holding.

A child may exert these same behaviors when they are unwell, teething, or experiencing a leap. In such cases, it is recommended to shorten your child's awake time slightly to avoid overtiredness.

Initial Tired Cues

- Rubbing eyes
- Yawning
- Red eyebrows
- Glazed eyes/staring into space
- Grizzly
- Loss of coordination/clumsiness (may have more falls or stumbles than usual)
- Loss of interest in what they were doing
- Lack of engagement
- Hiccups

- Nothing seems to make them happy—irrespective of changing their environment, activity, or offering comfort
- Clenching fists
- Jerky or sudden movements of arms and/or legs
- Pulling at ears; this can also signal teething or ear infection so best to check with a medical professional if you are uncertain
- Frowning, or a worried look on their face
- Fussiness with food, toys, or activities

Secondary Tired Cues

- Arching back or stiffening their body when you pick them up
- Constant crying or screaming
- Burying their head into your chest; this may also signal hunger
- Tantrums
- Some babies and children can become hysterical (crying or screaming as if they are in pain)

Other Tips

- **Some babies may not display definitive tired cues, which can be confusing for parents.** Where you are uncertain, attempt to follow the age-appropriate awake time guidelines as recommended in "Routines and Recommendations."

- **Tired cues seem to be a more accurate indication of the ideal sleep window in children under twelve months.** From twelve months onward, you may rely more on the average awake time to ascertain optimal sleep times.

- **The ideal amount of time for a child to fall asleep at**

naps and bedtime is between five and fifteen minutes.
Any longer suggests that you *may* have missed the sleep
window. Any less suggests a child may be sleep deprived.

- **Incorporating "wind-down time" before bed can
counteract overstimulation.** Try ten to fifteen minutes
prior to naps and twenty to thirty minutes before bedtime at
the end of the day. Include positive sleep associations such
as kissing family members good-night, dimming the lights,
closing the blinds, playing white noise, a swaddle or
sleeping bag, reading books, singing songs, and a cuddle.

- **Keep a sleep log.** If your child begins resisting sleep times
frequently (over a week or longer), start a sleep log to
ascertain if there is any regular pattern with their awake
time (i.e., whether there is an opportunity to reduce or
increase their awake window according to your findings).
*Record the total awake time—that is, from the time that they woke
from their previous sleep to the next time that they fall asleep.
Assume this awake time between their next sleep time.*

- **The ideal awake window between the last nap of the
day and bedtime can vary significantly between
children.** Some toddlers closer to twenty-four months may
sleep better overnight if they have less sleep during the day
(e.g., ninety minutes to two hours—rather than three
hours). While some may be content to fall asleep three
hours after they wake from their day nap, others may need
five to six hours of awake time, or they will passionately
resist bedtime! You may need to employ trial and error to
establish what is your child's ideal sleep window and their
sleep requirements during the day.

WHAT IS A DREAM FEED?

A dream feed is a method used to fill babies up with milk at night, without waking them. This feed is usually scheduled between 10:00 p.m. and 11:00 p.m. for children up to the age of six months and sometimes older—for example, at times of growth spurts and developmental change.

Why?

The intention of the dream feed is to minimize night waking due to hunger. Because the baby remains drowsy or asleep while feeding, the dream feed is one less feed they are waking for, which may increase overnight sleep duration between feeds and reduce habitual waking.

How?

If breastfeeding: gently lift your child up while they are still asleep and place them on the breast.

If bottle-feeding: place the bottle into your child's mouth while they remain in their sleep space or pick them up to feed them in your arms.

If your baby is too sleepy to feed, gently rub his or her cheeks to encourage them to rouse slightly and begin sucking. For particularly young and sleepy babies, changing their diaper before the feed may help.

Troubleshooting Tips

- Ensure the dream feed is adequate. The more milk that children consume during this feed, the longer they may be able to stretch in between overnight feeds.

- Formula is digested at a slower rate than breast milk, which means formula-fed babies may remain fuller for longer and require less frequent feeds than their breastfed counterparts —although this is not always the case.

The Dream Feed May *Not* Be Suitable for Your Child if:

- he or she starts waking at the time of the dream feed (or just before);

- he or she begins waking between one to two hours following the dream feed (when previously he or she slept); and/or

- he or she wakes completely during the dream feed and is difficult to settle back to sleep.

The first six to seven hours after a baby falls asleep is the most restorative sleep of the night. Sometimes, introducing a feed during this time, even if the baby remains asleep, can disrupt his or her natural sleep rhythm and may cause regression in overnight sleep. It may be a matter of trial and error to determine what is most suitable for your child.

When and How to Drop the Dream Feed

If your baby is at least six months and he or she can sleep through the night without any other feeds *for at least one week* (and this is not due to teething or illness), then you may consider dropping the dream feed. There are two ways I recommend you can do this:

1. **Bring the dream feed earlier by fifteen to thirty minutes over a few nights.** The final dream feed will be one hour after your child's usual bedtime—for example, if your baby is going to bed at 7:00 p.m., the last dream feed you will do before weaning completely will be at 8:00 p.m.

2. **Slowly reduce the amount of milk given at the dream feed.** If bottle-feeding, reduce the amount of milk given at each feed every one to two nights by 20–30 ml (0.5–1 oz). If your baby is drinking less than 60 ml (2oz) at the dream feed, you may consider eliminating this feed altogether. If breastfeeding (and your baby is feeding for longer than five minutes), gradually reduce the time you are feeding by one to two minutes each night over a few nights. When you are feeding for only five minutes at the dream feed, you can drop the feed altogether without reducing the time any further.

AVERAGE SLEEP REQUIREMENTS BY AGE

AGE	OVERNIGHT	NAPS	TOTAL (PER 24 HOURS)
Newborn to 2 months	8—9 hours	7—9 hours	16—18 hours
2—4 months	9—10 hours	4—5 hours (4—5 naps)	14—16 hours
4—6 months	10 hours	4—5 hours (3—4 naps)	14—15 hours
6—9 months	10—11 hours	3—4 hours (2—3 naps)	14 hours
9—12 months	10—12 hours	2—3 hours (2 naps)	14 hours
12—18 months	11—12 hours	2—3 hours (1—2 naps)	13—14 hours
18—24 months	11 hours	2 hours (1 nap)	13—14 hours
24—36 months	10—11 hours	1—2 hours (1 nap)	12—14 hours
3—5 years	10—13 hours	0—1 hours (0—1 nap)	11—13 hours

For premature babies, refer to their adjusted/corrected age for sleep requirements and routines. Some professionals recommend using adjusted/corrected age up to the age of two years.

You may be able to minimize overnight waking and bedtime resistance by adhering to the recommended nap hours and/or total sleep per twenty-four hours. Exceeding hours of day naps can compromise a child's overnight sleep duration.

BIRTH TO THREE MONTHS

General Recommendations

Respect your baby's need for a fourth trimester.
The transition from womb to world can be an intense and over-whelming time for infants, and therefore, it is extremely common for them to become overstimulated, fussy, and upset in the early weeks as they adjust to this change. To help them adapt to life on the outside, replicating the womb environment can work wonders to instill calm and encourage sound sleep. For nine to ten months, your baby has been accustomed to constant warmth, movement, noise, and the security of being snug in the confines of the womb. And since babies receive constant nutrition throughout this time via the bloodstream, the sensation of hunger following birth can be all-consuming for them. Consequently, newborns often become distressed when they are placed to sleep alone in a quiet room or are expected to adapt to a "parent-led" feeding and sleep schedule.

Solutions to ensure a peaceful transition include:

- white noise
- cosleeping
- swaddle (for sleep times)
- baby wearing
- follow a flexible age-appropriate awake time versus a strict routine
- minimizing stimulation such as bright lights, lots of visitors, and loud noises
- feed on demand
- plenty of love, cuddles, and connection
- a dark room is recommended for night sleep, and for day naps after six weeks of age

Breaking habits such as feeding to sleep or expecting your baby to self-settle efficiently at all sleep times is unrealistic. Babies in the first three months are particularly responsive to touch, movement, and sucking—for comfort, to satisfy neonatal reflexes and to fall asleep. Go with the flow in the early months, and focus on removing any negative or undesirable sleep associations (or habits) from six months of age using "The Sleep Play Love Method."

Your baby will cry a lot for many reasons. If there is a need that can be met, like hunger or the need for sleep, then it makes sense to respond accordingly. If your baby is crying and you can't discern an obvious reason, then it can be helpful to minimize environmental stimulation and just gently hold your child or lie down with them. Skin-to-skin, gentle movement while cuddling your baby in your arms, talking, or singing softly may help to comfort your baby. Babies will also cry to heal from trauma (especially from the birth process) and to efficiently release everyday stresses and tensions. If you have met your child's primary needs, then they may just need to cry in your loving arms for emotional regulation.

Colic and reflux are extremely common. Both can make sleep a challenge because of the discomfort they induce. Symptoms usually subside or clear altogether between four and six months. Introducing a pacifier for overly fussy babies can help them calm. Try to avoid overfeeding and overstimulation, which can exacerbate symptoms. Refer to "Common Sleep Difficulties and Solutions."

An infant's circadian rhythm (internal body clock) is not established until ten to twelve weeks. Consequently, catnapping, irregular sleep patterns (day and night), and day-and-night confusion are common. Regular sunlight exposure promotes melatonin production (sleep hormone), which is responsible for deciphering day from night. Maintaining a dark room at sleep times encourages the brain to release melatonin, therefore inducing sleep.

In the first few weeks, babies may experience day-and-night confusion. Because of their immature circadian rhythm, many babies will sleep for longer stretches during the day than overnight. It helps to wake your baby from their nap after a maximum of two hours during the day, and feed on demand (or every two to three hours) to avoid them waking so regularly overnight to feed. Sleep your baby (under six weeks) in a light room for naps (e.g., beside a window), and keep his or her room dark for all overnight sleep. From six weeks onward, sleep your baby in a dark room day and night. If your baby (six weeks and under) catnaps regularly during the day (e.g., twenty to thirty minute naps), experiment with maintaining a dark room for day naps rather than sleeping the baby in natural light. *Sleeping your baby in natural light following birth can also help to counteract common, mild jaundice.*

Catnapping is developmentally normal—expect naps anywhere from twenty to forty minutes. Ensure your baby is well fed, use white noise (to muffle household and outside noises), maintain a darkened room, follow an age-appropriate routine, keep them warm, and avoid overstimulation where possible. For additional information, refer to "Common Sleep Difficulties and Solutions: Catnapping."

Young babies spend 50 percent of their time in REM (light sleep), which explains why they awaken more easily—day and night— than older babies and toddlers. At six months, the overall time spent in REM sleep reduces to 30 percent, and you will generally notice daytime sleep patterns improve from this age.

Maintaining a structured or *consistent* routine is unlikely during the first three to four months. This is attributed to the drastic developmental changes and biological evolvement in sleep patterns from birth to three months. Don't be disheartened if your baby doesn't—or won't—sleep in his or her bassinet or crib for *every* sleep. Due to babies' short awake time, falling asleep in the car, carrier, swing, and stroller is inevitable throughout the day—especially when there are older siblings to care for. However, adhering to age-appropriate awake times (where possible) and implementing regular, positive sleep associations such as swaddle, white noise, dark room, cuddle, and a song cue your baby for bedtime and help them to feel safe and secure. You can expect more consistency with sleep patterns from six months of age.

Discomfort due to gas pain in their stomach or bowel is very common in the early weeks as babies adjust to digesting milk. This can cause squirming, crying, grunting, and long periods of wakefulness day—and night. Remember to always ensure your baby burps after feeds—or in between feeds if you are breastfeeding and have an oversupply or fast flow (to avoid your baby gulping and swallowing air). These symptoms may also resemble colic or reflux, so always seek medical advice where you are concerned.

Your baby may start to display symptoms of teething as early as three months. Although the average age to cut a first tooth is between six and seven months, all babies develop at varying paces.

Some babies are even born with teeth! Refer to "Common Sleep Difficulties and Solutions: Teething and Illness."

Developmental Milestones

- Your baby will have his or her initial growth spurt between one to three weeks—and another between six to eight weeks. Increased hunger, fussiness, cluster feeding, catnapping, and more frequent night waking are common.
- When his or her cheek is touched, a baby will turn to the same side to suckle.
- Can respond to sounds and may turn head toward noise.
- May smile between five to seven weeks (if not earlier).
- Mimics facial expressions and expresses emotions.
- By three months, can laugh and coo out aloud.
- Lifts head when prone (on tummy).
- Kicks legs vigorously by two months.
- Require three to five naps per day, a total of sixteen to eighteen hours sleep in a twenty-four-hour period.
- Refer to the Wonder Weeks for further information on developmental stages: mental leap one (four to five weeks), mental leap two (eight weeks), and mental leap three (twelve weeks).

Feeding and Nutrition

- Until your (breast) milk supply has been established— between six to eight weeks—feeding on demand is recommended. Expect to feed your infant anywhere between ninety minutes and three hours around the clock. Once your supply is established, feeding every two to three hours during the day, or three to four hours overnight, is average. A dream feed as per the routines in this book may help you achieve some extra mileage between feeds overnight. *At any age, your baby should be feeding more often during the day, than overnight. From four months, most babies can forego an additional thirty to sixty minutes between feeds overnight—when compared to their average daily feed intervals.*

- Encourage regular feeds during the day so that your baby is not compensating by waking frequently to feed overnight.

- Look out for hunger cues such as clenched fists, smacking or licking lips, opening and closing their mouth, sucking on lips/tongue/hands/fingers/toes/toys/clothing, rooting around for the breast, fussing, squirming, or crying.

- A sunken fontanelle and/or clenched fists may indicate that your baby is hungry or dehydrated. A satisfied baby will generally have loose fists, appear calm, and the soft spot on the top of their head will be flat or protruding, not sunken.

- Cluster feeding (i.e., a few hours of constant or close-together feeds—often in the early evening) is normal in the early weeks, the purpose of which is to stimulate milk production and to satisfy your child's evolving nutritional needs—especially during growth spurts (i.e., ten days to two weeks, three weeks, six weeks, and at three months). Albeit frustrating and exhausting, it is only temporary and will pass almost as soon as it began.

- Formula-fed babies will need around 150–200 ml (5–7 oz) per kilogram of body weight per day until six months of age.

- For parents who wish to introduce a bottle, it is recommended to wait until after breastfeeding has been established (between six to eight weeks). Refer to tips in "Managing Transitions: Introducing the Bottle."

- Your baby's only source of nutrition will be from breast milk or formula—that is, no water or solids until four to six months.

Settling Tips

- Address your child's primary needs such as hunger, comfort, thirst, pain, cleanliness, stimulation, and sleep—before reverting to settling techniques. If your baby continues to cry, consider his or her need to do so for stress relief or to heal trauma (e.g., prenatal stress, birth trauma, unfilled needs, overstimulation, developmental frustrations, and frightening events such as loud noises or parental separation).

- Harvey Karp's 5 Ss (i.e., swaddle, side/stomach position, shush, swing, and suck) can help to soothe overstimulated and fussy babies. More information at: happiestbaby.com

- Many babies of this age group will respond positively to a shush-pat, or gentle rocking from side to side—either in their parent's arms or positioned firmly on their side as they remain swaddled in their crib. *Young babies will often seek comfort in rhythmic patting on their bottoms. If you are concerned about this becoming a sleep crutch ongoing, experiment with resting your hand firmly on their bottom and/or removing your hand completely once your child appears to be close to—but not completely —asleep. You may recommence patting if they wake completely, repeating this process until they fall asleep.*

- Studies demonstrate that many young babies dislike the sensation of a light caress, preferring a firmer touch. Similarly, babies may also find it stressful to be touched in isolation, responding better to a multisensory experience (e.g., when touched in conjunction with a rocking movement, eye contact, and reassuring words from a familiar caregiver).

Settling tools can be extremely effective for soothing fussy, overtired, or sleepless babies. However, be mindful that when such methods are employed regularly (i.e., 80 percent of the time or more), these can develop into a "sleep need" or habit—interfering with a child's ability to self-settle and repressing emotions. Try to ascertain the root of the child's upset—reverting to settling methods once all other emotional and physiological needs have been satisfied. It is quite possible that a child may simply need to be held in their parent's loving arms while they cry to avail themselves of everyday stress, tension and frustration—or to heal from birth trauma.

Sleep Associations

- Realistically, at least 50 percent of the time you may have to hold, carry, or rock your child, or allow them to nap in the car, carrier, swing, or stroller to counteract overstimulation and other factors such as colic and reflux. This is often unavoidable—especially when parents have multiple children or busy lifestyles. Where possible, encourage day naps in your child's crib, cosleeper, or bassinet so the child becomes familiar with his or her sleep environment (this also becomes a sleep cue!). *Try to be patient and kind to yourself, as it is unlikely you will have a routine established until closer to six months.*

- Swaddle for all naps and bedtime—the exception being if your baby falls asleep in a baby carrier or car.

- The decision to use a pacifier is a personal one. If you

choose to do so, introduce the paci after breastfeeding has been established, and by one month of age—or your baby may resist taking to it.

Awake Times

Birth to One Month

Ensure the awake time does not exceed forty to sixty minutes. If your baby has only slept for twenty to thirty minutes at any one nap, place him or her back to sleep twenty to thirty minutes after waking. *Overstimulation and overtiredness can exacerbate colic and reflux symptoms—therefore, a shorter awake time may be necessary for children experiencing these symptoms (e.g., thirty to forty minutes).*

One to Two Months

Focus on a maximum awake time of one hour—or less if the baby's last sleep duration was less than one hour. *Lean toward forty minutes for babies with colic or reflux.*

Two to Three Months

Awake time is a maximum of one hour and fifteen minutes, or the duration of the last sleep time (if less than one hour). If colic or reflux is still an issue at this age, lean toward an awake time of one hour maximum.

Sample Routines

Routine for babies under three months: awake time and feed/play/feed/sleep

In the first three months, your baby is still establishing his or her circadian rhythm (internal body clock). Consequently, it is common to experience day-night confusion (i.e., sleeping all day and awake and feeding all night) and no regular wake or sleep times. It is not until *after* three months that I recommend focusing on regular nap and feeding times. For this age group, focus on an average awake time of forty to ninety minutes and a feed, play, feed, sleep routine.

Wake your baby to feed every two hours during the day (if they are still sleeping). This will help minimize day-night confusion. *For babies who only catnap, continue to place them back to sleep within the duration of their last sleep (i.e., if they only slept for twenty minutes, place him or her back to sleep after twenty to thirty minutes).* During the day, focus on **feed, play, feed, sleep:**

- **Offer a feed:** if breastfeeding, offer one side. For formula-fed babies, offer as much as they will take at the time.
- **Play:** change your babies' diaper in the middle of the feed to keep them from falling asleep, thus encouraging a more efficient feed. Lightly rubbing their cheeks or face can also help stimulate them and keep them awake to finish the feed.
- **Finish off the feed:** that is, offer the other breast if breastfeeding, or the remainder of the formula bottle if applicable.
- **Wind-down time:** burp, swaddle, draw blinds, turn on white noise, read a book, or sing a song.
- **Sleep:** place your baby back to bed for sleep.

Additional Routine Tips

- At nighttime, feed or resettle your baby straight back to sleep (i.e., no playing), maintain a dark and quiet environment, and keep interaction to a minimum.

- For babies with colic or reflux, stick to feed, play, and sleep (i.e., do not feed before sleep as this may exacerbate symptoms).

Routine

Three Months

Number of naps: four to five
Total nap hours: four to five hours
Awake time: ninety minutes

Option (a)
7:00 a.m.—Wake and milk
8:30 a.m.—Nap 1
10:00 a.m.—Wake and milk. *Allow your baby to sleep a maximum of two hours*
11:30 a.m.—Nap 2
1:00 p.m.—Wake and milk. *Allow your baby to sleep a maximum of two hours*
2:30 p.m.—Nap 3
4:00 p.m.—Wake and milk
5:30 p.m. to 6:00 p.m.—Nap 4: thirty-minute catnap
6:30 p.m.—Begin bedtime routine (bath, milk, swaddle, book, song)
7:30 p.m.—In bed, asleep
10:30 p.m.—Dream feed (schedule three hours from bedtime)

Option (b)
7:00 a.m.—Wake and milk
8:30 a.m.—Nap 1
10:00 a.m.—Wake and milk. *Allow your baby to sleep a maximum of two hours*
11:30 a.m.—Nap 2

1:00 p.m.—Wake and milk. *Allow your baby to sleep a maximum of two hours*

2:30 p.m.—Nap 3

4:00 p.m.—Wake and milk

5:30 p.m. to 6:30 p.m.—Nap 4

7:00 p.m.—Milk

8:00 p.m. to 8:30 p.m.—Nap 5: thirty-minute catnap

9:00 p.m.—Begin bedtime routine (bath, milk, swaddle, book, song)

10:00 p.m.—In bed, asleep

Additional Routine Tips

- Nap lengths are based on ninety minutes—if your baby only sleeps between thirty and forty minutes (or less), schedule his or her awake time earlier (e.g., one hour to one hour and fifteen minutes), dependent on the baby's tired cues. *In such cases, babies may have up to six or seven naps per day instead of four or five.*

- Milk feeds are scheduled approximately every three hours during the day. If your baby requires a top-up feed preceding bedtime (i.e., if they haven't fed substantially at their normal feed time), ensure the feed is at least twenty to thirty minutes prior to sleep times.

- As catnapping is still very common for this age group, timing milk feeds *before* sleep rather than upon waking may help to minimize premature waking because of hunger. If your baby is experiencing colic or reflux, then it is best to feed upon waking.

- It is acceptable to sleep your child in the stroller, car, swing, or baby carrier for the scheduled thirty-minute catnap—this may help counteract the overtiredness or fussiness that often presents at the end of the day.

- A dark room, warmth, and white noise are the key environmental factors that can improve catnapping at this age—refer to "Common Sleep Difficulties and Solutions: Catnapping."

- If your baby only catnaps (less than forty-five minutes) and you are unable to extend the nap, schedule additional naps throughout the day and a later bedtime—refer to routine option (b).

- As a guide, space overnight feeds three to four hours apart (resettle with alternative comfort or listening around this time).

- The three-month growth spurt may result in cluster feeding and more frequent overnight waking because of hunger. Maintain the dream feed. *Some babies may need to feed more frequently than three-hourly day and night temporarily.*

FOUR TO SIX MONTHS

General Recommendations

Alertness increases significantly as the fourth trimester ends.
Consequently, your baby may become distracted during feed times,
resulting in increased night waking due to hunger to compensate for
the lack of nutrition during the day. *Find a dark, quiet place for feeding
during the day, away from distractions and avoid over-scheduling.*

Separation anxiety can start as early as six months. This can be
attributed to the development of object permanence (i.e., the understanding that objects continue to exist—even when they cannot be
seen, heard, touched, smelled, or sensed in any way). Communicating
to your child when and where you are going (if leaving them
temporarily), and offering continual love and support, will encourage
your child's security and confidence.

**Sleep regression is particularly common at four months (the infa-
mous four-month sleep regression) and at six months.** This often

coincides with growth spurts, physical milestones (rolling and sitting up), transitioning out of the swaddle, increased motor skills, and object permanence. You may also notice that your baby wakes more often rolling in the crib. Respond to your children's needs during these times with love and patience—it is likely that they will require increased intervention and encouragement from you at sleep times, since insecurity and fear is synonymous with developmental change. While regression can last anywhere between two and six weeks, you can minimize the impact by maintaining a regular day-and-night routine, ensuring sufficient wind-down prior to sleep times, incorporating playtime in the child's room and crib, encouraging plenty of space and opportunity to practice their newfound skills during waking hours, and optimizing the sleep environment (particularly white noise, a darkened room, and warmth). Refer to recommendations in "The Seven Sleep Foundations: Developmental Stages, Milestones, and Transitions."

Most babies will cut their first tooth from six months of age. Sleep regression at these times is normal, and it is common to experience catnapping, bedtime resistance, heightened irritability, increased wakefulness, more frequent night waking, and early rising (even in babies who have previously been good sleepers). Teething may also affect a child's appetite, and consequently hunger can lead to disrupted day naps and night sleep.

Catnapping may persist well up to six or seven months and is developmentally normal as daytime sleep patterns are still establishing.

Awake time increases from ninety minutes to two hours.

Developmental Milestones

- Drop from four naps to three naps at around four months.
- May have five to six hours of unbroken sleep at night.

- Can express emotions and recognize familiar people, faces, and voices.
- Motor control and strength becomes more defined (e.g., reaching for objects, holding their head up, and sitting up with support).
- May begin rolling—which means transitioning out of the swaddle.
- Sleep habits (such as rocking, holding, and feeding to sleep) may begin to interfere with sleep quality and duration more noticeably closer to six months.
- Separation anxiety may start as early as six months. This can be attributed to object permanence. Clinginess, bedtime resistance, or increased night waking can be expected.
- A growth spurt at six months can cause increased hunger, crankiness, and regression in sleep patterns temporarily (e.g., frequent night waking and catnapping).
- Refer to the Wonder Weeks for further information on current developmental stages: mental leap four (eighteen to twenty weeks per four to five months) and mental leap five (six months).

Feeding and Nutrition

- Formula-fed babies: five to six bottles per twenty-four hours (150–240 ml, or 5–8 oz per feed).

- Breastfed babies: five to seven feeds per twenty-four hours.

- Some babies will show an interest in starting solids as early as four months. Follow your baby's lead as to his or her readiness: ability to sit up unassisted, good head-and-neck control, ability and willingness to chew, expressing interest when others are eating, reaching for food, and opening his or her mouth for food.

- It is recommended to begin solids by six months if you haven't already. This coincides with the age where your baby's iron stores begin to deplete, so his or her need for extra iron (among other vitamins and minerals) is increased. For a great reference on which foods and when, refer to Well Adjusted Babies (welladjusted.co).

Sleep Associations

- Swaddle for all sleep times—until babies show signs of rolling when swaddled, or you feel that they would benefit from having access to their hands at bedtime to self-soothe (e.g., to suck their hands for comfort).

- If you have introduced a pacifier, four months is the optimal time to consider weaning as this is the age when habits begin to override reflexes. If you choose to keep the pacifier, just ensure it is used *for sleep times only*, and your baby is not waking frequently overnight for you to replace it!

Routine

Four to Five Months

Number of naps: three
Total nap hours: four to five hours
Awake time: ninety minutes to one hour forty-five minutes

7:00 a.m.—Wake and milk
8:00 a.m.—Breakfast
8:30 a.m.—Nap 1: ninety-minute awake time
10:00 a.m.—Wake and milk. *Allow your baby to sleep for up to two hours*

11:00 a.m.—Lunch

11:45 p.m.—Nap 2: one-hour-forty-five-minute awake time

1:15 p.m.—Wake and milk. *Allow your baby to sleep up to two hours*

2:00 p.m.—Snack

3:00 p.m.—Nap 3: one-hour-forty-five-minute awake time

4:30 p.m.—Wake and milk

5:00 p.m.—Dinner

6:00 p.m.—Milk (*twenty to thirty minutes before bed*)

6:15 p.m. to 6:30 p.m.—In bed, asleep. One-hour-forty-five-minute to two-hour awake time

10:00 p.m./10:30 p.m.—Dream feed (schedule three to four hours from bedtime)

Additional Routine Tips

- From four months of age onward, try to resettle your child (for up to twenty minutes) if they have slept for *less than* forty-five minutes at nap time. Warm validation while sitting beside them, a gentle rock/jiggle from side-to-side while they remain in their crib, or holding your child to help them calm may be necessary. *Resetting for any longer than twenty minutes often becomes increasingly frustrating for parents and is, therefore, counterproductive when encouraging babies to fall back into a calm sleep state.*

- If your child has slept for less than forty-five minutes and you are unable to extend their nap, you may shorten the next awake time by fifteen to thirty minutes. Follow your child's tired cues and be mindful not to continually reduce their awake time—as this can promote further catnapping.

- If your child does not feed well upon waking at 7:00 a.m. (e.g., his or her last milk feed was 4:00 a.m. or later), offer them a top-up feed prior to nap 1. This may prevent catnapping due to hunger.

- The earliest time to schedule nap 1 *regularly* for babies who are five months and older is 8:00 a.m. If your four- to five-month-old is habitually rising early and you are regularly scheduling the first nap at 7:30 a.m., try gradually extending his or her awake time by ten minutes per day, over three days.

- Two to three overnight feeds are average (including the dream feed).

- Space overnight feeds three- to four-hourly. Resettle around this time by listening or offering an alternative source of comfort such as holding or rocking.

- Babies closer to five months may be capable of a two-hour awake window from nap 2 onward. I recommend maintaining a maximum awake time of one hour forty-five minutes for nap 1 until your child is closer to six months.

Routine

Five to Six Months

Number of naps: three
Total nap hours: four to five hours
Awake time: one hour forty-five minutes to two hours

7:00 a.m.—Wake and milk
8:00 a.m.—Breakfast

8:45 a.m./9:00 a.m.—Nap 1: one-hour-forty-five-minute awake time (extend to two hours from six months of age)
10:30 a.m.—Wake and milk. *Allow your baby to sleep up to two hours*
11:30 a.m.—Lunch
12:30 p.m.—Nap 2: two-hour awake time
2:00 p.m.—Wake and milk. *Allow your baby to sleep up to two hours*
4:00 p.m.—Nap 3: two-hour awake time
5:00 p.m.—Wake and dinner
6:30 p.m.—Milk (*twenty to thirty minutes before bed*)
7:00 p.m.—In bed, asleep. Two-hour awake time
10:30 p.m./11:00 p.m.—Dream feed (schedule three hours thirty minutes to four hours from bedtime)

Additional Routine Tips

- Follow your baby's lead as to his or her readiness for introducing solids: ability to sit up unassisted, good head-and-neck control, ability and willingness to chew, expressing interest when others are eating, reaching for food, and opening his or her mouth for food.

- If your child does not feed well upon waking at 7:00 a.m. (e.g., their last milk feed was 4:00 a.m. or later), offer them a top-up feed prior to nap 1. This may prevent catnapping due to hunger.

- The latest to wake your child from their last nap of the day is 5:00 p.m. (for a 7:00 p.m. bedtime).

- Some children may be capable of a longer awake window following a two-hour nap. If your child sleeps for two hours and constantly resists their next nap (within the two-hour awake window), you may extend their awake time by fifteen to thirty minutes.

- One to two night feeds are average (including the dream feed).

- Space overnight feeds three hours thirty minutes to four hours apart. Resettle around this time by listening or offering an alternative source of comfort such as holding.

Routine

Six Months

Number of naps: three
Total nap hours: four hours to four hours thirty minutes
Awake time: two hours

7:00 a.m.—Wake and milk
8:00 a.m.—Breakfast
9:00 a.m.—Nap 1: two-hour awake time
10:30 a.m.—Wake and milk. *Allow your baby to sleep up to two hours*
11.45 a.m.—Lunch
12:30 p.m.—Nap 2: two-hour awake time
2:00 p.m.—Wake and milk. *Allow your baby to sleep up to two hours*
4:00 p.m.—Nap 3: two-hour awake time
5:00 p.m.—Wake and dinner
6:30 p.m.—Milk (*twenty to thirty minutes before bed*)
7:00 p.m.—In bed, asleep. Two-hour awake time
11:00 p.m.—*Schedule the first feed (at least) four hours after bedtime*

Additional Routine Tips

- If your child does not feed well upon waking at 7:00 a.m. (e.g., their last milk feed was at 3:00 a.m. or later), offer them a top-up feed prior to nap 1. This may prevent catnapping due to hunger.

- If your child naps for two hours, you may be able to extend the awake time preceding their next nap (or bedtime) by an additional thirty minutes (e.g., an awake time of two hours thirty minutes).

- The latest to wake your child from their last nap is 5:00 p.m. (for a 7:00 p.m. bedtime).

- One to two overnight feeds are completely normal for this age group. From 7:00 p.m. (or bedtime), schedule any overnight feeds four to five hours apart. Resettle in between feed times—preferably by listening—or if you are unable to listen at every wake-up, alternate with holding or rocking. For assistance with scheduling overnight feeds, refer to "The Sleep Play Love Method: Scheduling Overnight Feeds (Six Months and Over)."

- Due to object permanence, some babies may become increasingly difficult to settle for sleep when they away from home. Where possible, aim to have most naps at home and schedule any appointments or outings around nap times.

- Daytime sleep patterns are generally not established until six to seven months—consequently, catnapping is common up until this age. Scheduling an additional/fourth nap and a later bedtime is preferable to extending children's awake time beyond their capability—as overtiredness is the main contributor to frequent night waking and early rising. Refer to "Routines and Recommendations: Average Sleep Requirements by Age" as a guide to how much sleep your child needs during the day, overnight, and in total over a twenty-four-hour period.

- The six-month growth spurt may cause some babies to feed more regularly than usual both day and night—and hence more frequent night-waking—due to hunger. You may choose to temporarily reintroduce the dream feed between 10:00 p.m. and 11:00 p.m.

SEVEN TO NINE MONTHS

General Recommendations

Babies commonly experience a growth spurt at nine months
causing increased hunger during these times. Sleep may naturally
regress for a few days, and babies may wake more frequently overnight
for milk. You may be able to help your child to sleep for longer
stretches overnight by: ensuring adequate solid meals and milk feeds
during the day, introducing a dream feed temporarily, and offering top-
up feeds before day sleeps.

**Sleep regression is particularly common between eight and nine
months.** This often coincides with growth spurts, separation anxiety,
physical milestones (rolling, sitting up, crawling, standing, cruising, or
walking), increased motor skills, and independence. As a result, you
may experience a disruption to your child's naps and overnight sleep
such as waking more frequently; rolling, standing, or rocking on all
fours in their crib. Respond to your children's needs during these
times with love and patience—it is likely that they will require
increased intervention and encouragement from you at sleep times,

since insecurity and fear are synonymous with change. While regression can last anywhere between two and six weeks, you can minimize the impact by maintaining a regular day-and-night routine, ensuring sufficient wind-down prior to sleep times, incorporating playtime in the child's room and crib, encouraging plenty of space and opportunity to practice his or her newfound skills during waking hours, and optimizing the sleep environment. Refer to recommendations in "The Seven Sleep Foundations: Developmental Stages, Milestones, and Transitions."

Teething can impact sleep either a little or a lot. Most babies will have cut their first tooth by seven months. Refer to "Common Sleep Difficulties and Solutions: Teething and Illness."

Developmental Milestones

- Awake time increases to between two hours thirty minutes and three hours.
- May have seven to ten hours of unbroken sleep overnight.
- Drop from three naps to two at nine months.
- Separation anxiety may start as early as seven months.
- Most babies will have cut their first or consecutive teeth.
- Fear of missing out (FOMO) peaks, which translates to increased difficulty sleeping when away from home.
- Can sit up unsupported.
- Start to crawl.
- Can clap and dance.
- Start babbling or may say some words.
- Fine-motor-control development (e.g., picking up and grasping objects and attempting to feed themselves).
- Stand with support.
- Cruising or walking by holding on to your hands or the furniture.

- Use pointing or gestures to communicate what they want.
- Can tolerate more substantial solids (e.g., meat, grains, pasta, dairy, and whole foods).
- A growth spurt at nine months may result in increased hunger, crankiness, and increased night waking.
- Nightmares can start as early as nine months.
- Refer to the Wonder Weeks for further information on current developmental stage: mental leap six (eight to nine months).

Feeding and Nutrition

- Formula-fed babies: four to six bottles per twenty-four hours (180–240 ml, or 6–8 oz per feed).

- Breastfed babies: five to six feeds per twenty-four hours.

- For an age-by-age guide to feeding your baby, refer to Well Adjusted Babies (welladjusted.co).

Routine

Seven Months

Number of naps: three
Total nap hours: three to four hours
Awake time: two hours to two hours thirty minutes

7:00 a.m.—Wake and milk
8:00 a.m.—Breakfast
9:00 a.m.—Nap 1: two-hour awake time
10:30 a.m.—Wake and milk. *Allow your baby to sleep up to two hours*
12:00 p.m.—Lunch
1:00 p.m.—Nap 2: two-hour-thirty-minute awake time

2:30 p.m.—Wake and milk. *Allow your baby to sleep up to two hours*
4:30 p.m. to 5:00 p.m.—Nap 3: between two-hour and two-hour-thirty-minute awake time
5:00 p.m.—Dinner
6:30 p.m./7:00 p.m.—Milk *(twenty to thirty minutes before bed)*
7:00 p.m./7:30 p.m.—In bed, asleep. Two-hour-thirty-minute awake time
11:00 p.m.—*Schedule the first feed no earlier than four hours after bedtime*

Additional Routine Tips

- If your child does not feed well upon waking at 7:00 a.m. (e.g., their last milk feed was 3:00 a.m. or later), offer them a top-up feed prior to nap 1. This may prevent catnapping due to hunger.

- If your child naps for two hours, you may be able to extend the awake time preceding their next nap (or bedtime) by an additional thirty minutes or more.

- Children between seven to eight months often begin resisting the third nap. This can be challenging as many are not capable of staying awake until bedtime without it—leading to excessive grumpiness, refusal to eat dinner, and consequently, frequent night waking from overtiredness and hunger.

- If your child constantly resists the third nap, you may try extending their awake time to somewhere between two hours thirty minutes to three hours (follow the eight to nine-month routine).

- If your child wakes from their second nap between 2:30 p.m. and 3:30 p.m. and refuses their third nap, opt for a 6:00 p.m. bedtime. If your child wakes from 3:30 p.m. onward, you can adhere to the two-hour-thirty-minute awake time—for example, a 3:45 p.m. wake would be a 6:15 p.m. bedtime, and a 4:00 p.m. wake would be a 6:30 p.m. bedtime, and so on.

- Wake your child no later than 5:00 p.m. from their third nap (for a 7:30 p.m. or 8:00 p.m. bedtime). If your child sleeps any longer, they may resist bedtime until much later. For a 7:00 p.m. bedtime, aim to wake your child no later than 4:30 p.m. from their last nap.

- One or two overnight feeds are still completely normal for this age group. From 7:00 p.m. (or bedtime), schedule overnight feeds between four to five hours apart. Resettle in between feed times—preferably by listening—or if you are unable to listen at every wake-up, alternate with holding or rocking. For assistance with scheduling overnight feeds, refer to "The Sleep Play Love Method: Scheduling Overnight Feeds (Six Months and Over)."

Dropping from Three Naps to Two

- Strive to maintain three naps until your child is capable of being awake for between two hours thirty minutes to three hours on a regular basis. Realistically, your child may not be capable of this until eight months of age.

- The latest time to wake your child from an afternoon nap is 4:30 p.m. (for a 7:00 p.m. to 7:30 p.m. bedtime) or 5:00 p.m. for a 7:30 p.m. to 8:00 p.m. bedtime. *Babies who sleep*

later than 4:30 p.m. may resist bedtime until 8:30 p.m. or 9:00 p.m.
You will need to employ trial and error for your child's specific
requirements.

- The earliest regular bedtime at night should be 6:30 p.m., and the latest is 8:00 p.m. A 6:00 p.m. bedtime may be necessary on days where children may skip (or resist) their afternoon nap—but this should be the exception rather than the rule.

- If your child can't quite make it through the day on two naps i.e., they are awake for between one to two hours beyond the suggested awake window toward the end of the day (leading to overtiredness and bedtime resistance), you have the option of keeping three naps and capping each at *one hour only* (e.g., **nap 1**: 9:00 a.m. to 10:00 a.m., **nap 2**: 12:30 p.m. to 1:30 p.m., and **nap 3**: 3:30 p.m. to 4:30 p.m. —with a 7:00 p.m. or 7:30 p.m. bedtime—*or* 4:00 p.m. to 5:00 p.m., with a 7:30 p.m. or 8:00 p.m. bedtime).

- To minimize overtiredness, you are best to schedule a later bedtime to accommodate for even a thirty-minute catnap in the afternoon if it means that (without it) your child is going to be awake more than one hour past their awake window. For example, if your seven-month-old wakes from his or her last nap at 3:00 p.m.—leaving no time for a third nap—I would advise a 6:00 p.m. to 6:30 p.m. bedtime. However, if the child wakes at 2:00 p.m., schedule another brief nap from 4:30 p.m. to 5:00 p.m., and a bedtime between 7:30 p.m. to 8:00 p.m.

- If your child is an early riser (before 6:00 a.m.), then you may need to keep three naps for a little longer or be persistent with resetting him or her until 7:00 a.m. so that you can make this transition easier.

- Albeit mostly capable of doing two naps, your child may have days where they will need three—especially at times where they have been especially active, woken earlier for the day, slept less than usual the previous night or during nap times, been away from home or out of routine, are teething, experiencing a leap, or unwell.

Routine

Eight to Nine Months

Number of naps: two
Total nap hours: three to four hours
Awake time: two hours thirty minutes to three hours

7:00 a.m.—Wake and milk
8:00 a.m.—Breakfast
9:30 a.m./10:00 a.m.—Nap 1: two-hour-thirty-minute to three-hour awake time. *Babies are more capable of a three-hour awake window for nap 1 from nine months.*
11:00 a.m.—Wake and milk. *Allow your baby to sleep up to two hours*
12:00 p.m.—Lunch
2:00 p.m./2:30 p.m.—Nap 2: three-hour awake time
3:30 p.m./4:00 p.m.—Wake and milk. *Allow your baby to sleep up to two hours*
5:00 p.m.—Dinner
6:00 p.m./6:30 p.m.—Milk (*twenty to thirty minutes before bed*)
6:30 p.m./7:00 p.m.—In bed, asleep. Three-hour awake time
11:00 p.m.—*Schedule the first feed no earlier than four hours after bedtime*

Additional Routine Tips

- If your child begins to resist nap 1, and/or only sleeps for a short time (i.e., forty-five minutes or less), you may try extending their awake time from two hours thirty minutes to three hours. Before changing the awake time, ensure that this resistance is a pattern over a few days or more, and not a result of a leap, developmental milestones, teething, or illness (catnapping and bedtime resistance is common during these times and may correct itself once your child has recovered—that is, it may not call for a change in routine).

- If your child naps for two hours, you may be able to extend the awake time preceding their next nap or bedtime by an additional thirty to sixty minutes.

- Some children between eight and ten months of age (on two naps) can thrive on a 2–3–4 "nap ladder" schedule. For example, **nap 1:** 9:00 a.m. (two-hour awake time), **nap 2:** 1:30 p.m. (three-hour awake time), and **bedtime:** 7:00 p.m. (four-hour awake time). Again, trial and error may be necessary to ascertain if this is suitable for your child.

- If your child begins a regular pattern of sleeping less overnight, waking more often, or rising early—and is not unwell, teething, or experiencing a leap—this may indicate a need for you to reduce their total nap hours (e.g., from four hours to three hours or three hours thirty minutes).

- One to two overnight feeds are still completely normal for this age group. From 7:00 p.m. (or bedtime), schedule any overnight feeds between four to five hours apart.

- Resettle in between feed times preferably by listening or

alternatively holding. For assistance scheduling overnight feeds, refer to "The Sleep Play Love Method: Scheduling Overnight Feeds (Six Months and Over)."

- The nine-month growth spurt may result in more frequent waking overnight because of hunger. You may choose to reintroduce the dream feed between 10:30 p.m. and 11:00 p.m., and some babies may need to feed more regularly than normal day and night (temporarily).

TEN TO TWELVE MONTHS

General Recommendations

Sleep regression is common at eleven to twelve months. This often coincides with growth spurts, separation anxiety, physical milestones (crawling, walking, standing, and cruising) and increased language skills and independence. You may also notice that your baby wakes more often distressed and standing in their crib. Respond to your children's needs during these times with love and patience—it is likely that they will require increased intervention and encouragement from you at sleep times, since insecurity and fear are synonymous with change. While regression can last anywhere between two and six weeks, you can minimize the impact by maintaining a regular day-and-night routine, ensuring sufficient wind-down prior to sleep times, incorporating playtime in the child's room and crib, encouraging plenty of space and opportunity to practice their newfound skills during waking hours, and optimizing the sleep environment. Refer to recommendations in "The Seven Sleep Foundations: Developmental Stages, Milestones, and Transitions."

Developmental Milestones

- Separation anxiety peaks between ten to eighteen months.
- Awake time increases to between three hours thirty minutes and four hours.
- Teething continues.
- Cruising, walking, or taking their first steps.
- Can say some words.
- Understand some simple instructions such as "Give me the cup" or "Put the cup down" if you show them what you want.
- Begin to link words with their meanings—for example, may recognize words like "ball" or "teddy," and look for these if you name them.
- Fine motor control develops further, enabling them to use their fingers to feed themselves at mealtimes and to hold a crayon to scribble.
- Most babies are eating the same foods as their family.
- Parents may notice that tantrums escalate as children begin to explore—and exert—their independence.
- Capable of sleeping ten to twelve hours overnight but may still wake during the night.
- Two naps are still recommended until approximately fourteen months.
- Refer to the Wonder Weeks for further information on current developmental stages: mental leap seven (ten to eleven months) and mental leap eight (twelve to thirteen months).

Feeding and Nutrition

- Formula-fed babies: three to four bottles per twenty-four hours (180–240 ml, or 6–8 oz per feed).

- Breastfed babies: three to five feeds per twenty-four hours.

Routine

Ten Months

Number of naps: two
Total nap hours: two to three hours
Awake time: three hours to three hours thirty minutes

7:00 a.m.—Wake and milk
8:00 a.m.—Breakfast
10:00 a.m.—Nap 1: three-hour awake time
11:30 a.m.—Wake and milk
12:30 p.m.—Lunch
2:30 p.m./3:00 p.m.—Nap 2: three-hour to three-hour-thirty-minute awake time
4:00 p.m.—Wake and milk (*wake no later than 4:30 p.m.*)
5:00 p.m.—Dinner
6:30 p.m./7:30 p.m.—Milk (*twenty to thirty minutes before bed*)
7:00 p.m. to 8:00 p.m.—In bed, asleep. Three-hour-thirty-minute awake time

Additional Routine Tips

- If your child sleeps for ninety minutes to two hours in the morning and constantly resists their afternoon nap—leading to bedtime resistance and/or increased overnight waking—experiment with capping their morning nap to between forty-five and sixty minutes and schedule their second nap at the usual time (i.e., three hours thirty minutes after waking). You may need to try this over a minimum of three days to gauge effectiveness.

- If your child naps for two hours, you may be able to extend the awake time preceding their next nap (or bedtime) by an additional thirty to sixty minutes.

- Unless your child is unwell, avoid letting them sleep for longer than three hours in total during the day—as this may result in bedtime resistance, increased night waking, and/or early rising.

- Breastfed and formula-fed babies are more capable of night weaning from this age.

- If you choose to continue to feed overnight, one feed scheduled after 11:00 p.m. should suffice. Alternatively, schedule overnight feeds five-hourly as a minimum.

Routine

Eleven to Twelve Months

Number of naps: two
Total nap hours: two to three hours
Awake time: three hours to three hours thirty minutes

7:00 a.m.—Wake and milk
8:00 a.m.—Breakfast
10:00 a.m.—Nap 1: three-hour awake time
11:30 a.m.—Wake and milk
1:00 p.m.—Lunch
3:00 p.m.—Nap 2: three-hour-thirty-minute awake time
4:00 p.m. to 4:30 p.m.—Wake and milk
5:00 p.m.—Dinner
7:00 p.m./7:30 p.m.—Milk *(twenty to thirty minutes before bed)*

7:30 p.m./8:00 p.m.—In bed, asleep. Three-hour-thirty-minute awake time

Additional Routine Tips

- If your child resists nap 1 and/or only sleeps for a short time (i.e., forty-five minutes or less), and this is a regular pattern over three days or more (not coinciding with a leap, developmental milestones, illness, or teething), try extending their awake time from three hours to three hours thirty minutes.

- If your child naps for two hours, you may be able to extend the awake time preceding their next nap or bedtime by an additional thirty to sixty minutes.

- If your child sleeps for two hours at their first nap, cap their second nap at one hour—for example, **nap 1**: 10:00 a.m. to 12:00 p.m., **nap 2**: 3:00 p.m. to 4:00 p.m. with bedtime of 7:30 p.m. *or* 3:30 p.m. to 4:30 p.m. and bedtime at 8:00 p.m.

- If your child continually resists an 8:00 p.m. bedtime with a 4:30 p.m. wake-up (i.e., three hours thirty minutes of awake time), be sure to wake them from naps no later than 4:00 p.m.

- The latest time to schedule bedtime is 8:00 p.m.

THIRTEEN TO EIGHTEEN MONTHS

General Recommendations

Sleep regression is particularly common at fourteen and eighteen months. This often coincides with separation anxiety, physical milestones (walking, cruising), and increased motor skills, language skills and desire for independence. There can also be many life transitions from twelve months onward, such as the birth of a sibling, potty training, parents returning to work, and starting childcare. Sleep regression at times of change is completely normal. Respond to your children's needs during these times with love and patience—it is likely that they will require more intervention from you at sleep times. Utilizing the connection tools such as quality one-on-one time, listening, and play, and maintaining a regular day-and-night routine with positive sleep associations will help you to avoid long-term regression. Refer to recommendations in "The Seven Sleep Foundations: Developmental Stages, Milestones, and Transitions."

Some toddlers may be ready to make the transition out of the crib and into a toddler bed. Refer to the "The Sleep Play Love Method" for recommendations and transition steps.

Developmental Milestones

- Walks without assistance.
- Separation anxiety is at its peak.
- Awake time increases to between four and five hours.
- Teething continues.
- Self-feeds with fingers and utensils.
- Imitates others.
- Likes to play games.
- Can identify body parts when prompted—for example, "Show me your nose! Where's your nose?"
- Can follow simple instructions.
- Uses a walker and can push and pull toys correctly.
- Temper tantrums are in full swing.
- Capable of sleeping eleven to twelve hours overnight but may still wake during the night.
- Drop from two naps to one between fourteen months and eighteen months.
- Refer to the Wonder Weeks for further information on current developmental stages: mental leap eight (twelve to thirteen months) and mental leap nine (fourteen to fifteen months).

Feeding and Nutrition

- Many professionals recommend transitioning to cow's milk (or milk alternative) from twelve months and the use of a "sippy cup" instead of a bottle.

- Formula-fed babies: three to four bottles per twenty-four hours (180–240 ml, or 6–8 oz per feed).

- Breastfed babies: three to five feeds per twenty-four hours.

Routine

Thirteen to Fifteen Months

Number of naps: one to two
Total nap hours: two to three hours
Awake time: three hours thirty minutes to four hours

7:00 a.m.—Wake (milk optional)
8:00 a.m.—Breakfast
10:00 a.m.—Milk
10:30 a.m. to 11:30 a.m.—Nap 1: three-hour-thirty-minute awake time. *Wake no later than 12:00 p.m., ideally 11:30 a.m. to ensure a second nap three hours thirty minutes later*
12:00 p.m. to 1:00 p.m.—Lunch
2:30 p.m.—Milk
3:00 p.m. to 4:00 p.m.—Nap 2: three-hour-thirty-minute awake time
5:00 p.m.—Dinner
7:00 p.m./7:30 p.m.—Milk
7:30 p.m./8:00 p.m.—In bed, asleep. Three-hour-thirty-minute to four-hour awake time

Additional Routine Tips

- The earliest *regular* bedtime at night should be 6:30 p.m., or 8:00 p.m. at the latest. A 6:00 p.m. bedtime may be necessary on occasion when your child resists their afternoon nap.

- Unless your child is unwell, avoid letting them sleep for longer than three hours during the day as this may cause them to resist bedtime, wake more frequently overnight, and/or rise earlier in the morning.

- The latest time to wake child of this age from their afternoon nap is 4:00 p.m. (for a 7:30 p.m. to 8:00 p.m. bedtime). Even a brief fifteen- to thirty-minute nap after 4:00 p.m. may result in bedtime resistance until much later at night. For this reason, it is best to avoid car trips after 4:00 p.m.

Dropping from Two Naps to One

This process can be an exhausting, frustrating, and lengthy one for parents (and children alike), taking anywhere between two to eight weeks—or more. Variables include the child's age, activity level, developmental stage, and general bandwidth. It is not uncommon at these times to experience sleep regression; bedtime resistance, increased night waking, and early rising due to too much or too little sleep during the day. The most challenging aspect of this transition is that many children are unable to regularly make it through to lunchtime (i.e., 12:00 p.m.) without a short morning nap.

General Tips

- The average recommended age to commence this transition is fourteen months.

- Until your child is fifteen to sixteen months old, he or she may require one nap on some days and two naps on others.

- Whether your child is having one nap or two, try to focus on a total sleep time of thirteen to fourteen hours in a twenty-four-hour period. The better your child is sleeping at night (i.e., closer to twelve hours), the more flexibility you will have with capping naps throughout the day.

- Focus on improving *night sleep first* before dropping or capping day naps.

Options to Maintain Two Naps

- Scheduling two naps may cause some children to resist consecutive naps and/or bedtime—irrespective of the awake time. To maintain two naps, 11:30 a.m. is the latest time to wake your child from their first nap, and the first nap should be no longer than one hour thirty minutes.

- Try capping each nap at forty-five minutes. It is recommended that your child is sleeping as close to twelve hours overnight *before* capping their total day naps to ninety minutes.

- Cap each nap to one hour. For example, **nap 1**: 10:00 a.m. to 11:00 a.m. or 10:30 a.m. to 11:30 a.m. and **nap 2**: 2:30 p.m. to 3:30 p.m. or 3:00 p.m. to 4:00 p.m. with a bedtime between 7:30 p.m. and 8:00 p.m.

- Allow your child to sleep for up to ninety minutes at nap 1, then schedule a thirty-minute power nap in the afternoon— for example, **nap 1**: 10:30 a.m. to 12:00 p.m., **nap 2**: 3:30 p.m. to 4:00 p.m. with a bed-time of 8:00 p.m. A drive in the car, walk in the stroller, or nap in carrier is acceptable for the last nap during this transition until you can stretch the morning nap out later on a regular basis.

- Cap nap 1 to between thirty and forty-five minutes and schedule your child's main nap three hours thirty minutes later—for example, **nap 1**: 10:15 a.m. to 10:45 a.m. or 10:30 a.m. to 11:00 a.m., **nap 2**: 2:30 p.m. until 4:00 p.m., and bedtime between 7:30 p.m. and 8:00 p.m.

Transitioning to One Nap

- It is unlikely children will transition from sleeping two to three hours over two naps—to sleeping one nap of three hours straightaway. For this reason, the earliest time I recommend starting their (one) nap is at 11:30 a.m. (for a minimum of ninety minutes).

- Bedtime will need to be at 6:00 p.m. if your child (under sixteen months) wakes earlier than 2:00 p.m. If your child wakes after 2:30 p.m., ensure a four-hour awake window before bedtime.

- Allow your child on one nap to sleep for up to three hours before waking them—any longer can impact the quality and duration of overnight sleep or result in bedtime resistance due to being undertired. Focus on a total of thirteen to fourteen hours of sleep per twenty-four hours.

- If your child regularly starts their first nap at 10:30 a.m. or 11:00 a.m. and they continue to sleep for longer than two hours, allow them to sleep for up to three hours and schedule an earlier bedtime (e.g., between 6:00 p.m. and 6:30 p.m.). If they wake any earlier than 1:00 p.m., then you may attempt a quick thirty-minute power nap approximately three hours later—for example, from 3:30 p.m. to 4:00 p.m. or 3:45 p.m. to 4:15 p.m., with bedtime scheduled four hours after waking. If unsuccessful, proceed with a 6:00 p.m. bedtime.

Routine

Sixteen to Eighteen Months

Number of naps: one
Total nap hours: two to three hours

    7:00 a.m.—Wake (milk optional)
    8:00 a.m.—Breakfast
    11:00 a.m.—Lunch
    11:30 a.m./12:00 p.m. Milk
    12:00 p.m. to 12:30 p.m.—Nap *(start nap any time between 12:00 p.m. and 12:30 p.m.)*
    3:00 p.m. to 3:30 p.m.—Wake
    5:00 p.m.—Dinner
    6:30 p.m./7:30 p.m.—Milk *(twenty to thirty minutes before bed)*
    7:00 p.m./8:00 p.m.—In bed, asleep

Additional Routine Tips

- Unless your child is unwell, avoid letting him or her sleep for longer than three hours during the day—as this may cause them to wake more frequently overnight or rise earlier in the morning.

- If your child begins a regular pattern of sleeping less overnight, waking more often, or rising early—and is not unwell, teething, or experiencing a leap—this may indicate a need for you to reduce the total nap hours (e.g., from three hours to between two hours and two hours thirty minutes).

- If your child is still having two naps, adhere to the routine and recommendations for the thirteen- to fifteen-month age group.

- Schedule your child's bedtime roughly four hours after waking from the day nap.

NINETEEN TO TWENTY-FOUR MONTHS

General Recommendations

Sleep regression is particularly common at twenty-four months often coinciding with separation anxiety, increased motor and language skills, and independence. There can also be many life transitions for children of this age group, such as the birth of a sibling, potty training, parents returning to work, and starting childcare. Sleep regression is completely normal. Respond to your children's needs during these times with love and patience—it is likely that they will require more intervention from you at sleep times. Utilizing the connection tools such as quality one-on-one time, listening, and play, and maintaining a regular day-and-night routine with positive sleep associations will help you to avoid long-term regression. Refer to recommendations in "The Seven Sleep Foundations: Developmental Stages, Milestones, and Transitions."

Developmental Milestones

- Capable of sleeping eleven to twelve hours overnight but may still wake during the night.
- Most children will be on one nap per day.
- Separation anxiety is at its peak.
- Temper tantrums continue as children exert their independence in daily tasks.
- Awake time increases up to six hours.
- Can scribble/doodle skillfully.
- Can brush teeth with your help.
- Can take apart and put together toys.
- Teething—especially two-year-old molars.
- May express shyness around people.
- Can identify body parts.
- Identifies likes and dislikes.
- May be ready for potty training or shows interest in going to the potty.
- Like helping their mom with chores around the house.
- Can link two or more words to express their feelings, desires, and needs—many can speak well enough to be understood.
- Can throw a ball.
- Can walk up and/or down stairs with support.
- Can identify people and objects in pictures.
- Start "mine" routine with objects.
- Love interactive games.
- Talk about themselves—often in the first person.
- Refer to the Wonder Weeks for further information on current developmental stages: mental leap ten (seventeen to eighteen months).

Routine

Nineteen to Twenty-Four Months

Number of naps: one
Total nap hours: two hours

7:00 a.m.—Wake
8:00 a.m.—Breakfast
12:00 p.m.—Lunch
12:30 p.m. to 1:00 p.m.—Nap (*start nap any time between 12:30 p.m. and 1:00 p.m.*)
3:00 p.m. to 3:30 p.m.—Wake
5:00 p.m.—Dinner
6:30 p.m./7:30 p.m.—Milk (*optional, twenty to thirty minutes before bed*)
7:00 p.m./7:30 p.m.—In bed, asleep

Additional Routine Tips

- Unless your child is unwell, avoid letting him or her sleep for longer than three hours during the day as this may cause them to wake more frequently overnight or rise earlier in the morning.

- If your child begins a regular pattern of sleeping less overnight, waking more often, or rising early—and is not unwell, teething, or experiencing a leap—this may indicate a need for you to reduce the total nap hours (e.g., from two hours to one hour thirty minutes).

- If your toddler regularly wakes early in the morning (before 6:00 a.m.), and this is not attributed to illness, teething, or developmental change, gradually extend his or her nap later by fifteen to thirty minutes—for example, from 12:30 p.m. to 12:45 p.m. *Remain persistent for three to four days to gauge effectiveness.*

- Schedule your child's bedtime roughly four hours to four hours thirty minutes after waking from the day nap.

- Milk is optional from this age; however, you may continue to breastfeed, or offer your child a sippy cup of milk or a milk alternative before bedtime. For assistance with weaning, refer to "The Sleep Play Love Method" or "Managing Transitions: Night Weaning and Weaning from Breastfeeding."

Feeding and Nutrition

Solids are more important at this age; however, between one and three breast or milk feeds per twenty-four hours is average.

TWENTY-FOUR TO THIRTY-SIX MONTHS

Developmental Milestones

- Have an established and reliable sleeping schedule.
- Are usually able to self-calm to fall asleep.
- Many children drop from one nap to none.
- Most children will be ready for potty training.
- Separation anxiety subsides for many children between two to three years.
- Express affection openly.
- Can make mechanical toys work.
- Identify common objects and pictures.
- Make themselves mostly understood by a stranger.
- Can take turns in simple games.
- Understand the meaning of "mine," "his," and "hers."
- Can walk up and down stairs alternating feet.
- Can pedal a tricycle.
- Can locate objects you are pointing to.
- Turn book pages one at a time.
- Can hold a pencil in the writing position.

Feeding and Nutrition

Babies will not require formula over two years of age; however, some children still enjoy a cup of milk at bedtime. If you decide to continue breastfeeding after two years of age, then how much and how often will be at your discretion.

Routine

Twenty-Four to Thirty-Six Months

Number of naps: one
Total nap hours: one to two hours

7:00 a.m.—Wake
8:00 a.m.—Breakfast
12:00 p.m.—Lunch
1:00 p.m. to 2:00 p.m.—Nap (*start nap any time between 1:00 p.m. and 2:00 p.m.*)
3:00 p.m. to 3:30 p.m.—Wake
5:00 p.m.—Dinner
6:30 p.m. to 7:30 p.m.—Milk (*optional, twenty to thirty minutes before bed*)
7:00 p.m./8:00 p.m.—In bed, asleep

Additional Routine Tips

- Avoid letting your child nap for longer than two hours as this may compromise his or her overnight sleep duration and quality.

- The latest to wake your child from his or her day nap is 3:30

p.m.—any later may result in bedtime resistance until 8:30 p.m. or 9:00 p.m.

- Schedule bedtime roughly four to five hours from waking from the day nap.

Dropping from One Nap to None

- Ideally, children will be on one nap until they are two and a half to three years old; however, some begin the process of dropping their day nap at around two years of age.

- Your child may still need to have one nap on some days, while on others, they can make it through the day without one at all. Variables include activity level, quality of overnight sleep, routine, stimulation, nutrition, developmental stage, and health (among other factors).

- If your child won't nap, incorporate some relax or wind-down time in the place of their afternoon nap. Ideas include quiet play in their bedroom, reading books, or a guided toddler meditation—our favorite is "New Horizon" children's meditations on YouTube.

- On "no nap days," schedule bedtime between 6:00 p.m. and 6:30 p.m. When children reach the age of three years, they may be more capable of stretching to a 7:00 p.m. bedtime without a nap.

- Ensure that your child does not nap for any longer than two to two and a half hours (for children aged two to two and a half years) and one to two hours (for children two and a half years and over). Any longer than this can compromise overnight sleep duration and/or result in a later bedtime, and bedtime resistance.

- Don't let the day nap extend any later than 3:00 p.m. if you intend on a 7:00 p.m. bedtime (assume a minimum four-hour awake window between waking from the day nap and bedtime).

- Scheduling your child's nap too early in the day can contribute to early rising. Ideally, a two-year-old will nap from 1:00 p.m. to 3:00 p.m./3:30 p.m., a two-and-a-half-year-old will nap from 1:30 p.m. to 3:00 p.m./3:30 p.m., and a three-year-old will nap from 1:30 p.m. to 2:30 p.m./3:00 p.m. *All children have individual needs. Trial and error may be necessary.*

- Avoid car trips after 3:30 p.m. Children are likely to fall asleep in the car when they are in the process of dropping naps. If your child falls asleep later than 3:30 p.m. (even just for a fifteen-minute car ride), bedtime resistance is almost inevitable—think 8:30 p.m. or 9:00 p.m.!

ROUTINE TROUBLESHOOTING

- All children have different capabilities with awake windows. The routines are an *average guide only*. If you know that your child can stay awake for less or longer than the recommended times for their age, follow the routine for the previous or the following age group or use a combination of awake windows.

- Adhering to awake windows (in combination with your baby's tired cues) is more important than attempting to keep to the specific feeding and sleep times outlined in the routines—these are a guide only and are based on recommended awake times, average feeding guidelines, and an "ideal" ninety minutes of nap time. Any parent can attest that this doesn't always go to plan!

- Feed times are scheduled from *the beginning of one feed to the next*—not from the time that you finished the feed to the next feed.

- If you are expressing breast milk, make a note of the time that you expressed when you are storing the milk. Due to hormone levels, expressed milk during the day should be fed to your baby during the day, and night-time expressed milk to be fed to your baby at night.

- Scheduling milk feeds twenty to thirty minutes *before* sleep times may help you to avoid a feed-to-sleep habit in the early months, or assist you in breaking an established feed-to-sleep pattern (refer to "The Sleep Play Love Method").

- The basic rule of thumb for overnight feeds is this: the length of time (hours) that a child can sustain between feeds during the day *should be the minimum* length of time for spacing overnight feeds. Most children can stretch *at least one hour more* at any age—for example, if your baby is feeding every four hours during the day, space the overnight feeds four-hourly at a minimum, or ideally, four and a half to five hours apart. For babies who are feeding every two to three hours during the day, try scheduling overnight feeds three-hourly to begin. *Growth spurts may demand additional day and night feeds to be scheduled temporarily (e.g., a week on average).*

- Many babies will benefit from a shorter awake time for their first nap when compared to the remainder of the day. You can stretch the awake time progressively over the day—for example, if the awake window for a seven-month-old is two hours to two hours thirty minutes, adhere to the two-hour window for the first nap of the day and two hours thirty minutes for the remainder of naps and bedtime. *Some babies may also need a shorter (or longer) awake time before bedtime, depending on quality and quantity of day sleeps. Trial and error may be necessary.*

- The first nap of the day is usually the most restorative and can set the tone for the remainder of the day. Try to stay at home for nap 1 where possible and venture out for any consecutive naps.

- For babies between five and eight months of age, the third nap of the day is usually the most challenging. Remember the 80/20 rule: what you do 80 percent of the time will create habits. Considering that this nap is the first to be dropped (somewhere between eight to nine months), do whatever is necessary to get your child to fall asleep at the time—for example, the baby carrier, swing (supervised), stroller, or car. It's always preferable that they do have a sleep as this will prevent an exceptionally early bedtime (e.g., 6:00 p.m.), or an extended awake time (which can lead to unsettledness, overtiredness, and consequently, bedtime resistance and frequent night waking owing to raised cortisol levels). Don't panic if your child eventually falls asleep for the afternoon nap later than anticipated, simply adjust their bedtime out to compensate for having a later afternoon sleep. *Remember this: 8:00 p.m. is the latest recommended bedtime for children six months and over, so it is best to work backward from this time when scheduling day naps.*

- Some babies eight months and older (on two naps) may respond well to a 2–3–4 "ladder" nap schedule. For example, assume a two-hour awake time between waking in the morning and nap 1; three-hour awake time between waking from nap 1 and nap 2; and four-hour awake time between waking from nap 2 and bedtime. *Trial and error may be necessary.*

- Introduce a predictable bedtime routine thirty to sixty minutes before sleep time at the end of the day. Avoid excess stimulation by means of electronics (TV, iPad, and phones), loud music, and bright (white) household lights.

- Some children instinctively navigate to roughhousing play before bedtime in their attempt to emotionally self-regulate and recover from any stored stress or tension from their day —or such feelings carried over from earlier life events. This vigorous and spontaneous play can be especially effective for children who experience anxiety at sleep times, and can also help both parent and child connect after any separation during the day (e.g., work and childcare) and the impending separation that bedtime presents. If this play proves counterproductive to your child's ability to fall asleep (i.e., they become hyperactive and resist bedtime), try incorporating this play earlier in the day, or spaced one to two hours from bedtime. For play ideas, refer to "The Seven Sleep Foundations: Emotional and Physical Well-Being."

- The actual "good-night" routine should be included in the overall sixty-minute bedtime routine and shouldn't be any longer than twenty minutes in total—enough time for one book with each parent, a brief recap of their day, and a kiss-and-hug good-night. The longer that parents *draw out* this process, the more likely it is that older children will make demands for *more books* or *more cuddles*. Short and sweet is preferable.

- If you are following a routine with two or more naps, don't let your child sleep for longer than two hours at any one nap (unless they are unwell). In my experience, this *almost always* leads to nap refusal for the proceeding nap and/or bedtime. Refer to the recommended total nap hours as outlined under each sample routine.

- If a child has slept for two hours at any one nap, they may be able to stay awake for an additional fifteen to sixty minutes before their next sleep time. Capabilities will vary per child and their age, and trial and error may be necessary.

- Attempt to be as regular as possible with your child's sleep times—this will help to regulate your child's body clock and promote more sustainable and desirable sleep patterns. The latest recommended time to wake your child in the morning is 7:00 a.m. (most babies will wake naturally sometime between 6:00 a.m. and 7:00 a.m.). Bedtime at the end of the day may vary more than the wake times, but ideally will be between 6:30 p.m. and 8:00 p.m. for most children. Variables may include transitioning between routines, dropping naps, and at times where children may nap for longer or less than usual (e.g., childcare, holidays, illness, teething, transitions, and milestones). Adhering to the age-appropriate awake times will ensure you stay on track and help you to minimize regression at times of change.

- The earliest time for children to start their day is 6:00 a.m. Avoid bringing your child into your bed for cuddles, offering breakfast, or starting playtime any earlier than 6:00 a.m., as this can promote habitual early rising. Always attempt to resettle your child if he or she wakes prior to 6:00 a.m., keeping them in their own bed or bedroom. If your child continually wakes early for a milk feed between 5:00 a.m. and 6:00 a.m. you can experiment with administering a dream feed at 5:00 a.m.—this may help them to sleep until 6:00 a.m. or later (considering that many children under twelve months will wake hungry in the early hours of the morning).

- When children have woken earlier than 6:00 a.m. and have not settled back to sleep, ensure that you schedule nap 1 within their age-appropriate wake window starting from 6:00 a.m. and no earlier; for example, for a six-month-old with a two-hour awake window, you would schedule his or her first nap *no earlier than* 8:00 a.m., even if the child woke at 5:30 a.m. or earlier for the day. *Additional rule of thumb:*

204

schedule nap 1 no earlier than 8:00 a.m. for babies on three naps; or 9:00 a.m. for babies on two naps.

- The earliest recommended (regular) bedtime for children six months and older is 6:30 p.m. In my experience, children who have a regular (early) bedtime of 6:00 p.m. commonly wake between 4:30 a.m. and 5:30 a.m. ready to start the day —or wake more frequently overnight. Try to schedule extra naps or resettle during shorter naps where possible. *A 6:00 p.m. bedtime may be necessary temporarily when dropping naps or on days when you are unable to schedule another nap and want to avoid an extended awake time before bed.*

- If your child begins waking regularly from a leaky diaper, this may indicate that you need to progress to the next size up. You may also try doubling their diaper for overnight sleep—use your normal size on the inside and a size larger on the outside to help prevent leaks and subsequently, less night or early-morning wake-ups.

- Focus on being *reactive* not *proactive* to your child's needs. Parental presence can overstimulate some children, so avoid your impulse to (regularly) rock, pat, shush, or sit beside your child to prevent them from crying, or to try to get them to fall asleep. Allow your child a little space at sleep times— while remaining close enough that you can see and/or hear them if they begin to struggle. Just one to two minutes can encourage children to develop their own coping and self-soothing strategies, so they may rely on you less over time. *Many children cry out while still asleep. Intervening to settle children too soon may either wake them up or inhibit their ability to self-settle in the long term. Wait until your child communicates that they need you—that is, the crying changes in volume, pitch, or becomes more persistent.*

- Remain responsive to your child and try to tune into what he or she is attempting to communicate in the moment. Not all crying must be stopped, nor does it always express the need to be rocked or fed. Offer your baby comfort when their cry changes from a *protest* (cries that change in pitch and volume, may stop and start, and/or sound more like a grizzle, fussing, or complaining) to an *emotional cry* (high-pitched, continuous crying that sounds stressful or urgent). Never ignore an emotional cry—or if you are uncertain.

- If resettling for day naps, ensure that you do so within five minutes—or a maximum of ten minutes if you anticipate that your baby may fall back to sleep on his or her own after this time. Any longer, and your baby may wake completely or become distressed and will be unlikely to fall back to sleep. Resettle your baby in the crib wherever possible—offering gentle validation and a hand on him or her for comfort (patting, or gentle rocking) as required. Holding the baby should be the last resort, and you will do so if he or she is unable to calm down without being physically close to you. *Because of an infant's needs for coregulation, babies under four months may need to be held to help them calm when compared to children six months and over.*

- To encourage self-settling, place your child into bed *at the beginning* of all sleep times while he or she is still awake. Drowsy is acceptable, but sometimes there is be a fine line between drowsy and asleep! If your child is under six months and still having difficulty linking sleep cycles during the day, or self-settling overnight, then it's okay at times to rock, hold, pat, or feed *back to sleep* when they wake midnap or overnight. Just ensure that your child is falling to sleep independently at the *beginning* of the sleep cycle—and remember the 80/20 rule for creating and breaking habits. Refer to "The Sleep Play Love Method" as necessary.

- Keep overnight settling calm, dark, and quiet. Avoid changing the environment or engaging in any stimulating play or activity.

- If your child must sleep away from home, I recommend that you take their creature comforts and maintain all sleep associations (e.g., blankets, white noise, swaddle or sleep bag, and lovely or pacifier).

- Plan any extended car trips at the start of your child's scheduled nap time to ensure that your child can sleep in transit. If you are traveling only a short distance, try to arrive at your destination when your child is scheduled to have their nap—where you can place the child to sleep in either the stroller, pack 'n play, or baby carrier. While away from home, some hands-on assistance to help your child fall asleep (such as pacifier, milk, or movement) is acceptable—remember, 80/20!

- If your child falls asleep in the car before their nap time for any less than twenty minutes, you may attempt to transfer them into their crib when you arrive home. If this is unsuccessful, keep them up for a brief play (e.g., forty-five to sixty minutes), and attempt nap time after this.

- If your child has slept for twenty minutes or more in transit (e.g., the car or stroller), a successful transfer is often unlikely. Where possible, keep driving or walking so that your child can remain asleep for at least one sleep cycle (i.e., forty-five to fifty minutes). If your child has slept for forty-five minutes or less, you can shorten the awake time preceding your child's next nap by fifteen to thirty minutes.

- If you have a day out of routine, don't panic—simply plan to be at home for your child's naps on the following day so that you can get back on track. It usually takes three days or more of being out of routine for regression to occur.

- At times of growth spurts (i.e., three, four, six, and nine months), you may consider introducing, or reintroducing, a dream feed temporarily for one week or so. This may help you to achieve longer stretches of sleep overnight and rule out hunger as a catalyst for night waking.

- If your child starts to resist their morning and/or afternoon nap, take longer than twenty minutes to fall asleep, or sleep for shorter intervals—and this is a regular pattern over the course of three to seven days—try extending their awake time by fifteen to thirty minutes or proceed to the next routine to see if this makes a difference. You will need to persevere for a minimum of three days to ascertain effectiveness. *Before making changes to awake time, ensure that resistance or catnapping is not temporarily an outcome of teething, illness, transitions, or milestones.*

- Teething, illness, life transitions, leaps, and developmental milestones can impact sleep a little—or a lot—and regression at such times is normal. It is common to experience catnapping, early rising, nap and bedtime resistance, increased night waking, general unsettledness, and an increased reliance on parental intervention to fall asleep—and settle back to sleep. Regression at these times may seem to appear overnight, whereas disruption to sleep habits that arise from being "out of routine"—or requiring a change to routine or environment—usually takes longer to impact sleep patterns (e.g., three days or more). Respond to your child's needs appropriately during these times and seek medical attention if you are concerned about your child's health.

- Holding babies close helps to raise their antibody production and temperature—essential for fighting off illness. This explains why many children become clingy when they are ill or teething. Children may have increased sleep needs and/or require more hands-on intervention at such times—undoubtedly impacting on your regular sleep routine. Baby wearing and cosleeping may be effective solutions in the interim, and you can proceed with your usual routine once your child has recovered.

SECTION V
THE SLEEP PLAY LOVE
METHOD

ABOUT THE METHOD

Why the Sleep Play Love Method?

The Sleep Play Love Method is an emotional well-being strategy rather than a "behavioral" approach or a "sleep-training" technique. This process encourages self-settling in a gentle and respectful manner, helping you, the parent or caregiver, to overcome negative sleep patterns (or control patterns) such as feeding, rocking, holding, or patting to sleep. At the heart of this method are the philosophies of Aware Parenting and Parenting by Connection, which support our children in expressing—not suppressing—their emotions. Releasing emotions in the nurturing, calm presence of a parent or caregiver (pre-dominantly through crying and tantrums) strengthens the child's sense of connection, security, and safety, which is essential for long-term healthy and sound sleep.

What Can I Use This Method For?

- Breaking habits such as rocking, feeding, holding, or patting to sleep.

- Transitioning children from cosleeping into their own room and/or crib.
- Transitioning children from a crib to a toddler bed.
- Weaning from the pacifier, breastfeeding, or the bottle.
- Night weaning.
- Alleviating a child's reliance on a caregiver to fall asleep.
- Children six months and over.

Although this method may be used for babies as young as four months, biological inconsistencies with sleep patterns (and heightened need for coregulation) in infants under six months of age can make breaking habits and implementing *long-term* changes to sleep patterns more challenging. In my experience, results are increasingly varied in children under six months.

Identifying the Problem to Find a Solution

It is imperative to recognize that children don't form sleep habits or control patterns independently of their parents. We must assume personal responsibility and acknowledge our role in the sleep difficulty if we intend to find a solution.

Not all habits translate to sleep issues; I have known some babies who can happily feed to sleep, self-settle, and sleep through the night.

However, for the majority of children who are rocked, held, fed, or patted-to-sleep—or rely on the pacifier, a lovey, or parental presence to fall asleep—this often inhibits their self-settling ability and fosters codependency rather than promoting sleep independence. This commonly translates to increased parental intervention not only to *get* to sleep at the start of naps and/or bedtime but also to fall *back* to sleep when they wake prematurely from day naps or overnight—sometimes as regularly as every one to two hours.

The inability to self-settle is often the catalyst for habitual catnapping and frequent, irregular overnight waking—often accompanied by crying and/or screaming because the child is unable to link sleep cycles without help. This is often an exhausting and frustrating process for parents, which can take its toll on the entire family unit.

One aim of the Sleep Play Love Method is to create some mindfulness around our children's control patterns and enable them to offload their feelings at appropriate times by supporting their tears and tantrums—instead of continually suppressing them with the breast, pacifier, bottle, lovey, or movement.

Begin by taking note of how your child communicates their needs. Any sudden, frantic, full-blown cry is likely to be a control pattern—and is often witnessed when we attempt to break sleep patterns such as rocking, feeding, or holding to sleep. For example, if we place our awake child in their crib without engaging in these actions to help them fall asleep, we will commonly witness them go from "zero to hero" in the volume stakes. There will likely be an outburst of emotion: lots of tears, trembling, and physical thrashing. This is their way of letting you know they are not happy and/or are feeling uncomfortable with the change to their routine. The key emotions that underpin such behavior are *almost always* fear and insecurity, as a direct result of removing the child's control pattern/sleep need that they have become accustomed to—often for their entire lives.

Seek comfort in the knowledge that it is okay for your children to experience these intense feelings. In fact, it is a healthy part of life. If you can support them through this difficult time by offering your presence, love, and reassurance, the results are often astounding.

Thankfully, babies are fast learners, and provided you are persistent and committed to at least three to four days, you will see an improvement in your child's ability to self-settle at the start of bedtimes and overnight, if not a complete transformation.

Offering Comfort in Other Ways

You might be thinking, "What is wrong with offering comfort to my child when they need it?" To which the answer is this: absolutely nothing. *It's our intention—that is, the what, why, when, and how we soothe our children, which makes the difference.*

> *While all children need to be comforted when they cry, there is a difference between comfort that represses emotions and comfort that allows for emotions to be felt and released.*
> - Aletha Solter

You can still hold, rock, or pat your child for comfort, just be mindful that this is not performed with the intention of stopping him or her from crying or getting them to fall asleep (all the time).

The habits that we encourage during the day (80 percent of the time, or more) usually become our children's sleep needs too. For example, if you resort to movement (e.g., walking, bouncing, rocking, the stroller, car, or swing) to soothe your child every time they fuss or cry throughout the day, chances are they will need some form of movement to fall asleep and remain asleep. In such cases, consider an an alternative to soothe your child during the day—such as holding your child in your arms (without movement).

When you are intending to break a certain control pattern or sleep need, then it may also be helpful to stop engaging in that specific action *immediately* before sleep. You can always reach for an alternative to help soothe your child before sleep times and overnight if you wish to transition him or her gradually toward independent sleep.

CONTROL PATTERN	REPLACE WITH
Feeding	Holding in arms, or rocking/patting/jiggling—either in arms or crib
Rocking	Holding in arms, or patting/rocking/jiggling while the child remains in their crib
Holding	Patting, jiggling, or resting a firm hand on the child while they remain in their crib
Patting	Resting a firm hand on the child's back, side, bottom, or stomach (without movement)—or on the mattress beside them (without touch)

When you are attempting to change a certain control pattern, it is important to keep in mind that even though you are still offering your loving presence and comfort in another way (such as holding instead of rocking), your child may still become upset, as it is not the comfort they are seeking (or rather have become accustomed to "needing").

Feeding is the one exception. We must feed our babies when they are hungry but abstain from feeding *frequently* for comfort or to distract our children from their physical or emotional hurts, frustrations, or boredom—that may otherwise be more efficiently supported (and/or healed) by holding and listening. *Emotional eating in young children can lead to comfort eating as adults (among other destructive behavioral patterns).* Comfort and snack (breast or bottle) feeding can also mean smaller and more frequent milk feeds throughout the day, less solids consumption, and consequently, increased overnight waking for longer or more substantial milk feeds.

It can also make it more difficult to stop feeding your child to sleep —and back to sleep overnight—while continuing to cosleep. You may experience heightened resistance if you attempt to offer another method of comfort when your child is used to being physically close to you and feeding frequently throughout the night (seeing as cosleeping and breast sleeping and/or feeding to sleep tend to coexist). See steps as follows for options to gently and respectfully transition your cosleeping child to independent sleep.

It is important to be aware of our inclination (as parents) to replace one control pattern with another—rather than to completely "heal" the pattern. For example, we may be successful in helping our child to overcome their dependence on breastfeeding (during the day and at sleep times) only for them to develop a reliance on an alternative source of comfort—or distraction—such as the pacifier, hair twirling, finger sucking, resting their hands in their mother's cleavage, or handholding. Although these newly acquired patterns may appear to make the transition easier for parents temporarily (and can serve as a bonding experience at times), they are neither empowering nor sustainable for the child if he or she becomes reliant on these actions to fall asleep—and back to sleep—in the long term. Such circumstances may present the opportunity for a parent to set a firm, yet loving, limit around the new habit—before it develops into another control pattern or sleep crutch. For guidance on establishing limits, refer to "The Seven Sleep Foundations: Emotional and Physical Well-Being."

PREPARING FOR CHANGE

1. You as the parent/s must be ready and committed to creating change. Most of the time it is us who get in the way of our child being able to sleep well: our agendas, and the things we do and don't do. Your young child will never come to you and say, "Hey, I think it's time we stop sleeping together!" So, you must be firm in your conviction and be prepared to persistently set the boundaries in order to facilitate the necessary change in sleep patterns and/or routine. The success of this method is directly proportionate to the readiness of you, the parents, and your commitment and consistency in executing its steps. If you are uncertain or are not in the right mindset to calmly respond to your children as they offload some intense emotions, I recommend waiting until a more suitable time. The decision to move forward must come from you, so get ready, emotionally and physically, and feel confident that you have a plan in place.

2. Ensure your child is in "reasonable" health before making changes to their (sleep) routine. When experiencing teething, an illness, allergies, or medical conditions, children generally don't sleep as well as they can. They may have a greater need for comfort or require increased parental intervention at sleep times—and therefore an increased reliance on their control pattern or sleep need. It is important to remember that breastfeeding to sleep can be a particularly challenging pattern to change at such times, as it can be a natural pain reliever for teething babies, and children may have a genuine, increased need for overnight feeds (for nutrition and hydration) if they are potentially "off" their food during the day (which often coincides with teething and/or illness). It is common for children at these times to resist nap and bedtimes, have shorter naps, and to wake more frequently overnight—so it is best to wait until they are in better health before making changes to routine or breaking sleep habits if you wish to optimize cooperation, ease, and sustainability.

There will always be something happening at any one time in the first one to three years, such as developmental changes, leaps, teething, or illness. It would be unreasonable to expect that you will ever have "all your ducks lined up" or experience consistency in the true sense of the word, as our children are forever growing, changing, and evolving. Provided that your child is in relatively good health and spirits, then I recommend starting the process—*a good indication of the level of health or readiness of your child is this: Would you be prepared to place them in the care of others (e.g., childcare), in their current state of health? If children are in "reasonable" health to be left in the care of others (and the parents feel confident to do so), they can be considered well enough to begin this process.*

> **Note:** Stress-relief crying can be effective for pain relief and may help to alleviate any associated frustration and discomfort that a child experiences when teething, unwell, or in pain. At times where your child is experiencing pain or discomfort because they are either teething or ill—and you have taken appropriate measures to minimize the pain/discomfort through homeopathic or pharmaceutical remedies—supporting your child to offload his or her frustrations and upset can expedite the recovery process and contribute toward better sleep.

3. Clear your calendar. It usually takes between three and seven days to experience definitive progress with this method. I usually recommend either starting over a weekend or having your spouse, family member, or friend available to support you *for the first three days at least (in my experience, it is nights one to three that are the most challenging).* Attempt to stay home for all naps and overnight sleep for a minimum of one week while everyone adjusts to your new sleep routine.

4. You can't pour from an empty cup, so take care of yourself first. This method can be emotionally intense for all involved, and therefore, it is imperative that you have appropriate support in place, like a spouse, family member, or friend who can listen to you if this process triggers some uncomfortable memories or feelings from your past or upbringing. It also helps to have someone who can take over from you if and when the going gets tough and you can no longer listen to your child as he or she cries. Refer to recommendations for self-care rituals and listening partnerships outlined in "The Seven Sleep Foundations: Emotional and Physical Well-Being."

5. Implement a regular age-appropriate routine with associated awake times as per "Routines and Recommendations." If time allows, I recommend doing so at least one week before starting this process, to ensure your child is well rested (and not overtired). When a child becomes overtired, his or her cortisol levels rise—cortisol is a stress hormone that has a more potent stimulant effect than caffeine. As a result, you may notice that your child gains a "second wind" and becomes hyperactive or erratic, despite being overdue for sleep. Overtiredness can also present as crying, distress, thrashing, or tantrums. You also want to avoid an undertired child by placing him or her down to sleep before they are "ready." If your child is undertired, you may notice that he or she stalls at bedtimes (particularly in older children), or remains awake in bed talking, laughing, babbling, or is just generally unsettled. The child may escalate to a frustrated or angry cry as time progresses, but he or she won't *usually* become too distressed or hysterical. An overtired or undertired child will rely more heavily on his or her control pattern or associated sleep need to fall asleep, and may wake more often. Missing the child's ideal sleep window almost always results in heightened resistance and/or behavioral difficulties at bedtimes—meaning it will take the child longer to eventually fall asleep (anywhere from thirty minutes to two hours, or more), and making him or her far less accepting of any change to their routine.

6. Optimize the sleep environment. Ensure the environment is not too hot or cold, your child's sleep space is darkened, white noise is playing indefinitely (i.e., is not set to a timer), and the room is free from toys, distractions, and clutter. You may opt for a small salt lamp to help you to navigate your way to your child for settling overnight—as red light is less disruptive to the circadian rhythm. For children who are moving into a new room, it may be a welcome touch to place some family photos on the wall beside the child's bed or crib, as this can increase familiarity and security at sleep times and help ease separation anxiety. For further environmental and bedding recommendations, refer to "The Seven Sleep Foundations: Environment."

7. Include quality one-on-one time into your day. Incorporate a minimum of five to ten minutes of distraction-free time with your child every day. Refer to "The Seven Sleep Foundations: Emotional and Physical Well-Being."

8. Introduce regular roughhousing play. Aim for at least five to ten minutes per day. This vigorous, spontaneous play can help children sleep better as it encourages them to release any built-up stress or tension from their day—which may otherwise surface as night waking. Although many children respond positively to roughhousing play before bedtime—and it can in fact minimize bedtime resistance and aid sounder sleep—you may want to avoid this at least twenty to thirty minutes preceding bedtimes if you notice that your child becomes hyperactive or has difficulty falling asleep afterward. Refer to "The Seven Sleep Foundations: Emotional and Physical Well-Being."

9. Observe your child during the day, noting his or her behavior (e.g., tears, whines, and tantrums), and try to become attuned to your child's *real* needs versus control pattern(s). If we can observe *what things* our children request during the day when they are upset and what *we do* to soothe them, then we can make a conscious effort to *listen* to our children as they offload their feelings during the day—instead of trying to prevent them from surfacing with the intention of avoiding conflict. Some examples include a pacifier or lovey, television, comfort or snack feeding (e.g., feeding children when they are physically hurt, upset, or bored), or picking up babies every time they crawl to our legs or begin to grizzle or whine. Sometimes babies are communicating a real need (e.g., a desire for stimulation or a change in scenery), so become aware of this—before offering their control pattern. *The safer and more supported children feel to offload feelings during their waking hours, the less likely they will be to wake overnight to do so. Every tantrum is an opportunity to either connect and heal or disconnect and repress.*

10. Be prepared for a little, or a lot, of crying. There is no such thing as a no-cry solution when changing sleep patterns, and nor would we want there to be—as crying is the primary way in which children communicate their needs to us, and their main avenue to release any stored or present stress and tension.

Babies rarely relinquish their favorite things without a fight, so you can expect some screaming, thrashing, and potentially aggressive behavior—especially in toddlers and older children (aggression is a by-product of fear). Albeit difficult for parents to experience, this is a normal emotional process for change. *Remember that the underlying emotions for all children when experiencing change or life transitions are fear (sometimes terror if there has been early trauma) and insecurity. Anger and frustration will arise and subside, sadness and grief will take over, and the healing process will begin.*

Your role is to hold a loving and supportive presence throughout this process. Children can only avail themselves of stress and, therefore, heal from upset and trauma if they are held in their parents' loving arms or within their supportive and calm presence—as opposed to being left to cry alone through "cry it out" sleep-training methods, which instead *creates* a stress response.

Assuming there are no underlying medical conditions, illnesses, or allergies, most children respond rather quickly to this technique. How long your child cries will be dependent on any associated trauma and/or how long any habits or patterns have persisted. The longer a habit or sleep pattern has been present, the longer it may take to change, although this is not always the case. I have known babies to cry for anywhere between ten minutes to over an hour. However, if you remain persistent with this approach and continue to listen, validate, and support them through this difficult time, the length and intensity of crying will decrease as the days progress.

11. **Nights first, then days.** Lack of sleep during the day can lead to overtiredness, increased bedtime resistance, and difficulty adapting to changes in routine. An overtired baby will *almost always* require more parental intervention to fall asleep (e.g., rocking, feeding, or holding), and hence it may become more challenging to change these patterns. Albeit every family circumstance is unique, I most often advise to keep days the same, temporarily. For example, if you are feeding to sleep for days and nights, *focus on first breaking this association for nights.* This way, you can ensure that your child continues to have uninterrupted day sleep(s), and that he or she is well rested and ready to tackle the bedtime change. This also makes it more "digestible" for parents, as it can be overwhelming breaking habits for days and nights at the same time—especially if there is a lot of crying and not a lot of sleep! Once your child has successfully learned to self-settle at the

beginning of bedtimes, then you can either focus on one nap at a time or all naps.

12. If you are transitioning your child into a crib, toddler bed, or new room, prioritize the transition into the child's new sleep space. Therefore, you will start with days *first*. Begin this process during the day so that your child will have their day nap(s) in their new sleep space. Avoid making their first sleep in their new bed and/or room at nighttime as this usually creates more anxiety. One option is to position the child's crib next to the parents' bed, but where possible, I recommend that you move them into a separate sleep space altogether—preferably their own room. If you are also feeding, rocking, holding, or patting to sleep, you will continue to do so for the first three to six days. You can commence the process of breaking this pattern once you have successfully transitioned your child into their own sleep space for days and nights. *If you are cosleeping with your child and making this transition, refer to "The Sleep Play Love Method: Recommended Transition from Cosleeping (and Feeding, Rocking, Holding, or Patting to Sleep) to Independent Sleep."*

13. If you plan to transition your child into a crib, a toddler bed, and/or their own room, introduce some playtime in the child's new sleep space three to seven days* before the big move. Room and crib (or bed) play will create some safety and security for children as they become familiar with their new sleep space. Some games you can play to help your child bond with their new bed and/or room include hide-and-seek, catchy with a soft ball (in and around their bed), gentle pillow fights, or roughhousing play. Peekaboo (i.e., placing your child in their bed and hiding underneath or beside it) is especially effective for working with fears and anxiety around separation. You may also try some creative role-playing; for example, place your child in the crib or bed and have some fun with what is usually a highly emotive experience—for instance, instruct your child to lie down on the mattress, "It's bedtime now, which means you must lie down and go to sleep!" If you're child tries to get out of the bed or stands up in the crib, assume a stern look and with some playfulness point your finger at the child or place your hands on your hips and say, "I told you to lie down and go to sleep. Do you know what happens to cheeky little monkeys who don't go to sleep or do as they're told? They are punished with kisses and cuddles!"—you would then proceed to jump on the child and kiss and cuddle them. If you can encourage some giggles, engagement, and laughter, you're on the right track! Laughter is essential for releasing fear (in this case, separation from you and the adjustment to a new sleep environment) and ultimately encourages connection, safety, and a bond with the new sleep space. New bedding, toys, furniture, or room decorations may empower and/or excite older children and help them view this move more positively—that is, as a "rite of passage" rather than an "eviction." Transitional items such as an old T-shirt or a lovey (with breast-milk and/or mom's scent infused) can be an effective, temporary solution to help children adapt with greater ease.

Although three to seven days is ideal, one or two days will suffice if you have time constraints.

14. Avoid making too many transitions at once—focus on one change at a time. When making changes to sleep patterns, fostering safety and security is paramount, as is ensuring that we prepare our child in a respectful manner that encourages connection and cooperation. With any life transition such as starting childcare, introducing a new sibling, transitioning from a crib to a toddler bed, potty training, or weaning (from the pacifier, bottle, breast, or parental presence at bedtimes), feelings of insecurity and fear are always heightened. Focusing on one change at a time will help prevent further grief, trauma, or upset, and ensure a smoother transition—with the opportunity to strengthen the parent-child bond in the process.

WHEN YOU ARE READY TO START

1. Choose a slightly earlier bedtime on nights one to three. Aim for fifteen to thirty minutes earlier than usual to accommodate for any tears or resistance. This can also help minimize overtiredness and consequently, overnight waking.

2. Introduce wind-down time and positive sleep associations. Commence these ten to fifteen minutes before nap time and thirty to sixty minutes before bedtime. The actual bedtime routine (e.g., milk and sleep associations), should be no longer than twenty to thirty minutes to avoid stalling and second winds. Suggestions include white noise, a dark room, swaddle or sleep bag, cuddle, book, song, debrief of the day (for older children), and a kiss-and-cuddle good-night. The only variables may be bath and massage at nighttime. Holding, rocking, feeding, patting, and the pacifier should be avoided as sleep cues. For recommendations, refer to "The Seven Sleep Foundations: Positive Sleep Associations."

3. Make one small change to the bedtime routine at a time. Take one small step first by removing—or changing—one thing your child relies on to fall asleep (e.g., sleep space, movement, pacifier, bottle, or breast). For example, if your child has a pacifier *and* relies on either motion or parental presence to fall asleep, using the Sleep Play Love Method, focus on removing the pacifier first (over three or so days), then you may remove your intervention by either listening or using gradual withdrawal. Similarly, if you are transitioning your child from a crib to a toddler bed (or a new room), focus on the change at hand—removing any control patterns once you have successfully moved your child into their new sleep space.

4. Communicate your intentions in advance. Children thrive on connection, love, and predictability. When making changes to sleep routines, or amid life transitions, it is important that we communicate openly and respectfully to children about the change *before* making it. Babies and children understand more than we give them credit for—even if they don't understand each and every word you use, they may identify with certain words, and/or the overall tone and intention. When you have your child's cooperation and understanding, the results can be remarkable. This also makes for a deeper parent-child connection and a more effective and sustainable outcome when making changes to sleep patterns.

5. Explain to your child what their new routine will look like. For example, "Darling, tonight I am not going to feed you until you fall asleep. We will have milk, a book, and a cuddle, and then I am going to tuck you into your bed to fall asleep. I will be right here if you need me. You are safe, and I love you." Encourage any crying, resistance, or upset as it arises and hold a loving space for your child to express their feelings as they arise during the day—this will prevent them from "bottling up" and releasing their tension at nighttime (i.e., bedtime resistance, night waking, and nightmares).

6. Make the desired changes to your child's sleep routine. Before proceeding, ensure that you have implemented the steps in "Preparing for Change."

If you are feeding to sleep:

Option A: *Proceed to step 7.*

Option B: Schedule milk feeds twenty to thirty minutes before sleep associations (i.e., switch up the order of things so that feeding is the *first thing* you do at bedtime—followed by a sleeping bag, book, and kiss-and-cuddle good-night). You can also feed your child in another room in the house or in their room with the light on so they are less inclined to fall asleep on the breast or bottle. *Either proceed to step 7, or with "Option D" as follows.*

Option C: Continue to feed before sleep, but "break the attachment" (i.e., remove your child from the breast or bottle) before they fall completely asleep. If your child begins to wake, fuss, or root around for the nipple once you have removed it from their mouth, you have the option to (a) replace the nipple (breast or bottle) into their mouth and repeat this process until you can place them into their crib while drowsy, but awake; (b) proceed to rock or hold your child to sleep, or until they are drowsy enough to place into their crib; or (c) proceed with steps 9 to 12 and refer to *"Troubleshooting Tips for Listening"* as necessary.

Option D: Gradual withdrawal. Revoke your intervention every two to three days, for up to eighteen days. For example;

Nights one to three: rock your child to sleep in your arms.
Nights four to six: hold your child to sleep in your arms.
Nights seven to nine: pat, jiggle, rock, or gently rub your child's

torso/side/back/bottom until they fall asleep—as your child remains in their crib or bed.

Nights ten to twelve: rest a firm hand on your child's torso/side/back/bottom without movement—as your child remains in their crib or bed.

Nights thirteen to fifteen: rest your hand on the mattress beside your child (slight touch, no movement).

Nights sixteen to eighteen: kneel beside your child's crib or bed without touch, using warm validation and encouragement as necessary.

If your child is still reliant on your presence to fall asleep after this time, you can employ "check-ins" i.e., reassure your child that they are safe and loved. Tell them that you will be leaving the room for only a short while to wash the dishes (as an example) and you will return after this time to kiss/cuddle/tuck them in for bed again. Begin with one minute, and then increase time increments over one or more night(s).

If your child becomes uncomfortable, or begins to cry as you withdraw your intervention during any step of this process, proceed with steps 8 to 12, and refer to "Troubleshooting Tips for Listening" as necessary. *Remember to communicate each change with your child in advance to foster safety and encourage their cooperation.*

> **Note:** Dependent on temperament and age, some children may become too stimulated by patting or certain touch, in which case parental presence may be sufficient—trial and error will determine this. Exercise your intuition as to the most suitable way to proceed with gradual withdrawal for your child.

Option E: If breastfeeding, replace the breast with a bottle of expressed milk, formula, cow's milk, or milk alternative (ensure that the milk source is age-appropriate). Continue to feed before sleep for three days. On day four, proceed with either option A, B, C, or D.

What to do when your child wakes?

Proceed with your choice of method when children wake midnap or during the night—unless your child is due for a milk feed, in which case you can feed them and place them back to sleep. Your child will most likely fall asleep while feeding at these times—this is okay.

Although listening is preferable (as this supports children to effectively heal from their dependence on you and the feelings of fear surrounding the change to their sleep routine), we must consider our current physical and emotional state—or limitations. If you have listened intensely to your child at the start of their sleep time and you find that you are unable to listen any further when they wake, you do have the option of a limited cry approach for any subsequent wake-ups (e.g., rocking, holding, patting, or resting a hand on your child until they fall back to sleep—or even listening at every other wake-up).

The most integral part of this process is *how* your child is falling asleep at the *beginning* of sleep times. If you can encourage self-settling by removing your intervention—and especially by eliciting an emotional release—your child will naturally wake less over time because they have the confidence and skill (and feel safe enough) to transition from one sleep cycle to the next independently.

> **Note:** It is also important to remember that regular milk consumption overnight (i.e., out of habit or for comfort, and not for nutrition) can prevent children from entering a deeper state of sleep as their digestive system is constantly activated to process the milk.

For assistance with scheduling overnight feeds when breaking a feed-to-sleep pattern, refer to "Scheduling Overnight Feeds (Six Months and Over)."

If you are rocking to sleep:

Option A: *Proceed to step 7.*

Option B: Hold your child before sleep *without* rocking or movement. *Proceed with steps 8 to 12, and refer to "Troubleshooting Tips for Listening" as necessary.*

Option C: Rock your child before sleep—but rock/jiggle them while they remain lying in their crib (not in your arms). Continue for a maximum of three days, and then proceed with either option A, D, or E.

Option D: Continue to rock your child before sleep either in your arms or in the crib, but cease any movement before they are completely asleep:

1. If you are rocking the child in their crib, transition to resting your hand firmly on their torso/side/back/bottom (without movement).
2. If you are rocking the child in your arms, transition to holding in arms, or attempt to place them in the crib while they are still awake or drowsy.

If your child begins to wake, fuss, or cry once out of your arms, or when you have ceased movement, you have the option to (a) resume rocking your child and repeat this process until they can fall asleep in their crib with little-to-no movement; or (b) proceed with steps 8 to 12 and refer to *"Troubleshooting Tips for Listening"* as necessary.

Option E: Gradual withdrawal. Revoke your intervention every two to three days, for up to fifteen days. For example;

Nights one to three: hold your child to sleep in your arms.

Nights four to six: pat, jiggle, rock, or gently rub your child's torso/side/back/bottom until they fall asleep—as your child remains in their crib.

Nights seven to nine: rest a firm hand on your child's torso/side/back/bottom without movement.

Nights ten to twelve: rest your hand on the mattress beside your child (slight touch, no movement).

Nights thirteen to fifteen: kneel beside your child's crib or bed without touch, using warm validation and encouragement as necessary.

Nights sixteen and onward: check ins as required.

If your child becomes uncomfortable, or begins to cry as you withdraw your intervention during any step of this process, proceed with steps 8 to 12, and refer to "Troubleshooting Tips for Listening" as necessary. *Remember to communicate each change with your child in advance to foster safety and encourage their cooperation.*

> **Note:** Dependent on temperament and age, some children may become too stimulated by patting or certain touch, in which case parental presence may be sufficient—trial and error will determine this. Exercise your intuition as to the most suitable way to proceed with gradual withdrawal for your child.

What to do when your child wakes?

Proceed with your choice of method when children wake midnap or during the night—unless your child is due for a milk feed, in which case you can feed them and place them back to sleep.

Although listening is preferable (as this supports children to effectively heal from their dependence on you and the feelings of fear surrounding the change to their sleep routine), we must consider our current physical and emotional state—or limitations. If you have listened intensely to your child at the start of their sleep time and you find that you are unable to listen any further when they wake, you do have the option of a limited cry approach for any subsequent wake-ups (e.g., rocking, holding, patting, or resting a hand on your child until they fall back to sleep—or even listening at every other wake-up).

The most integral part of this process is *how* your child is falling asleep at the *beginning* of sleep times. If you can encourage self-settling by removing your intervention—and especially by eliciting an emotional release—your child will naturally wake less over time because they have the confidence and skill (and feel safe enough) to transition from one sleep cycle to the next independently.

If you are holding to sleep:

Option A: *Proceed to step 7.*

Option B: Continue to hold your child before sleep, but place them into their crib before they fall completely asleep. If your child begins to wake, fuss, or cry once out of your arms, you have the option to (a) pick them up and repeat this process until you can place them into their crib while drowsy, but awake; or (b) proceed with steps 8 to 12 and refer to "*Troubleshooting Tips for Listening*" as necessary.

Option C: Gradual withdrawal. Revoke your intervention every two to three days, for up to twelve days. For example;

Nights one to three: pat, jiggle, rock, or gently rub your child's torso/side/back/bottom until they fall asleep—as your child remains in their crib.
Nights four to six: rest a firm hand on your child's torso/side/back/bottom without movement.
Nights seven to nine: rest your hand on the mattress beside your child (slight touch, no movement).
Nights ten to twelve: kneel beside your child's crib or bed without

touch, using warm validation and encouragement as necessary. **Nights thirteen and onward:** check ins as required.

If your child becomes uncomfortable, or begins to cry as you withdraw your intervention during any step of this process, proceed with steps 8 to 12, and refer to "Troubleshooting Tips for Listening" as necessary. *Remember to communicate each change with your child in advance to foster safety and encourage their cooperation.*

> **Note:** Dependent on temperament and age, some children may become too stimulated by patting or certain touch, in which case parental presence may be sufficient—trial and error will determine this. Exercise your intuition as to the most suitable way to proceed with gradual withdrawal for your child.

What to do when your child wakes?

Proceed with your choice of method when children wake midnap or during the night—unless your child is due for a milk feed, in which case you can feed them and place them back to sleep.

Although listening is preferable (as this supports children to effectively heal from their dependence on you and the feelings of fear surrounding the change to their sleep routine), we must consider our current physical and emotional state—or limitations. If you have listened intensely to your child at the start of their sleep time and you find that you are unable to listen any further when they wake, you do have the option of a limited cry approach for any subsequent wake-ups (e.g., holding, patting, or resting a hand on your child until they fall back to sleep—or even listening at every other wake-up).

The most integral part of this process is *how* your child is falling asleep at the *beginning* of sleep times. If you can encourage self-settling by removing your intervention—and especially by eliciting an emotional release—your child will naturally wake less over time because they have the confidence and skill (and feel safe enough) to transition from one sleep cycle to the next independently.

If you are patting, resting a hand on your child, or holding their hand until they fall asleep (either in their crib or bed):

Option A: *Proceed to step 7.*

Option B: Cease patting, or remove your hand/touch before your child falls completely asleep. If your child begins to wake, fuss, or cry once you have stopped patting or removed your hand, you have the option to (a) resume patting or return your hand to your child and repeat this process until they fall asleep with little-to-no touch or movement; or (b) proceed with steps 8 to 12 and refer to "*Troubleshooting Tips for Listening*" as necessary.

Option C: Gradual withdrawal. Revoke your intervention every two to three days, for up to fifteen days. For example, if you are patting your child to sleep;

Nights one to three: transition to resting a firm hand on your child, or holding their hand (without movement). *You can either sit beside your child on their bed, or kneel/stand beside their crib.*
Nights four to six: rest a firm hand on the mattress beside your child, or if they are in a bed, you may sit beside them with your hand or body only *slightly* touching them.
Nights seven to nine: kneel beside your child's crib or bed, or sit at the end of your child's bed without touch. Use warm validation and encouragement as necessary.
Nights ten to twelve: Sit halfway between the child's crib/bed and the bedroom door (either on a chair or the floor). *You can experiment with moving varying distances away over a few nights for a more gradual approach.*
Nights thirteen to fifteen: option to either (a) sit just inside the

bedroom door—on a chair or the floor; (b) proceed with check-ins; or (c) alternate between sitting inside the doorway, and leaving the room for short bursts of time.

If your child becomes uncomfortable, or begins to cry as you withdraw your intervention during any step of this process, proceed with steps 8 to 12, and refer to "Troubleshooting Tips for Listening." *Remember to communicate each change with your child in advance to foster safety and encourage their cooperation.*

> **Note:** Dependent on temperament and age, some children may become too stimulated by certain touch, in which case parental presence may be sufficient—trial and error will determine this. Exercise your intuition as to the most suitable way to proceed with gradual withdrawal for your child.

What to do when your child wakes?

Proceed with your choice of method when children wake midnap or during the night—unless your child is due for a milk feed, in which case you can feed them and place them back to sleep.

Although listening is preferable (as this supports children to effectively heal from their dependence on you and the feelings of fear surrounding the change to their sleep routine), we must consider our current physical and emotional state—or limitations. If you have listened intensely to your child at the start of their sleep time and you find that you are unable to listen any further when they wake, you do have the option of a limited cry approach for any subsequent wake-ups (e.g., rocking, holding, patting, or resting a hand on your child until they fall back to sleep—or even listening at every other wake-up).

The most integral part of this process is *how* your child is falling asleep at the *beginning* of sleep times. If you can encourage self-settling by removing your intervention—and especially by eliciting an emotional release—your child will naturally wake less over time because they have the confidence and skill (and feel safe enough) to transition from one sleep cycle to the next independently.

If the child relies on a parent in the room to fall asleep (i.e., you are lying or sitting beside the child until he or she falls asleep without hands-on touch or movement):

Option A: *Proceed to step 7.*

Option B: Continue to lie or sit beside your child until they are almost, but not completely asleep. If your child begins to wake, fuss, or cry when you attempt to leave their bedside, you have the option to (a) resume your position beside your child and repeat this process until they are drowsy (but awake) and you can leave the room; (b) proceed with "check-ins" as per "Option D" below; or (c) continue with steps 8 to 12 and refer to "*Troubleshooting Tips for Listening*" as necessary.

Option C: Attempt to find the "sweet spot" between staying in the room for reassurance and moving just the right distance away from your child's crib/bed with the intention of eliciting an emotional release—*without* giving into your child's control pattern or sleep need (which in this case will be lying, sitting, or kneeling beside them). Experiment with standing or sitting at varying distances away from your child while remaining in the room and using warm and loving validation and reassurance to let them know they are loved, safe, and that you are there to help them get through this difficult time. *Proceed with steps 8 to 12, and refer to "Troubleshooting Tips for Listening" as necessary.*

Option D: For children twelve months and over, you have the option of employing check-ins. For example, if your child cries, protests, or says "don't go" or "stay," when you attempt to leave the room, give them a hug and a kiss, reassure them that they are safe and loved, and that you will be right back to check on them in two minutes (or less): "I am going to wash the dishes, and I will be back to tuck you in and give you another kiss and cuddle really soon." You can increase the increments of time over one to three nights—or longer if necessary—until your child feels safe enough to fall asleep without you in the room. *Proceed with steps 8 to 12, and refer to "Troubleshooting Tips for Listening" as necessary.*

Option E: Gradual withdrawal. Revoke your intervention gradually every two to three days for up to nine days. For example, if you are lying beside your child;

Nights one to three: kneel beside your child's crib or bed, or sit at the end of your child's bed (without touch). Use warm validation and encouragement as necessary. *You can experiment with moving varying distances away over a few nights for a more gradual approach.*
Nights four to six: Sit halfway between the child's crib/bed and the bedroom door (either on a chair or the floor). *You can experiment with moving varying distances away over a few nights for a more gradual approach.*
Nights seven to nine: option to either (a) sit just inside the bedroom door—on a chair or the floor; (b) proceed with check-ins; or (c) alternate between sitting inside the doorway, and leaving the room for short bursts of time.

If your child becomes uncomfortable, or begins to cry as you withdraw your intervention during any step of this process, proceed with steps 8 to 12, and refer to "Troubleshooting Tips for Listening" as necessary. *Remember to communicate each change with your child in advance to foster safety and encourage their cooperation.*

Option F: Install a safety gate.* Some older children who have transitioned into a toddler bed may begin venturing out of their bed and/or bedroom multiple times at sleep times and during the night. A safety gate at the bedroom door can help children stay in their room (and may prevent potential injury). The child's perceived lack of freedom in this scenario can quite often lead to emotional release—particularly anger and frustration—so be prepared to listen and offer appropriate comfort as necessary. *Use in combination with Option A, B, C, D, E, or F; or proceed with steps 8 to 12 and refer to "Troubleshooting Tips for Listening" as necessary.*

A gate should be introduced to children as a "safety measure" rather than a perceived punishment. Empowering toddlers to decorate their own gate with stickers, streamers, or even paint can alleviate fear and ensure their cooperation as much as possible.

What to do when your child wakes?

Proceed with your choice of method when children wake midnap or during the night—unless your child is due for a milk feed, in which case you can feed them and place them back to sleep. Children often become rather upset when you move a further distance away from their bedside, so some intense listening can be anticipated. I recommend preparing as best you can with the action steps within "Preparing for Change"—especially listening time for parent and child, quality one-on-one time, crib/room play, roughhousing, and role-playing. *Proceed with steps 8 to 12, and refer to "Troubleshooting Tips for Listening" as necessary.*

If your child relies on the pacifier to fall asleep:

Option A: Cold turkey. *Proceed to step 7.*

Option B: Allow your child to keep the pacifier for their day nap(s) on the day you start. Proceed with option A, C, or D for their night sleep.

If your child also relies on their pacifier outside of sleep times, then you may decide to limit the pacifier *for sleep times only* for the first three to seven days before commencing the weaning process for sleep times.

Option C: Allow your child to fall *almost* asleep with the pacifier, removing it from their mouth before they are completely asleep. If your child begins to wake, fuss, or root around for the pacifier once you have removed it from their mouth, you have the option to (a) replace the pacifier into their mouth and repeat this process until they can fall asleep without it; (b) proceed with "Option D" below; or (c) continue with steps 8 to 12 and refer to *"Troubleshooting Tips for Listening"* as necessary.

Option D: Replace the comfort of the pacifier with your presence in the following ways:

1. Holding or rocking your child in your arms until they fall asleep. *Do this for no longer than three nights, and proceed with listening or gradual withdrawal from day four.*
2. Rocking, patting, or jiggling your child while they remain in their crib. *Do this for no longer than three nights, and proceed with listening or gradual withdrawal from day four.*
3. Lying or sitting beside your child with limited or no touch. *Do this for no longer than three nights, and proceed with listening or gradual withdrawal from day four.*

What to do when your child wakes?

Proceed with your choice of method when children wake midnap or during the night; however, the weaning process is most effective if you can listen to your child as they cry and release their feelings of dependence and stored emotions.

If you are unable to listen any further, you can try either holding or rocking them to sleep, or you may offer your child their pacifier. Let them know that they have done a great job and that you will both pick up where you left off tomorrow. You may continue to do this for days or weeks, depending on your bandwidth and individual circumstance.

Contrary to existing belief systems, you *won't be creating bad habits* because this is an emotional process—and method, not a behavioral one. Listening—even just for five minutes—to your child as they express their uncomfortable feelings through tears, crying, trembling, or thrashing is far better than repressing the feelings altogether by offering the pacifier (or any associated control pattern) as soon as your child begins to cry. *This transition can take much longer for some children —sometimes even months, depending on their age, degree of attachment, and stored feelings enabled by the pacifier.*

If you are transitioning your child into a new bed (e.g., crib to toddler bed) and/or a new room:

Between two and a half to three years of age is ideal for this stage (unless the child is climbing out of their crib—which would require parents to make this transition sooner for safety reasons). Remember to start with the day nap(s) first! *If you are also feeding, rocking, patting, or holding to sleep—or you are cosleeping prior to making this transition —follow the steps in "Recommended Transition from Cosleeping (and Feeding, Rocking, Holding, or Patting to Sleep) to Independent Sleep."*

Option A: *Proceed to step 7.*

Option B: "Camp out" in your child's room.

Nights one to three: sleep on a mattress on the floor beside your child's bed for the whole night.
Nights four to six: sleep on the mattress only until your child falls asleep, and if/when they wake overnight—returning to your own bed to sleep for the remainder of the night.
Nights seven to nine: remove the mattress from your child's room.

You may sit on, or beside their bed until they are asleep *or almost asleep* before leaving the room.

Night ten and onward: check ins as required.

If at any time your child becomes uncomfortable with you leaving the room, or begins to cry as you move away from them, proceed with steps 8 to 12, and refer to "Troubleshooting Tips for Listening" as necessary. *Remember to communicate each change with your child in advance to foster safety and encourage their cooperation.*

Option C: Gradual withdrawal. Revoke your intervention gradually every two to three days for up to nine days. For example;

Nights one to three: sit beside your child's bed until they fall asleep.
Nights four to six: sit beside your child's bed until they are *almost* asleep before leaving the room.
Nights seven to nine: you have the option of (a) moving further away from your child while you remain in their room (e.g., sitting on a chair halfway between their bed and the door—or on the floor beside their doorway); (b) employing check-ins; or (c) combining both over the period of three to seven days.

If your child becomes uncomfortable with you leaving the room, or begin to cry as you move away from them in any step of this process, proceed with steps 8 to 12, and refer to "Troubleshooting Tips for Listening" as necessary. *Remember to communicate each change with your child in advance to foster safety and encourage their cooperation.*

What to do when your child wakes?

When your child wakes overnight, assume your same position as per the beginning of bedtime—for example, on the mattress or sitting on a chair in their room. Ensure that you remove your intervention slightly every three-or-so days to prevent your presence becoming a sleep crutch. A safety gate (as outlined previously) may be necessary—as a temporary measure—if your child proceeds to venture out of their bed/room at bedtime and/or overnight.

> **Note:** Although listening is preferred (for time efficiency, sustainability, and emotional well-being), gradual withdrawal options in step 6 above have been included to give parents an alternative if they do not feel comfortable with listening straightaway. Results with a gradual withdrawal approach can be varied and may not be as efficient, nor effective at producing the same long-term results as listening. Many children will resist alternative methods of comfort if they have been accustomed to a specific sleep need (e.g., feeding) and will continue to cry regardless of whether a parent is still offering his or her warm attention and physical closeness—say, by holding. Keep in mind that you may default to listening irrespective of your best intentions to implement gradual withdrawal, and for this reason, I recommend familiarizing yourself with the steps in "Preparing for Change" and "When You Are Ready to Start" prior to commencing any change to your child's sleep routine.

7. Following the bedtime routine (a maximum of twenty to thirty minutes), place your awake child in his or her crib/bed. Reaffirm to your child, "It is time for sleep, sweetie. You are safe, and I love you. I am going to leave the room now, but I will be right here if you need me." If your child does not become immediately hysterical, leave the room, and remain responsive to his or her needs (or cries).

Proceed with steps 8 to 12, and refer to "Troubleshooting Tips for Listening" as necessary.

8. If your child begins to protest or cry, tune into what they are

trying to communicate, and remain responsive. Is the cry emotional or urgent? Frustrated or angry? A grizzle or hysterical? Are you confident that you have met all your child's basic needs (i.e., hunger, temperature, clean diaper, or discomfort/pain)? This must take priority before moving forward.

If your child is still having milk, ensure that they have had an adequate feed before bedtime to eliminate the possibility of hunger—especially important when breaking a feed-to-sleep pattern.

If your child becomes immediately upset when you place him or her in their crib awake, move away from their bedside, stop rocking them, or remove them prematurely from the breast, bottle, or pacifier before they are completely asleep, chances are they are crying to express their grief, anger, frustration, fear, insecurity, or confusion around the change to their routine—that is, the absence of their control pattern (as opposed to calling out for an immediate need to be met).

Toddlers and older children who are reliant on a caregiver to fall asleep may stall the bedtime process with last-minute requests such as asking to use the bathroom, something more to eat, milk, water, one more book, or another cuddle. In such instances, it may be an idea to cover all bases at least thirty minutes before bedtime—for example, "It's bedtime soon, darling; do you need to use the bathroom, or would you like anything more to eat or drink before we read our books and say good-night?" Keep a sippy cup of water beside their bed for them to access themselves as required—so that this is one less thing to wake you for overnight.

Use your intuition to determine if their request is genuine, and your discretion as to whether you accommodate them. Otherwise, it may be an opportunity for you to set a limit—for example, "There are no more books tonight, sweetie; we can read some more tomorrow. It's bedtime now." Setting limits often inspires tears and/or tantrums —these are generally better out than in and better out before bedtime than in the middle of the night! *Proceed with steps 9 to 12, and refer to "Troubleshooting Tips for Listening" as necessary.*

9. Be reactive, not proactive, to your child's needs. If the cry is not emotional and you are certain that their immediate needs have been met, then you may leave your child's room to give them the space and opportunity self-settle. If your child escalates from "zero to hero," becoming really upset immediately—and you don't have the chance to leave the room—stay with them, and proceed to step 11.

Parental presence can overstimulate some children, making this process more challenging. In many cases, it's us (the parents) who have a more difficult time breaking sleep habits, as these habits have also become ours. We lack confidence and become doubtful that our children can fall asleep without us—and with this thought process, we also cannot help but feel somewhat anxious, which our children sense immediately, making sleep a further challenge.

> *I have known children who have coslept and fed to sleep for over twelve months, yet when afforded the space at bedtime without a parent beside them, they have rolled over and fallen asleep independently on night one! Respect your children's ability and resilience, affording them the benefit of the doubt that they are capable of making these changes with ease, grace, and velocity. I have been privy to many families who have experienced life-changing results in the first one to three days (irrespective of the habit or how long it has persisted), which is testament to the fact that it doesn't always have to be a difficult or lengthy process. Usually, if it is, then it's the parents who are getting in the way—either because of lack of support, commitment, confidence, direction, and follow-through, or because of emotional state such as worry, stress, or anxiety.*

When you have tucked your child in, tell them, "I am leaving the room now. You are safe, I love you, and I will be right back if you need me." Try to allow at least one to two minutes before returning, unless they become hysterical, in which case you would attend to them immediately and listen—and/or provide appropriate comfort. If this is in the middle of the night, and the cry is off and on, then you may employ check-ins every five to ten minutes until they either (a) fall back asleep, or (b) their cries escalate. *Proceed with steps 10 to 12, and refer to "Troubleshooting Tips for Listening" as required.*

> **Note:** It is most important that you encourage self-settling *at the beginning* of nap and bedtimes. If you choose to feed or hold your child to help them resettle overnight, it is less important to get them back into their sleep space awake. In other words, if they fall asleep on the breast overnight, do not wake them up to put them back in their crib. Rocking, holding, or swaying for comfort is fine; just be mindful of engaging in any activity to stop the crying. The aim is to encourage your child to release any uncomfortable feelings this process evokes in them, or which have been stored away in their emotional backpack over time. *Remember this: children heal and recover by crying while in the loving presence of their parents—either in arms or a short distance away (but still in full sight).*

Once children are capable of self-settling at the beginning of bedtime and nap times *without parental intervention,* the number of times they wake expecting to be fed, rocked, held, or patted back to sleep will naturally decrease.

10. If your child continues to be unsettled (but is not overly upset), always attempt to settle them while they remain in their crib or bed. Don't intervene unnecessarily by picking your child up and/or offering their control pattern—proceed with your chosen option for settling in step 6.

If your child is sitting, rocking, crawling, or standing in their crib, your first option may be to encourage them to lie on their side or tummy and rub their back gently while using reassuring words until they are calm (or asleep) and you are able to leave the room. Another less hands-on option is to kneel beside their crib and tap the mattress to persuade them to lie back down. Use gentle words of validation and encouragement such as, "It's sleep time, darling. I know you are having a hard time getting to sleep. I am right here, I love you, you are safe, and I will stay with you until you close your eyes/fall back asleep." If your child responds by lying down and settling, you can use your touch until they are close to falling asleep or completely asleep—just be sure to remove your intervention every two to three days to avoid developing a new sleep crutch. *Refer to options for gradual withdrawal under step 6.*

This step can be especially challenging if your child has become accustomed to you being in the room while they fall asleep (without direct touch). Unlike feeding to sleep, rocking to sleep, or patting to sleep, there are limited options to gradually withdraw your intervention *without* increasing the physical distance between you and your child. You may choose to employ brief check-ins by leaving the room for short bursts of time (even thirty to sixty seconds) while continuing to remain responsive to your child's cries. *Repeat steps 9 through 12 as necessary, and refer to "Troubleshooting Tips for Listening."*

11. If your child will not settle in their crib/bed (i.e., they become immediately upset before you have left the room or become progressively upset after you have left), then either hold them or sit by their bedside using warm validation. If your child stops crying when you hold them, give them a quick cuddle and kiss, let them know that they are safe and loved, and tell them that you are going to place them back in their crib/bed. Reaffirm that it is sleep time. Some children who are conditioned to holding or rocking at sleep times may stop crying and settle immediately when picked up. In this case, you may need to employ trial and error to ascertain the "sweet spot" whereby you are still present and providing some comfort, but not giving into your child's control pattern/sleep need that you are intending to break (refer to the gradual withdrawal suggestions in step 6). You may experiment with positioning yourself at varying distances away from your child if they are not reliant on touch or movement (i.e., you are lying or sitting beside them at sleep times). Remember that our intention is not to stop the crying, but to encourage an emotional release so that our children can heal from their associated control pattern and transition toward independent sleep—that is, without their reliance on *you* to fall asleep and stay asleep.

If your child remains "relatively" calm, you may leave the room or proceed with check-ins as necessary. If they continue to appear unsettled or upset, resume your position close by, using reassuring words and intermittent touch for comfort as required. Once settled or asleep, leave the room, and repeat steps 8 through 12 as necessary.

Physical comfort (such as holding) should be the "go to" in cases where the child has become very upset and continues to cry even when the child is being held —that is, the comfort does not act to repress the crying by satisfying a control pattern.

12. If your child will not settle when held (i.e., they continue to cry), hold your child and listen lovingly. Refer to "Troubleshooting Tips for Listening" as necessary. You should stay with your child and hold them for as long as it takes for them to either calm down enough to place them back to sleep, or to fall asleep in your arms—*for as long as you can withstand without attempting to stop the crying.* This can be quite confronting for parents, as it feels counterintuitive to listen to our children cry without actively trying to stop them. *If you can remain calm, confident, and strong, the healing process will begin. There can be a fair amount of grief experienced when we take away something that children have become attached to over a period of time, and unburden them of their dependence on us or a particular sleep prop. Progression can be rather rapid and efficient if you can commit to—mostly listening for—at least three nights. If you reach the point of emotional release with your child (crying, screaming, and thrashing), this is where the magic happens. It is through intense emotional release that we can truly recover from hurt and trauma.*

TROUBLESHOOTING TIPS FOR LISTENING

- Listening partnerships and regular self-care is paramount to a parent's ability to remain calm, listen, and support their children appropriately as they navigate change—in any area of their lives. Regular listening time will help parents to heal from their own hurts and emotional triggers, enabling them to be more "available" and present to support their children as necessary through this process. Refer to "The Seven Sleep Foundations: Emotional and Physical Well-Being."

- How long or how intensely your child cries will be dependent on several factors:

  · Associated early trauma.
  · The parent's emotional state and the level of warmth and connection they can bring to their child while listening.
  · The regularity of connection tools in the child's routine (i.e., listening, play, and quality time).
  · How much listening the parents have previously

engaged in with the child—in general and/or with respect to the specific emotional project at hand.
- · The frequency of use of the control pattern to repress emotions, hence the degree of "stored" feelings.
- · How long any habits/patterns have persisted.

Generally (although not always), the longer a habit or sleep pattern has been present, or the more attached the child has become to the action or object that you are removing, the longer it may take to experience change. I have known babies to cry for anywhere between ten and ninety minutes. However, if you persist with this approach over time and continue to listen, validate, and support your child through this difficult time, the length and intensity of crying will decrease as the days progress.

- Maintain eye contact where possible and refrain from offering the pacifier, breast, bottle, lovey, distracting, or changing the environment while listening; this would only serve to inhibit the healing process by stopping the crying. We can only do what we are capable of at the time, so don't be too hard on yourself if you resort to doing this once the crying has become too much, or if you don't have the support you require to proceed with listening.

- You may gently rock, sing, sway, or walk with your child during this process if you feel it will soothe him or her, but avoid rocking, shushing, patting, feeding—or engaging in any action with the intention to stop or repress the crying. Remember, you want to allow your child to heal and recover by freely expressing his or her full spectrum of emotion.

- Warmly validate your child's feelings. For example, "I know this is hard for you darling. You really want milk right now– but I am holding you; you have me. You can have milk next time you wake (or in the morning/tomorrow)."

- For children and who have endured some degree of early trauma (e.g., premature birth, hospitalization, surgery, or illness), using language—while listening—to acknowledge their experience in that early memory can accelerate the (past and present) healing process. For example, for a child who was separated from their mother at birth, reassurance such as; "I am here now sweetie, I won't let anything happen to you again" or; "I won't leave you. You are safe to go to sleep now, I'll be right here" can be effective. *Where there has been early trauma, expect that a child may need to cry harder, and for longer periods over a few days (or more) to lighten the load in their "emotional backpack" with respect to the feelings that this process triggers from the earlier life event(s).*

- If you are withholding milk (either by breast or bottle) and you are unsure whether your child is genuinely hungry or thirsty during this process, offer water or milk in a cup. Know that if you are helping your child meet his or her needs for emotional release (e.g., dependency, loneliness, grief, and desperation), the child will most likely cry harder and angrily reject your offer. Feel confident knowing that he or she has your attention, warmth, and love and that his or her primary needs for hunger, thirst, and closeness have been met.

- If you know that your child is currently teething or unwell —and you have taken appropriate pain relief measures— the listening process can still be effective for alleviating any associated frustration, tension, or pain. Some parents may feel uncomfortable listening to their children during these times—this is okay. In such circumstances, you may choose to listen for a shorter period of time and/or comfort your child—as necessary—until they are settled enough to fall asleep. Use warm words of validation to acknowledge their discomfort such as; "I know it must hurt having your teeth coming through darling, I am here for you, and I love you."

- If you need a break from listening to your child, you can leave the room for a few minutes. Communicate that you will be leaving briefly, that you love them, and that you will be right back. Preferably, ask your spouse or partner to take over from you temporarily.

- Remain as calm as you can for as long as you are able to. Parental frustration and anxiety are counterproductive to instilling calm, confidence, and security in your child at these times. The moment you begin to feel triggered while listening to your child, it may be best to cease listening, or ask someone to take over the listening for you. Despite your best intentions to help your child release and recover from their hurts, your feelings will subconsciously create a disconnect between you and your child—exacerbating insecurity and inhibiting progress.

- If you do not have anyone to take over from you and you are unable to listen any further, let your child know that you are unable to listen anymore right now. Congratulate them on how well they have done. You may proceed with feeding, rocking, holding, or patting to sleep, or offering the pacifier. Let them know you will pick up again the next time they wake overnight, or tomorrow.

- Don't be hard on yourself if you choose the path of least resistance (e.g., by rocking or feeding to sleep when you are unable to continue with listening). Contrary to what we are led to believe through traditional behavioral methods, you will not be "giving in" to your child's demands or creating bad habits in the long term. You do not have to be *consistent* so much as *persistent* with the timing or length of listening.

Emotion overrides behavior, and therefore, any feelings you have supported your child to release (even if just five to ten minutes at a time) is better than nothing and will contribute to an overall difference in his or her ability to overcome the associated control pattern.

- Your child may fall asleep in your arms after crying. This is okay, and you will not be creating a crutch of holding to sleep. Again, any emotion they have been supported to release will contribute to better long-term sleep patterns. You can place your child into their sleep space once they have fallen asleep.

- If your child is crying in their crib/bed but ceases crying the moment you pick them up, then this may indicate that there is nothing physically threatening to them (i.e., they are not in pain or discomfort). In such cases, give them a brief hug and a kiss and reassure them that you love them and that they are safe. Proceed by placing them back in their bed or crib and support them through any emotional release by kneeling or sitting beside them. You can place a hand on, or beside them and use warm words of validation. Avoid your impulse to pick them up or to hold them—unless you are unable to effectively listen anymore. For children who need to be held (rocked or patted) to fall asleep, it is necessary to remove the degree of physical touch in order to elicit an emotional release—and consequently, heal the grief and dependence attached to that need, so that they can transition more efficiently toward independent sleep. Aim for the "sweet spot" between offering some level of comfort (this may simply be your presence and warm reassurance) and encouraging emotional release. *It's the release of feelings that provides the opportunity for your child to move forward and create change.* Trial and error may be necessary for this. If you are unsure, the sweet spot is usually where they become uncomfortable and begin to protest or cry.

- The more that children thrash or the harder they cry, the more intense the feelings are that they are offloading. This is actually a positive sign, as it indicates progress. If at any time you feel you may be injured or you could drop your child during a thrashing episode, calmly place them in the crib, sit beside them, and use reassuring words until you feel you can hold them again.

- If children feel cold and clammy to the touch during a thrashing or crying episode, they are likely to be working on releasing stored and/or momentary fear. If they are hot and sweaty, then the feeling released is most likely to be anger. In both cases, it is reasonable to expect that the child may seek some distance from you. Don't take this personally. Stay close (but not too close) and continue to provide reassurance and warm, loving validation.

- Vomiting can be a emotional reaction for some children, especially where they have experienced early trauma (terror). Although unnerving for parents, this is simply another form of intense emotional release; that when supported appropriately, and with love, can expedite the healing of past and present fears. Ensure that your child—and their clothing and bedding—is clean. Offer as much physical comfort and warm validation as necessary, and proceed with listening when you feel comfortable to do so.

- While some parents may feel that the listening process resembles a "cry it out" approach, *I can guarantee you nothing is farther from the truth.* A cry-it-out, or controlled-crying method, is just that: withholding attention, and controlling your responsiveness on the basis of increments of time—

which actually generates a *stress response*. When children are supported to cry in the loving presence of their parents, crying serves as *stress relief*, enabling children to recover from the emotions and negative patterns that are burdening them and inhibiting their true potential.

- Know that you're not withholding your love, closeness, or intimacy during this process; you're only withholding your child's control pattern—the action that has tampered down their emotions until this current time. Stored emotions have nowhere to go but out—once we remove the very thing that has kept them "in check" (in some cases, for months or years). If you pour in as much love and warmth as you can, your child will feel your presence and attention—and this will allow them to shift their disempowering emotions that have been potentially holding back their confidence—and ability—to sleep well. In the days or weeks to follow, it is not unusual to witness dramatic leaps in developmental, cognitive, and verbal progress—as well as increased confidence and happier overall disposition.

SCHEDULING OVERNIGHT FEEDS
(SIX MONTHS AND OVER)

Most of the time, children who are fed to sleep also wake multiple times per night to be fed back to sleep—in my experience, the average occurrence lies between two and six times per night. Therefore, when breaking a feed-to-sleep pattern, you might also make gradual changes to reduce the number of times your child is fed overnight. Some options to achieve fewer night feeds (for babies six months and older) or night weaning (for babies nine months and older) include the following:

1. Create some mindfulness about how quick you may be to settle your baby overnight. Many babies cry out in their sleep but don't necessarily require parental intervention to fall back to sleep. Some babies may cry or grizzle for five to ten minutes and then fall back to sleep independently. *It is important that you honor children with some space overnight and afford them the chance to self-settle.* Tune into their cries, because if they desperately need your help to fall back to sleep, they won't hold back! You may be able to reduce overnight wakes by 50 percent simply by listening to see if you are really needed before taking action.

Many parents are concerned that allowing their child to cry overnight will wake other family members. Minimize the disturbance to your spouse (or partner) by encouraging him or her to wear earplugs. Even in a room-sharing scenario, children can generally sleep through more noise than we may think. If you are concerned that your crying baby may wake his or her sibling(s), introduce some white noise. For guidelines and recommendations, refer to "The Seven Sleep Foundations: Environment."

2. Keep a log for one to three nights detailing how many times your child is feeding overnight and how long they feed for each time. This can help you discern the nutritive feeds from the comfort feeds. The general rule of thumb assumes that; if your breastfed child is only feeding for five minutes or less, it is more likely to be a comfort or habitual feed rather than nutritive. If your child is feeding for longer than five minutes, you can gradually reduce the time you are feeding by one to two minutes over a week. If your baby is formula fed and is drinking less than 60 ml (2 oz) at any overnight feed, then you can consider eliminating this feed altogether. If your baby is consuming more than 60 ml (2 oz), you may reduce the amount of milk given in the bottle at each overnight feed every one or two nights (e.g., by 20–30 ml/0.5–1 oz, until the last feed given is 60 ml/2 oz). *For most babies between nine and twelve months, overnight feeds will be mostly habitual—or for comfort—rather than nutritive.*

3. Replace comfort feeds with alternate comfort (e.g., cuddles and holding) or listening. You have the option of holding or rocking your baby when they wake (instead of feeding), or if they are crying and upset and unable to be soothed with physical closeness, proceed with listening.

4. Feed every *second* time your child wakes rather than *every* time. Offer alternative comfort such as holding and cuddling when your child wakes outside of feeding times. If your child becomes upset when you refuse to give him or her the breast or bottle—and physical comfort is not enough—proceed with listening; refer to "Troubleshooting Tips for Listening."

5. Space out otherwise-regular overnight feeds. Between four and six months, babies can generally forgo an additional hour between feeds overnight than during the day (e.g., if you are feeding your child four-hourly by day, schedule overnight feeds between four- to five-hourly). For babies who are feeding two-hourly or less overnight (i.e., they are fed upon each wake-up), start by spacing feeds out three-hourly (as a minimum)—for example, after a 7:00 p.m. bedtime, the first feed of the night would be no earlier than 10:00 p.m. Each subsequent feed would then be scheduled no sooner than every three hours. Listen to your child lovingly if, and when he or she wakes outside of scheduled feeding times—or use an alternative source of comfort such as holding, patting, or rocking. If your child is only waking once for a feed, try, if possible, to schedule this feed after 12:00 a.m. and try to gradually extend this later by one hour each week, over a three- to four-week period. Babies who have been accustomed to being fed every time they wake overnight (sometimes as often as every one or two hours) will no doubt have some hard feelings about this change. They will thrash, cry, and scream to communicate they are not happy or are feeling uncomfortable with this. Know that this reaction is normal and in fact essential for long-term progress. The more you can support your child to release this stress and tension (and consequently, feelings of frustration, grief, sadness, and confusion surrounding the change to their routine), the more effective and efficient this process will be. *It is useful to note that most newborns feed every three to four hours around the clock, so beginning on a three-hourly overnight feeding schedule for a child (six months and over) is kind, gentle, and gradual—and won't be expecting too much from your little one when commencing this transition.*

6. Gradually curtail overnight feeds each week by extending the time elapsed between feeds by one hour per week. Increase the intervals between night feeds over a period of three weeks (e.g., **week one**: three-hour intervals; **week two**: four-hour intervals; and **week three**: five-hour intervals). These intervals refer to the time elapsed since the start of the previous feed to the start of the following feed. Resettle if your baby awakens during these intervals by offering an alternative method of comfort such as holding, gentle rocking—or listening.

7. Substitute breastfeeding with an alternative source of nutrition or hydration (e.g., formula, water, or milk). This can help you differentiate hunger from comfort. Many children breastfeed regularly overnight to keep stored feelings under control, not because they are hungry. Therefore, children will most likely refuse a bottle or cup (unless of course they are genuinely hungry or thirsty). *Cow's milk should be avoided for infants under twelve months. Water should not be introduced earlier than four to six months.*

8. If you are feeding your child every time they wake overnight, try fading out feeds gradually over a week. For example, **night one**: introduce a dream feed three to four hours after bedtime and avoid feeding your child if they wake before the dream feed. Feed your child each time they wake after the dream feed. **Night two**: resettle the first time your child wakes after the dream feed. Feed upon any consecutive waking(s). **Night three**: resettle for the first two wakes following the dream feed and feed upon any consecutive waking(s). **Night four**: resettle for the initial three wakes following the dream feed, feed upon any consecutive waking(s), and so on. The intention is to slowly schedule overnight feeds later and later, until the last feed you are doing is at 5:00 a.m. Once children are capable of sleeping through continually for one week, you can wean them from the dream feed completely—either by feeding them less at the dream feed over a few nights or scheduling the time of the dream feed *earlier* by thirty minutes over three nights.

9. Gradually replace feeds with listening or alternative comfort such as rocking, holding, or patting. For example, **night one**: resettle your child the first time they wake (e.g., 10:00 p.m.) and feed every other time thereafter. **Night two**: hopefully they will wake a little later (e.g., 11:00 p.m.)—so continue to resettle for the first wake and feed upon every other waking thereafter, and so on.

10. Use the "core night method." Once your child has demonstrated that he or she can sleep for a certain length of time throughout the night (e.g., 10:30 p.m. to 3:00 a.m.), and does so for three to seven nights consecutively, you will no longer feed him or her during this span of time. Ideally this method should be considered when your child is still waking in the night looking for a feed but only feeding for a short time and/or refusing the milk feed upon waking for the day.

Ensure that your child has received an adequate milk feed before sleep times so you can be assured that they are not waking hungry. The age of your child must be considered when deciding what is "fair and reasonable" for scheduling overnight feeds. Most babies from six months of age are capable of sleeping through the night with between one to two feeds (spaced four to five hours apart). In consideration of growth spurts, night weaning is easier and more sustainable after nine months.

At any age, your child should always be feeding more during the day than overnight. Most babies who are fed to sleep are often fed back to sleep multiple times per night, resulting in more milk consumption overnight rather than during the day. A gradual approach to reducing night feeds ensures the transfer of feeds from night into day to restore this balance and ensures you are not elimi-

nating feeds completely (most important for babies under twelve months). Gradually reducing overnight feeds can also prevent potential onset of mastitis, or uncomfortable engorged breasts.

RECOMMENDED TRANSITION FROM COSLEEPING* (AND FEEDING, ROCKING, HOLDING, OR PATTING TO SLEEP) TO INDEPENDENT SLEEP

Cosleeping can be a mutually rewarding, bonding, nurturing, and loving experience for both parent and child. However, for many parents, cosleeping is a last desperate attempt to clutch at whatever sleep they can, having felt as though they have exhausted all other options.

Cosleeping and feeding to sleep, or "breast sleeping," are almost always synonymous. Rare is the family I have worked with who are only cosleeping in the absence of feeding to sleep—or feeding regularly overnight—unless in the case of an older child who has previously been weaned from the breastfeeding or child who is formula fed. And, if it's not feeding to sleep, then it will most likely be that the child relies on parental presence—or intervention of some description—to fall asleep, and remain asleep.

This process may also be applicable if you are feeding, rocking, patting, holding —or lying with— your child until they fall asleep and wish to transition them from either (a) bassinet to crib; (b) crib to bed and/or; (c) their own room—i.e., not necessarily cosleeping.

The decision to end your cosleeping journey is entirely personal. However, when the difficulties of sleeping together outweigh the advantages, you may consider moving your child to his or her own crib or bed.

Below is my step-by-step recommendation for slowly transitioning children toward independent sleep—moving them out of the family bed and into their own sleep space, and encouraging them to self-settle without the reliance on breastfeeding or parental intervention such as rocking, holding, patting, or lying beside the child to help them sleep.

This is a gradual approach, with an average timeline of three to ten days—dependent on how quickly you wish to progress through the steps. I have also included some options for parents who wish to speed up, or slow down, this process.

Prior to making this transition, follow the steps outlined in "Preparing for Change" and "When You Are Ready to Start."

Days One to Three

Transition your child into their crib/bed for day naps.

- Incorporate crib/bed play (outlined in "Preparing for Change") for a few days beforehand and continue this for one to two weeks.
- If your child is already sleeping in their own crib/bed and/or room for day naps, but overnight you are cosleeping, proceed to "Nights Four to Six."
- If you are also feeding, rocking, patting, holding—or lying with—your child until they fall asleep, continue to do so as per normal.

Option A: Crib/bed in the child's own room.

Option B: Crib or mattress positioned beside parents' bed.

Nights One to Three

Continue to cosleep, and feed/rock/hold/pat/lie with your child until he or she falls asleep.

Be mindful about *how often* your child is waking overnight, and *how you are responding each time*—this is the key to your progress. Where possible, aim to schedule feeds at a minimum of three- to four-hourly—or at least attempt to feed every second time your child wakes, rather than each time. Offer cuddles in between overnight feeds to help your child settle. When cosleeping, keep in mind that the biggest challenge can often be observing the time as well as remembering to wake up to settle at every second feed. This may be especially demanding if you are accustomed to placing the breast in your child's mouth each time he or she stirs overnight. Try to tune into your child's cries overnight. He or she may still be asleep, in which case a feed or cuddle may not even be necessary! *Refer to "Scheduling Overnight Feeds (Six Months and Over)."*

Option: Proceed to "Nights Four to Six."

Days Four to Six

Transition your child into their own crib/bed and room (if you haven't done so already).
Continue to feed, rock, hold, pat, or lie with your child until they fall asleep.

Nights Four to Six

Transition your child into their own crib/bed and room.

- Continue to feed/rock/hold/pat/lie with your child until they fall asleep.
- Proceed with spacing out overnight feeds. Refer to options in "Scheduling Overnight Feeds (Six Months and Over)."

Option A: Crib or mattress positioned beside parents' bed.

Option B: You may sleep on a mattress in your child's room and either cosleep with him or her on the mattress or have your child sleep in their crib/bed with you on the mattress. You will proceed to sleep the whole night with your child in his or her room.

Days Seven to Nine

- Continue to sleep your child in their own room.
- Continue to feed, rock, hold, pat, or lie with your child until they fall asleep.

Option: Cease the feed—or hold/rock/pat/lie-to-sleep association for nap time(s). Refer to step 6 in "When You Are Ready to Start" and "Troubleshooting Tips for Listening" as necessary.

Nights Seven to Nine

Cease the feed—or hold/rock/pat/lie-to-sleep association for bedtime.

- Revisit step 6 in "When You Are Ready to Start" and "Troubleshooting Tips for Listening" as necessary.
- For scheduling overnight feeds, refer to options in "Scheduling Overnight Feeds (Six Months and Over)."

If your child has been sleeping in a crib or on a mattress in the parent's bedroom until now, proceed with option (b) as per "Nights Four to Six."

If you have been sleeping on a mattress in your child's room for nights four to six, you may sleep on the mattress *only* until he or she falls asleep (i.e., at the start of bedtime), and you may resume your position on the mattress when your child wakes overnight if your intervention is required. You will return to your own bed once your child is asleep. If you have been cosleeping on the mattress with your child from nights four to six, then from nights seven to nine, you may sleep on the mattress, and your child can sleep in their crib or bed; in such instance, you can sleep positioned next to the child for the entirety of the night.

Days Ten to Twelve

If you have been able to successfully wean your child from their associated sleep need for nights, use the same process to cease this pattern for day naps—if you haven't already organically done this.

Option: If your child is having more than one nap, you can break the associated sleep pattern one nap at a time, if you would prefer not to tackle both simultaneously.

Nights Ten to Twelve

Continue as per nights seven to nine.

If you have been sleeping on the mattress in your child's room for nights four to nine, you will now need to remove the mattress from his or her room. If your child still needs you to fall asleep at bedtime, then you may kneel on the floor or sit on a chair next to their crib/bed and provide loving validation: "You are safe. I love you; I am right here for you. I will stay with you until you fall asleep." Try to minimize the degree of touch. A hand resting beside the child (on the mattress) or a firm hand on his or her back or bottom until they become drowsy is sufficient. If you are using touch to help your child fall asleep, do so a little less over a three-day period, until the child is self-settling—revisit step 6 in "When You Are Ready to Start" and "Troubleshooting Tips for Listening" as necessary.

Days Thirteen to Fifteen

By this stage, your child will hopefully be falling asleep independently, and in his or her own sleep space—for day naps at least. If you are still having trouble with this, revisit steps in "When You Are Ready to Start" and repeat as necessary.

Nights Thirteen to Fifteen

Ideally, you will have removed yourself from your child's room, and they will be capable of self-settling at bedtimes. If they still need a little help, you have the option of employing check-ins: instead of kneeling beside their crib or bed to help them fall asleep, tuck them in, let them know that they are safe, and that you love them. Then say, "I just need to go and brush my teeth [or any other activity]. I will be back in two minutes to check on you/tuck you in/give you another cuddle-and-kiss good-night." If your child starts to cry or protest as you make to leave, proceed with step 8 to 12 in "When You Are Ready to Start" and repeat steps as necessary.

If your child remains relatively settled, leave the room, and return in two minutes, as promised. If they are still awake when you return, tuck them in again, give them a kiss good-night, remind them that it is time for sleep, and let them know you will be back again soon if they need you. If they remain settled, you may increase the check-in intervals by one to two minutes. Repeat this process until your child falls asleep.

> **Note:** In my experience, long-term improvements with sleep patterns occur more steadily once children are sleeping in their own room. If you wish to continue to cosleep while breaking a feed-to-sleep (or other) association, follow the appropriate steps as per "Preparing for Change," "When You Are Ready to Start," and "Scheduling Overnight Feeds (Six Months and Over)."

This process is most successful when used for babies six months and over. I recommend considering the timing of this transition if your baby was born prematurely, had a traumatic birth experience, has digestion issues, is underweight, or suffered early trauma. In these cases, he or she may benefit from the reassurance of a few more months of sleeping next to you.

SECTION VI
MANAGING TRANSITIONS

Irrespective of the timing or scale of the transition—or the age of your child, connection is key when helping children adapt with greater ease and cooperation. By implementing the connection tools into your daily routine (as outlined in the "Seven Sleep Foundations: Emotional and Physical Well-Being") you will be establishing a solid foundation of trust and safety to ensure a smoother process for the whole family.

In preparation for any transition, refer to "The Sleep Play Love Method: Preparing for Change, steps 1–10."

COMMENCING CHILDCARE

Because this transition usually coincides with parents returning to work, it can be an emotional and exhausting time for the family unit. The overall change to a child's routine, environment, and carers—not to mention the increase in stimulation—can lead to the onset of sleep regression and behavioral challenges.

Tips for a Smooth Transition

- **Choose a childcare facility with caregivers who you feel confident and comfortable with,** as well as the center's philosophy, reputation, staff-to-child ratio, and overall "feel."

- **Attend an orientation.** This is a great way for you to witness the interaction between your child and their carer(s)—and with the other children.

- **Be specific with your child's routine, diet, and special**

needs so that the center can maintain some consistency to what your child is accustomed to at home.

- **If your chosen childcare has specified nap times (and these are within your child's age-appropriate awake windows), try adjusting your routine at home to reflect this for consistency.** If you are aware of the schedule before commencing, try implementing these routine changes at home in advance.

- **Take your child's creature comforts and sleep associations with you:** sleeping bag, swaddle, lovey, pacifier, milk bottle, blanket, and water bottle. A family photo may also help ease the pain of separation at times when your child may be missing you.

- **Make allowances for your child to be emotional and overtired, and for sleep to regress temporarily.** An earlier bedtime between 6:00 p.m. and 6:30 p.m. may be necessary while your child adjusts. Try not to plan any extracurricular activities on child-care days and avoid long trips or holidays within the first month.

- **Overcome any sleep habits prior to starting childcare.** That is, anything the staff will be unable to replicate, such as feeding or rocking to sleep; refer to "The Sleep Play Love Method."

- **Ask your center to keep a log of your child's daily activities:** water consumption, sleep times, food intake, physical play, and emotional state. This can help with determining the root cause and potential solution if sleep is disrupted at home.

- **Ensure that the staff responsible for looking after your** child are aware of any specific parenting practices that you adopt at home. For example, any words, actions, or activities that help to calm your child when he or she is upset or distressed.

- **Connect.** Quality one-on-one time is particularly effective when done before *and* after childcare. Anywhere between five to twenty minutes in the morning before your child leaves for the day can work wonders to help ease the child's fears around the impending separation. Another five to twenty minutes when your child returns home in the afternoon is beneficial to help them to recover and heal from any unreleased upsets during their time away from you— and often contributes toward better sleep.

- **Incorporate some roughhousing play before bed.** Vigorous and spontaneous play is especially effective at the end of the day to release any residual physical or emotional stress or tension that may otherwise present as nightmares and disturbed sleep. Don't be surprised if laughter turns to tears—this is all a part of the process! Be prepared to listen lovingly as necessary.

- **Be patient.** Depending on your child's temperament, it may take some time for them to bond with his or her new caregivers and peers, and adjust to a new routine away from home and away from you.

- **Attachment bridging, connection, and honest communication in advance are key.** Refer to tips for dealing with separation anxiety in "Common Sleep Difficulties and Solutions: Separation Anxiety."

NIGHT WEANING

Many professionals claim that a baby is physiologically "ready" to sleep through the night without feeds from six months of age. Professionally, I find that this largely depends on the children—their current health, weight, developmental stage, whether they are breastfed or formula fed, if they were born premature, if solids have been well established, and if they are consuming adequate milk and solids in their waking hours to accommodate for night weaning. It also very much depends on you—the parent. There are no hard-and-fast rules with when or how to wean; if it's not a problem for you, it's not a problem!

While it is extremely natural and developmentally "normal" for a child of six months and beyond to still have one or more milk feeds overnight—and this can be an extremely bonding and nurturing experience between parent and child—habitual night waking to feed for comfort (or to help a child link sleep cycles) can take its toll on the whole family. Sleep deprivation can lead to deterioration of physical and mental health, relationship breakdowns, and depression. It's usually under these circumstances that I recommend parents assess their options for scheduling fewer night feeds, or eliminating feeds altogether—especially if no one in the family is getting the sleep that they need. Although feed-related sleep difficulties are more prevalent in breastfed babies, it can also affect formula-fed babies.

Average Number of Night Feeds by Age

Birth to three months: feed every two to three hours, on demand.
Three to four months: two to three feeds per night or every three to six hours, on demand.
Five to six months: one to two night feeds.
Seven to nine months: one or maybe two night feeds.
Ten to twelve months: sometimes one feed overnight.
Twelve months and over: generally no feeds.

The above is only an average. Irrespective of age, some children may require additional feeds during growth spurts, or at times of illness, teething, or developmental milestones—where daytime feeds are inadequate from loss of appetite, distraction, and/or discomfort. Premature babies may also have additional feeding needs up to twelve months and beyond.

How Do I Know When My Child May Be Ready to Night Wean?

- Your child is at least six months or older and solids have been well established.
- Your child was not premature and is not underweight.
- Night feeds are habitual or for comfort rather than nutritive —that is, your child breastfeeds for less than five minutes or consumes less than 60 ml (2 oz) of formula and falls straight back to sleep.
- There is no pattern to overnight feeds—that is, the number of wakes and times can vary from one night to the next.
- Your child is feeding more overnight than during the day.

- Regular night feedings are draining mom's energy and the overall enjoyment of feeding—and/or parenthood.
- Your child has previously been able to sleep through without feeds and/or has slept through with only a dream feed for a period of three or more days in a row, and this is not related to illness or teething.
- Your child is feeding once overnight (e.g., between 3:00 a.m. and 4:00 a.m.) and regularly refuses his or her morning feed.

At six months of age, you can expect a growth spurt, a developmental leap, and changes in overnight sleep patterns. While you may attempt to night wean your child from this age, the outcome may be dependent on factors outside of your control. I recommend waiting until closer to ten months before making this transition—this also accommodates for any regression at the mercy of the nine-month growth spurt.

The most effective way for you and your family to approach this transition will be dependent on the age of your child and the frequency of overnight feeds. A gradual process is recommended both from an emotional well-being perspective and to avoid such health problems as mastitis and painful engorged breasts due to cutting out too many feeds, or too quickly.

Preparing to Night Wean

Follow the recommendations as per The Sleep Play Love Method in "Preparing for Change" and "When You Are Ready to Start" prior to undertaking this transition. Refer to "Scheduling Overnight Feeds (Six Months and Over)" for options when commencing the weaning process.

Tips for Cosleeping Families

- **If you are breastfeeding, change your sleeping arrangements temporarily.** Create a distance between your child and yourself in the bed (e.g., have dad sleep beside him or her, place a lovey between you, or sleep on a mattress).

- **Shorten the nighttime feeds** by reducing formula amount, the length of breastfeeding time, and/or removing the milk before your child falls back to sleep.

- **Stop feeding a sleeping baby.** Don't breastfeed or offer the bottle every time your baby stirs overnight. It is natural for babies to cry out in their sleep multiple times a night—so wait until they are in fact awake and calling out for you before feeding.

Something to Consider Before Weaning

There are many benefits to feeding overnight. In addition to melatonin, evening and nighttime breast milk is rich with other sleep-inducing and brain-boosting amino acids (breast milk varies in its composition during the day when compared to at night). Overnight feeds also promote milk supply and may encourage the development of your baby's circadian rhythm in the first three months of life.

WEANING FROM BREASTFEEDING

Some babies may wean themselves from the breast on their own after they begin consuming solids between four and six months. If you are considering weaning your child *under* the age of twelve months, it is recommended that breast milk be substituted for formula until they turn one, as this will remain their main source of nutrition. From twelve months, some babies are more interested in solid food than breast milk or formula—after they have tried a variety of foods and can competently drink from a cup. At this age, children may be weaned safely from breastfeeding or formula—with the option of weaning completely or offering a milk alternative.

The weaning process may be more challenging when the decision is instigated by the parent, and this can be a particularly emotive transition—for both parent and child alike—irrespective of the child's age. There can be many reasons a mother may choose to end her breast-feeding journey. Some of these include pregnancy, returning to work, exhaustion, low milk supply, lack of enjoyment in feeding, and/or resentment because a child is habitually feeding on demand all day and night. Parents may also decide to wean their older child (e.g., two years and older) after a mutually rewarding breastfeeding relationship because they feel that it is "time." It may take some delicate planning and support to make this transition respectfully with the emotional well-being of parent and child of utmost importance.

Tips for a Smooth Transition (Parent-Led Weaning)

- **Plan ahead.** Ensure you have an appropriate support network in place, your child is in good health, and be prepared for some big feelings to surface—both for you and your child. *Follow the appropriate steps in "The Sleep Play Love Method: Preparing for Change."*

- **Avoid other transitions and choose your timing wisely.** Do not attempt to wean your child if he or she is already experiencing other major milestones, transitions, or change such as separation anxiety, potty training, a new sibling, or starting childcare. Similarly, you may have more success with this process if you wait out any developmental change such as learning to walk or teething. Such transitions increase a child's vulnerability and heightens his or her sense of insecurity—so focus on one change at a time.

- **Communicate your (weaning) intentions with your child.** Let him or her know that your breastfeeding journey has come to an end; when you will be making this change, how things will be different for them, and whether you decide to replace the breast with anything else such as cuddles, the bottle, or a milk alternative.

- **Keep a feeding log** of the times and length of breastfeeds during the day (and overnight if applicable) to discern comfort feeds from nutritive feeds. Usually, feeds that are less than five minutes in duration are considered to be for comfort (and/or habit) and, therefore, may potentially be eliminated without reducing the time of the feed any further. If your child is twelve months or over, and feeding for ten minutes or longer at any one feed, you may gradually reduce the feeding time by one to two minutes each day. *Demand feeding children (six months and older) during the day often promotes the cycle of demand feeding overnight—owing to inadequate consumption of solid food (and habit).*

- **Be mindful of *when* you feed your child during the day.** Most often breastfeeding becomes a control pattern, and children will seek out the breast when they are bored, upset, in pain, feeling off track, or frightened. Try to avoid feeding your child if they are not hungry, as this can lead to repression of feelings and a host of behavioral difficulties. Instead, tune into what your child is attempting to communicate to you: Do they have a genuine hunger? And if so, can this be better satisfied with a healthy meal or snack rather than the breast? Are they perhaps thirsty? Do they need a cuddle? A change in scenery? Connection? *When feeding has been used habitually to store uncomfortable feelings over time, withholding the breast when your child is seeking comfort may be met with much resistance. Expect erratic (and potentially aggressive) behavior—thrashing, hitting, screaming, crying, and trembling—as your child attempts to heal from the associated addiction and dependence. Be prepared to set some warm, yet firm, limits and listen lovingly. Refer to "The Sleep Play Love Method: Troubleshooting Tips for Listening."*

- **Adhere to the average number of feeds per age** as per "Routines and Recommendations" to ensure that your child under twelve months is consuming the recommended amount of milk per twenty-four hours.

- **Offer a substitute** for the breast or bottle. If your child is under twelve months, you may replace breast milk with formula. If your child is twelve months and over, try cow's milk or nondairy alternative.

- **It may be useful to focus on breaking any feed-to-sleep association or comfort-feeding pattern before weaning completely.** Follow the appropriate steps as outlined in step 6 in "The Sleep Play Love Method."

- **Focus on scheduling overnight feeds further apart over a period of a week or more before weaning completely for days too.** Refer to the options in "The Sleep Play Love Method: Scheduling Overnight Feeds (Six Months and Over)." Focus on night weaning completely before ceasing all day feeds.

- **Establish connection and safety.** For many children, breastfeeding is a primal source of comfort, safety, and connection. Continuing to offer this closeness in other ways will help ensure that your child does not feel rejected. Quality one-on-one time, building laughter through play, and listening are valuable tools to assist your child through this process. Refer to connection tools as detailed in "The Seven Sleep Foundations: Emotional and Physical Well-Being."

- **For older children (i.e., two years and older), do something special to celebrate this milestone.** Ideas include taking them for their "last feed" in a special place, cooking them their favorite meal or treat, or spending some quality time together to mark the end of your bonding breastfeeding journey.

- **Gradual is key.** Begin by cutting out just one (day) feed every three to seven days (or whatever you feel most comfortable with). This will give your child (and your breasts) time to adjust to the change in feeding schedule— helping you to avoid potential blocked ducts or infection.

INTRODUCING A NEW SIBLING

Introducing a new baby to the family can be a major transition for everyone. With the sudden shift in family dynamics, parent's attention, and the shake-up to day-to-day life, it's no wonder many older children struggle with feelings of insecurity, grief, sadness, anger, frustration, confusion, hurt, and loss. And, for us, to witness such struggles for our children can also be one of the biggest challenges we face throughout our parenting journey.

At these times, increased behavioral issues, sleep- and potty-regression can be common. Tantrums, crying, aggression (toward the baby or a parent), resistance, and defiance are just a child's way of trying to connect, gain attention, and express his or her mixed feelings surrounding the change. While it can all seem too difficult at times, there are some simple things that you can do to guide your child through this transition as smoothly as possible.

Tips for a Smooth Transition

- **Prepare your child for the change.** Toddler-friendly books such as *My New Baby* and *Hello Baby* can be an effective way to prepare children for the arrival of a new sibling.

- **Role-playing** with dolls, talking about the birth process, and encouraging children to communicate and express any big feelings that they have can make them feel more comfortable with the impending change.

- **Establish a "connection plan."** With all the pouring over a newborn baby from family and friends, it is only natural that older children will feel some degree of disconnect. The outcome is often undesired "button-pushing" behavior for—positive or negative—attention. Plan to allocate *at least* thirty minutes per day for connection time with your older children (i.e., play, listening, and quality one-on-one time). This could be thirty to sixty minutes spent together while the baby is napping, or a block of ten to fifteen minutes throughout the day. Each day may look very different, and this is okay. Where possible, schedule this time in your diary as you would any other appointment. Remember this: as you invest in your child's "emotional bank account", ultimately your child will feel more secure and loved—consequently alleviating the off track (and insanity-provoking!) behavior that arises from lack of connection time.

- **Quality one-on-one time.** Aim for at least ten to twenty minutes of quality time per day where you can be truly present. Let your child choose the activity; use plenty of eye contact, physical play, hugs, and kisses to remind your child that he or she is still very loved and special to you. Encouraging laughter through play and listening during these special moments will allow them to feel safe and connected enough to release any fears or insecurities he or she may be harboring with this transition. Your older child may desire to be treated like a baby again (e.g., wanting to have a pacifier, lovey, breast/milk, wear a diaper, be worn in a carrier, or sleep in a crib). Indulging these requests—where you feel comfortable and appropriate—during quality time (i.e., role-playing that they are a baby) can help your child adapt to the role of big brother/sister with greater cooperation.

- **Validate their emotions.** Often all that our children desire is to feel heard and understood. Acknowledging our children's emotions (whether positive or negative) helps them to normalize certain feelings without shame or judgment. For example, "I know being a big brother/sister can be hard sometimes. It's normal to feel upset. Mommy and Daddy love you very much."

- **Set firm, loving limits.** Children feel more secure and confident when they know that they can expect consistency with our responses and reactions, with obvious "no-go zones," including physical harm (or the threat of). Off-track behavior and subsequent "broken thinking" results from a broken connection. What children need more than anything at these times is their parent's love and attention to restore their confidence and security. *Setting limits often leads to emotional release, so this is a perfect opportunity to pour in your love and warmth and listen. This enables your child to effectively recover from any big feelings—past or present—triggered by such a significant life transition.*

- **Support tears and tantrums.** Your child is no doubt feeling an uncomfortable mix of emotions: grief, sadness, confusion, and anger—much of this attributed to the loss of their parent's attention, which they have now been forced to share with a new baby. Many of these feelings will be expressed through tantrums, screaming, limit-testing behavior, and aggression toward a parent or the baby. It is important that we provide a safe, judgment-free space to encourage healthy expression without shame, punishment, or blame. Offering regular cuddles and telling your child often that you love them can help them feel more confident and secure and help to minimize off-track behavior.

- **Create a safe space.** Establish a safe space in your house where your older child can be free to explore, play, and be away from the baby. This is one less thing that they are expected to "share" with their sibling and can be their go-to haven when they feel like jumping, being loud, or making a mess—where they are not at risk of hurting the baby or being scolded by a frustrated parent. Equally important is having a safe space for the baby, which is away from the prying hands of older siblings—such as a playpen, crib, or bassinet.

- **Maintain a regular routine.** A regular day-and-night routine (including awake times, mealtimes, nap times, wind-down time, and bedtime) helps children to feel more confident and safe. If your older child is having adequate night sleep and day rest, they will be more capable of managing their impulses. Tantrums, limit-testing behavior, and aggression commonly escalate when children are overtired, hungry, or dehydrated. If your older child is no longer napping, ensure that they (at very least) have stimulation-free downtime during the day (e.g., quiet play in their bedroom, reading books, or puzzles). Maintaining blood sugar levels with regular healthy meals and snacks and hydrating with plenty of water throughout the day can also do wonders for balancing moods—refer to "The Seven Sleep Foundations: Nutrition."

- **Avoid other transitions.** Adjusting to the role of big brother or sister is one of the biggest transitions our children will experience. Keeping everything else in their lives as steady and predictable as possible will help them adapt with greater ease and cooperation. This is not the time to begin potty training, moving them into a big-kid bed, night weaning, increasing childcare days, weaning from the pacifier/bottle/breast/lovey, or sleep training. Try to make these changes at least two to three months either side of the arrival of a new baby and keep in mind that; during times of insecurity, your child will rely more heavily on their comfort source. This serves as a reminder to be patient, accepting, and loving toward our children's "vices"—which, in all fairness to them, we are responsible for creating. *For tips on transitioning your child to independent sleep and removing their reliance on various sleep needs, habits, or control patterns, refer to "The Sleep Play Love Method."*

- **Don't expect too much.** When you have a new, tiny, dependent baby, it is easy to forget that our older children— albeit enormous by comparison—are also still somewhat babies. Many of us subconsciously place expectations on them to cope, adjust, "grow up," or accept new responsibilities prematurely. The sudden change in family dynamic can be a difficult adjustment for many children, so exercising patience, love, and compassion—without expectation—can make for a happier transition and experience for everyone.

- **Include your child as you go about your day.** Including your child in the day-to-day routine care for a newborn (e.g., fetching diapers and books) and chores around the house is one way to make him or her feel loved and important. It may backfire with a defiant "no" at times, but provided that there is no expectation, you will be empowering your child to make his or her own decisions with respect to their level of involvement.

- **Encourage independent play.** Encouraging children to play independently in a safe place is integral to their development, confidence, and security. Focus on simply observing your child play. Try not to interrupt them while they are concentrating on a task, or by being too quick to jump in and "fix" their problems when they become frustrated—this can deprive them of vital learning opportunities. Your presence and availability is enough. Trust in your children's choice of activity and their ability to problem solve without your intervention. *Accepting your child's struggles and frustrations as they arise throughout the day by listening can encourage these feelings to be released momentarily, instead of accumulating—which may otherwise escalate to behavioral and sleep difficulties.*

- **Be prepared for any "honeymoon period" to end.** Even if an older child has provided the most loving reception toward their younger sibling, understand that the honeymoon phase most commonly ends around the three-month mark. This is when many children experience the epiphany that their baby brother/sister is here to stay and not just a temporary novelty. Parents who know this can prepare with extra quality time and support from loved ones.

POTTY TRAINING

Learning to use the toilet is a process that takes time. Rather than push or manipulate your child by giving him treats such as candy or a special reward for something that he will learn to do on his own, trust that he will learn when he is ready. Respect is based on trust.

—Magda Gerber

Similarly, with other milestones such as crawling, walking, and talking, children will learn to use the toilet at their own individual pace (commonly between the ages of eighteen months to three years). There are three aspects of children's development that we must take into consideration before assessing their readiness for potty training;

Cognitive readiness: Children's understanding of the (parents') expectations of them with respect to using the toilet.

Physical readiness: Children's body awareness (i.e., knowing when they need to go to the toilet, being able to physically hold off going to the toilet, and being able to pull their own pants up and down).

Emotional readiness: Children's willingness to let go of the comfort of using a diaper (which has been their trusted toilet until this time), and to part with their bodily functions (which they still perceive as being inseparable from their bodies).

Signs That May Indicate Your Child's Readiness

- He or she shows an interest in going to the toilet with you, or sitting on the potty.
- He or she can tell you when they have done a pee or poop in their diaper.
- He or she is competent in taking their own pants off.
- He or she dislikes being in their diaper and/or continue to take their diaper off.
- He or she regularly wakes up in the morning with a dry diaper.
- He or she demonstrates an increased awareness of bodily functions (e.g., will hide or reside to a "favorite spot" to do a poop).

Tips for a Smooth Transition

- **Attempt to remain neutral with both expression and language when changing your children's diaper.** Refrain from commenting on the smell or appearance or saying things like "Ewww" or "Yucky poo." Despite our best intentions (usually to make our child laugh), this can subconsciously instill embarrassment, insecurity, and shame around the toileting process, making this transition more challenging.

- **Children's books** such as *The Potty Book* can help ease children into this transition.

- **If the process seems overwhelming, begin with one hour of dedicated "diaper-free time" per day.** Choose a time each day where you can engage the help of your spouse, and/or are least likely to be stressed or distracted with household chores or family commitments. You can gradually increase increments of time as necessary over a few weeks or more.

- **Where possible, start in the warmer months** so that children can run around comfortably without clothes or a diaper on—making the toileting process easier.

- **Let your child choose their own underwear.** This can be empowering for children and help them feel a part of the process.

- **Let your child come with you when you go to the toilet** so that poop or pee is normalized, not "taboo."

- **Floating toilet targets** are available online for boys and girls and can create some fun—converting toilet time into "target practice."

- **Avoid punishments or time-outs for accidents.** A gentle reminder that your child is to use the potty or the toilet works just fine.

- **A potty may be a smoother transition to begin with —rather than a toilet seat**, as this can be overwhelming for little children who may be afraid of "falling in"!

- **Help your children decorate their potty** with stickers or paint.

- **Attune to your children's cues.** If you notice that your child appears as though they need to go to the toilet (e.g., holding themselves or legs together or a "suspect/funny face"), you might say, "It looks like you need to go to the toilet. Do you want me to help you?"

- **Refrain from using extrinsic motivation tools such as rewards, manipulation, and bribes.** This process is best trusted to the children and their individual readiness, and most children will be responsive when we provide a relaxed and supportive presence.

- **Offer plenty of positive reinforcement and encouragement when children are successful at using the potty or toilet.** Hugs, high fives, singing, and dancing are a great way to celebrate this milestone of independence.

- **Offer children the option of using the toilet or potty instead of wearing a diaper**—if, and when your child resists having their diaper changed.

- **Encourage children to use the toilet before the bath, when they wake up in the morning (and from naps), and at bedtimes.** These are common times that children will need to use the bathroom.

- **Ensure children have access to a potty in the lounge room or play area.** This will encourage your child to experiment unprompted and in their own time—without pressure or expectation.

- **Don't force the process.** Trust that your child will be ready to tackle this transition in their own time. The more we try to control, the more likely that children will experience regression or feel like a failure if they have an accident.

- **Role-playing can be an effective way to dispel any fears surrounding this transition.** For example, using reverse psychology (or role reversal), begin jumping around the room holding your crutch or bottom. With desperation in your voice, say "I really, really need to pee/poop—help!" Allow your child to assume the upper hand by guiding you to where the toilet is. When you get there, act as if you are afraid to use it—for example, "Oh no, I don't want to go in there!" You can continue to jump around and play with this idea for as long as it takes to create some laughter. This can be really empowering for children and work wonders to propel them forward by creating safety and increased confidence.

INTRODUCING THE BOTTLE

Whether you wish to introduce a bottle to give mom some flexibility or decide to introduce formula feeds, the following suggestions may help.

To Continue Breastfeeding

- **Wait until your baby is at least one month old and breastfeeding has been well established.** This can help to avoid nipple confusion.

- **To maintain the breastfeed, use a breast pump at the time you feed your baby the bottle.** Breastfeeding works on supply and demand; therefore, any feed you discontinue will compromise your supply.

- **Get someone else to do the feed.** Babies will be more inclined to feed from the bottle (and from someone else) if they can't smell or see their mom.

- **If you are replacing feeds with formula, or weaning from breastfeeding to formula feeding, you might need to express your milk sometimes to prevent engorgement or mastitis.** Express just enough for comfort —if you express too much, you will stimulate an increase in supply.

Tips for a Smooth Transition

- **Validate your child's frustrations, confusion, and disappointment** that may arise with this transition. Offer your love and be prepared to listen to some tears in the process.

- **Try a few different bottle and nipple types.** Some babies prefer nipples that most closely resemble the shape of their mom's nipple.

- **Slow-flow nipples are recommended** to begin with.

- **If your baby takes to a pacifier, you might try to select a nipple with a similar shape** to that of the pacifier.

- **Express some breast milk** on the nipple.

- **Experiment** with different milk temperatures.

- **Try different holding positions.** Again, it is best if mom isn't the one doing this!

- **Offer the bottle when it is milk time**, when your baby is hungry.

- **Let your baby hold and play with the bottle during the day.** Allow your baby to suck on the nipple and play with it in his or her mouth.

- **The age of your baby will determine whether to replace the breastfeeds with infant formula, cow's milk, or milk alternative.** Babies younger than twelve months shouldn't be offered cow's milk, so they must be either fed expressed breastmilk or formula.

TRANSITIONING OUT OF THE SWADDLE

Swaddling is a safe and effective way to respect your baby's need for a fourth trimester in the first three months. Wrapping a baby encourages security and warmth, and effectively switches on his or her "calming reflex." Swaddling may also encourage sounder, longer sleep as it helps to muffle a child's Moro reflex—preventing him or her from startling themselves awake mid-sleep-cycle.

Many parents attest that their "stubborn," "spirited," or "strong-willed" baby continually breaks free from the swaddle, or demonstrates a keen dislike of being wrapped. Before discounting swaddling altogether, I recommend trying either a Love to Dream (zip-up swaddle) or the Baby Loves Sleep Koala Hugs wrap (with hidden arm pockets). Both swaddles are made with stretch fabric, enabling baby's arms to be positioned up for more flexible movement—as opposed to the traditional "strait jacket" style. This can be especially soothing for young babies, considering that many of them have been accustomed to having their hands up beside their face in the womb. In addition, the zip-up/pocket feature helps to keep babies' arms contained, preventing the all-too-common Houdini-style breakouts.

Signs That May Indicate Readiness

- Your baby has started rolling and attempts to roll swaddled.

- Your baby continually breaks out of the swaddle (may also
  be solved by a better wrapping technique or by using a zip-
  up swaddle instead of a wrap).

- Your baby regularly fights the swaddle. *Remember, an overtired
  or overstimulated baby will naturally resist being swaddled.
  However, in many cases, it may help to calm the baby's overactive
  nervous system and promotes longer, sounder sleep.*

- Your baby is between three and four months, has lost his or
  her startle reflex, and/or seeks comfort/self-settles by
  sucking his or her hands at sleep times (which he or she
  would be unable to do if swaddled).

How to Make This Transition

There are many ways to transition out of the swaddle. Some
prefer unswaddling the legs first (keeping the arms secure). My only
concern with this is that; if babies start rolling at an early age (e.g.,
four months), where full head control is not yet developed, they may
have difficulty moving their head to the side or rolling back over
if they are unable to use their arms. *For safety reasons, I always recommend
arms first.*

1. Keeping legs and one arm wrapped, leave one arm out for
   three nights.
2. Two arms out with legs still wrapped for nights four, five,
   and six.
3. Release legs on night seven.

What to Expect

It is common to experience some degree of sleep regression or change in sleep patterns when making this transition. At the beginning, your baby may resist bedtimes, catnap, or wake more frequently than normal. He or she may also be more irritable or unsettled in general. It may take between three to seven nights as your baby adjusts to his or her newfound freedom and mobility without the swaddle.

Transitional Products

- **Love to Dream 50/50 swaddle or ergoPouch swaddle and sleep bag in one.** A swaddle with shoulder studs/zips that allow for babies' arms to be released one or two at a time, while keeping their body contained.

- **The Magic Sleep Suit, Zipadee-zip, and the Sleepy Hugs Sleep Suit.** Halfway between a swaddle and sleep bag, these suits help to muffle the startle reflex by keeping babies' hands contained but with enough freedom to move them— helping babies to feel secure and cozy, and sleeping for longer.

Tips for a Smooth Transition

- **Keep a regular day-and-night routine.** Well-rested babies (i.e., neither under- nor overtired) will adapt to changes in their routine and environment with greater ease and cooperation.

- **Optimize the sleep environment.** Refer to "The Seven Sleep Foundations: Environment."

- **Engage in plenty of crib and bedroom play throughout the day.** Focus on having your child play or lie in bed outside of sleep times (unswaddled) to build their comfort and security.

- **Increase wind-down time before sleep times.** Aim for ten to fifteen minutes before naps and thirty to sixty minutes at the end of the day.

- **Establish positive sleep associations.** Refer to "The Seven Sleep Foundations: Positive Sleep Associations."

- **Be prepared to spend extra time sitting beside your child's bed** to help them to fall asleep as they adjust to their newly found freedom. A hand resting on them for extra reassurance may be necessary in the interim.

- **Listen.** If your child becomes increasingly upset at sleep times and has difficulty settling without the swaddle, hold him or her and allow them to cry in your arms as you listen lovingly. Refer to "The Sleep Play Love Method: Troubleshooting Tips for Listening."

- **Avoid sleep training or other transitions.** Ditching the swaddle can be a major transition for many babies. Avoid any other changes in routine until your baby can sleep without being wrapped.

MOVING HOUSE

Moving house can be a major adjustment for little people, especially if you are moving from the only home that they have ever known. Children thrive on routine, and moving house disrupts just about everything that makes them feel safe and secure—i.e., a new room, new neighborhood, and (potentially) new childcare, friends, activities, and inevitably a new routine.

Tips for a Smooth Transition

- **Communicate when, why, where, and how the move will happen.** Tip: little boys will love to hear about the big truck on moving day!

- **Let your children go shopping with you** to select new bedding or something special for their new room.

- **Give your children the grand tour of the new house and neighborhood.** Show them where their bedroom will be and create some excitement around new activities that you will do together when you move—e.g., building a cubby house, planting a flower or vegetable garden, climbing a tree, or special places that they can explore. Show your child some local parks or attractions and drop in to see their new childcare center or preschool.

- **Encourage your children to help you pack** so that they feel empowered and a valuable part of the process.

- **On moving day, say good-bye to each room of the old house** for closure.

- **Once you arrive at the new house, set up your children's room first.** It helps if you can set up the bed and furniture in a layout similar to that of the old house. Unpack all boxes, put away clothes and toys, and make their bed so that their room is complete.

- **Maintain sleep associations and nap, meal, and bedtime routines.** Keep familiar objects (bedding and special toys) on hand and accessible during the move.

- **Daily crib-play/play in your children's new room** will encourage safety and familiarity.

- **Family photos placed on the wall in your children's room** may help to reduce anxiety at sleep times.

- **Take some time off work** to unpack and help your children adjust after the move.

- **Avoid scheduling any holidays, major appointments, or other transitions**—such as moving your child from crib to bed, weaning of any kind, or potty training—for at least a few weeks so that you can focus on getting back into a routine and properly settling into your new home.

TRAVEL

Whether you are traveling away from home by a little or a long distance, inevitably being out of routine and away from your creature comforts can create some degree of apprehension and insecurity—and consequently, sleep may regress temporarily. To minimize the disruption on sleep and behavior, the following tips may help.

General Tips

- **Replicate your home sleep environment as much as possible.** Pack all the essential creature comforts and sleep associations such as sleeping bags, swaddles, special toys, bedding, white noise, pacifiers, and bedclothes.

- **Pack family photos to place up beside your children's bed for travel.** This can help them feel more secure at sleep times.

- **Maintain a dark sleep environment.** To maintain a dark room for sleep times when away from home, take some foil or a travel blackout blind with you to place on the windows.

- **If your child will be sleeping in a pack 'n play while you are away, try to set one up at home three to seven days prior to traveling.** Encourage some playtime in the pack 'n play during the day and aim to have some naps and overnight sleeps in it before you leave to increase familiarity and reduce any anxiety while away.

- **Maintain your regular routine (meal, nap, and bedtimes) as much as you can.** The main catalyst for regression following holidays is jet lag/travel across time zones, inconsistency with bedtime at night (usually later when on holidays) and wake time in the morning (usually earlier due to later bedtime and overtiredness).

Tips for Flying with Children

- **For international flights, a late afternoon or early evening departure is ideal.** This way, you can encourage your children to sleep on the plane when they would normally be sleeping, and most of the flight time will have elapsed overnight.

- **When booking your tickets, order a specialized meal option**—e.g., vegetarian or baby. This way you're guaranteed to get your meals first—a definite perk if wrangling hungry toddlers.

- **Obtain airport lounge membership before you travel.** Nothing compares to the comfort of the lounges, food, and drinks—and some even have a play area for children.

- **For long international flights, stop overs can help to avoid—or minimize jetlag.** Where possible, select a halfway point to stay for one to three nights on your way to and/or from your destination.

- **Organize your hotel transfers in advance.** Ensure your method of transport can accommodate your family, luggage, and a stroller. Most transfers are arranged through your hotel, so be clear on your specific requirements when you book.

- **Children under two travel free if they are on your lap or if you book a bassinet.** If you're traveling on a long flight with an infant, request a bassinet. This way, your baby gets a place to sleep, and you get your hands (and lap) free for at least part of the flight at no extra cost. Availability is not always guaranteed, as bassinets are limited and priority is often given to the youngest children on board. Check the guidelines with your airline before you fly, as qualifying age can vary from six months to two years, and there may be specific height and weight requirements. *There are no bassinets on domestic or short-distance international flights.*

- **If traveling to another time zone, transition to the new time zone as soon as you step onto the plane or you arrive at your destination.** Adhere to the new time for all mealtimes, nap times, and bedtimes. Exposure to as much natural sunlight as possible during the day will help to stimulate your child's circadian rhythm and speed up the adjustment process. It is equally important to keep the environment dark for sleep times. Resist the temptation to let your child sleep for longer than usual during the day, or later in the morning—this will undoubtedly result in long stretches of wakefulness overnight! *Breastfed babies may take a* *few more days to adjust because their mother's milk supply must also adjust to the new time zone.*

- For other time zones that may only differ by a couple of hours from home, you may slowly adjust to the new time zone by moving nap times, mealtimes, and bedtime gradually—i.e., forward or backward by fifteen to thirty minutes per day over a few days before your departure —refer to sample transition steps as per "Standard Time and Daylight Savings."

- Feed young children on takeoff and landing—or offer them a pacifier. The sucking motion can minimize the pressure for little ears. If you are using formula, the airline can heat bottles for you—just be sure to ask well in advance so they can accommodate your request.

- Pack the essentials in your carry-on. Useful things to pack in include essential oils, water mist spray, diapers, baby wipes, moisturizer, baby bottom balm, a couple of changes of loose and comfortable clothing (in case of accidents), plenty of snacks, formula, bottles, muslin swaddle blankets, a warmer sleeping blanket, swaddle or a sleeping bag, lovey or special toy, pacifiers, sippy cups, entertainment for older children (books, cards, movies, toys, games, and coloring), a baby carrier (for the sometimes-lengthy immigration process), iPad, phone charger, and junior headphones.

- Bring your stroller. Most airlines allow you to take your stroller to the boarding gate, and you can either collect it when you step off the plane or it will be available in oversized luggage. Check with your airline as to their policy and where to collect once you arrive at your destination.

STANDARD TIME AND DAYLIGHT SAVINGS

Although this transition involves moving the clock forward or back-ward by *only one hour*, the change to routine and the body clock can impact children and parents for weeks. I recommend a gradual transition to and from standard time and daylight savings time, and this is done by moving bedtime, nap time(s), and mealtimes fifteen minutes later or earlier each day over a *four-day period*. You also have the option of doing this over three days (i.e., moving times earlier/later by twenty minutes per day), or more gradually (e.g., ten minutes earlier/later per day over six days, or cold turkey). However, the latter can be more disruptive for children who are less adaptable.

Daylight Savings (DT) to Standard Time (ST)

TIMING	TRANSITION STEPS	DT	ST
Four Days Prior	- Usual wake time, mealtimes, and nap time(s) - Move bedtime later by 15 minutes	7:00 a.m. 7:15 p.m.	6:00 a.m. 6:15 p.m.
Three Days Prior	- Wake your child up 15 minutes later in the morning - Move mealtimes and naptime(s) later by 15 minutes - Move bedtime later by 30 minutes	7:15 a.m. 7:30 p.m.	6:15 a.m. 6:30 p.m.
Two Days Prior	- Wake your child up 30 minutes later in the morning - Move mealtimes and naptime(s) later by 30 minutes - Move bedtime later by 45 minutes	7:30 a.m. 7:45 p.m.	6:30 a.m. 6:45 p.m.
One Day Prior	- Wake your child up 45 minutes later in the morning - Move mealtimes and naptime(s) later by 45 minutes - Move bedtime later by one hour	7:45 a.m. 8:00 p.m.	6:45 a.m. 7:00 p.m.
Standard Time Takes Effect	- Regular waking time, mealtimes, naptime(s), and bedtime	8:00 a.m. (does not apply)	7:00 a.m.

The above assumes a 7:00 a.m. to 7:00 p.m. schedule. If your child is on a 7:30 p.m. or 8:00 p.m. to 7:30 a.m. or 8:00 a.m. schedule before this transition, the above steps need not apply. *It is especially important to follow the above steps if your child is already an early riser (i.e., he or she wakes earlier than 6:00 a.m.), or you may experience that your child's new wake-up time will be 5:00 a.m. or earlier!*

Standard Time (ST) to Daylight Savings (DT)

TIMING	TRANSITION STEPS	ST	DT
Four Days Prior	- Usual wake time, mealtimes, and nap time(s) - Move bedtime earlier by 15 minutes	7:00 a.m. 6:45 p.m.	8:00 a.m. 7:45 p.m.
Three Days Prior	- Wake your child up 15 minutes earlier in the morning - Move mealtimes and naptime(s) earlier by 15 minutes - Move bedtime earlier by 30 minutes	6:45 a.m. 6:30 p.m.	7:45 a.m. 7:30 p.m.
Two Days Prior	- Wake your child up 30 minutes earlier in the morning - Move mealtimes and naptime(s) earlier by 30 minutes - Move bedtime earlier by 45 minutes	6:30 a.m. 6:15 p.m.	7:30 a.m. 7:15 p.m.
One Day Prior	- Wake your child up 45 minutes earlier in the morning - Move mealtimes and naptime(s) earlier by 45 minutes - Move bedtime earlier by one hour	6:15 a.m. 6:00 p.m.	7:15 a.m. 7:00 p.m.
Daylight Savings Takes Effect	- Regular waking time, mealtimes, naptime(s), and bedtime	6:00 a.m. (does not apply)	7:00 a.m.

The above assumes a 7:00 a.m. to 7:00 p.m. schedule. It is common for children to begin waking anywhere between thirty to sixty minutes earlier a week or so before this change takes place. In such circumstances, or if your child is already waking early (i.e., before 6:00 a.m.) you may only need to transition out the naptime(s), mealtimes, and bedtimes—not the wake-up times.

REFLECTION

Sleep difficulties are very *rarely* ever just about sleep, and the catalysts for such challenges can be varied and complex. Albeit often only temporary—attributed to variables such as teething, developmental milestones, illness, habit, and environment—ongoing sleep regression (or issues) usually manifest when parents lack the confidence, awareness, knowledge, support, or bandwidth to make the required changes to their child's routine.

Babies and children are continually developing and changing—and as such, their sleep needs and reliance on us (as their parents) also continues to change. Our challenge is to accept the fickle landscape of our children's sleep patterns—letting go of our attachment to how we expect (or want) them to sleep and/or comparing them to others. We must learn to adapt to our children's evolving needs, instead of expecting our children to fit *our* ideals or agendas—because this is only ever a recipe for angst and discontent.

Children's ability to sleep (well) is directly proportionate to their perceived level of safety, and the opportunity they are afforded to regularly heal their fears, upsets, and insecurities in the supportive and loving presence of a caregiver. Implementation of "The Seven Sleep

Foundations"—and most importantly, parent-child connection tools—is the cornerstone to healthy, sustainable sleep habits.

Like our children, we too are forever learning and growing—and as such, our parenting toolbox and confidence also continues to expand. It's impossible to have all the answers, all the time. However, by holding the loving intention to gently and respectfully assist your child to sleep better—and arming yourself with a support network and the knowledge that feels intuitively right for you and your family—you will ensure your long-term success.

Raising little humans and all the challenges that come with this ever-changing territory is no small feat—it's exhausting, confusing, and overwhelming. But on the flipside, it can also be joyful, rewarding and enlightening. As parents, we are all doing our best, and our best needs to be enough. Enough for now.

ABOUT THE AUTHOR

Sophie Acott is a mother, certified sleep consultant, parent coach, homebirth enthusiast, and conscious parenting advocate. After working with families for many years using traditional behavioral methodologies, Sophie recognized that something was amiss. Mainstream cry-it-out and popular sleep-training techniques lacked sustainability and failed to acknowledge the inextricable link between the parent-child connection and sleep challenges. On the contrary, the trend toward attachment parenting and no-cry approaches—while a move in the right direction—ignored the fundamental function of crying to help children release everyday stress and heal from trauma. Sophie conceptualized the Sleep Play Love method from her desire to empower parents with the tools and confidence to overcome sleep challenges as their children evolved beyond babyhood. Sophie shares her wealth of sleep experience and knowledge via her growing Facebook community of thousands of parents, and her Sleep Play Love blog. Born and raised in Australia, Sophie now resides in San Diego, California, with her husband and four young children.

Made in the USA
Middletown, DE
28 April 2020